DYING of MONEY

*Lessons of the Great
German and American Inflations*

Jens O. Parsson

© 2011 Jens O. Parsson (Ronald H. Marcks)
All Rights Reserved.

No part of this publication may be reproduced, stored in a retrieval system, or transmitted, in any form or by any means, electronic, mechanical, photocopying, recording, or otherwise, without the written permission of the author.

First published by Wellspring Press 1974 Boston
Published by Dog Ear Publishing 2011
4010 W. 86th Street, Ste H
Indianapolis, IN 46268
www.dogearpublishing.net

ISBN: 978-145750-266-8

This paper is acid free and meets all ANSI standards for archival quality paper.
Printed in the United States of America

The cover motif is a piece of old German money. It is a Reichsbanknote issued on August 22, 1923 for one hundred million marks. Nine years earlier, that many marks would have been about 5 percent of all the German marks in the world, worth 23 million American dollars. On the day it was issued, it was worth about twenty dollars. Three months later, it was worth only a few thousandths of an American cent. The process by which this occurs is known as inflation.

A few years before, in 1920 and 1921, Germany had enjoyed a remarkable prosperity envied by the rest of the world. Prices were steady, business was humming, everyone was working, the stock market was skyrocketing. The Germans were swimming in easy money. Within the year, they were drowning in it. Until it was all over, no one seemed to notice any connection between the earlier false boom and the later inflationary bust.

In this book, Jens O. Parsson performs the neat trick of transforming the dry economic subject of inflation into a white-knuckles kind of blood-chiller. He begins with a freewheeling account of the spectacular inflation that all but destroyed Germany in 1923, taking it apart to find out both what made it tick and what made it finally end. He goes on to look at the American inflation that was steadily gaining force after 1962. In terms clear and fascinating enough for any layman, but with technical validity enough for any economist, he applies the lessons gleaned from the German inflation to find that too much about the American inflation was the same, lacking only the inexorable further deterioration that time would bring. The book concludes by charting out all the possible future prognoses for the American inflation, none easy but some much less catastrophic than others.

Mr. Parsson brings much new light to bear on this subject. He lays on the line in tough, spare language exactly how and why the American inflation was caused, exactly who was responsible for causing it, exactly who unjustly benefited and who suffered from the inflation, exactly why the government could not permit the inflation to stop or even to cease growing worse, exactly who was going to pay the ultimate price, and exactly what would have to be done to avert the ultimate conclusion.

This book packs a wallop. It is not for the timid, and it spares no tender sensibilities. The conclusions it reaches are shocking and are bound to provoke endless dispute. If they proved to approximate even remotely the correct analysis of the American inflation, hardly any American citizen could escape being the prey of inflation and no one could afford not to know where the inflation was taking him. In the economic daily lives of everyone, nothing will be the same after this book as it was before.

Contents

Foreword 7

PROLOGUE
The German Inflation of 1914–1923

1 The Ascent 15
2 The Descent 21
3 The Gains and Losses 26
4 The Roots 30
5 The Great Prosperity of 1920–1921 37
6 Politics 42
7 The Lessons 46

ACT ONE
The Rise of the Great American Inflation

8 The War 53
9 Grappling with Stability 59
10 The Great Prosperity of 1962–1968 64
11 The Inflationary Syndrome 70
12 Culprits and Scapegoats 85
13 The Open Questions 93

Contents

INTERLUDE
The General Theory of Inflation

14	Welcome to Economic Theory	97
15	Prices	99
16	Inflation	106
17	Velocity	112
18	Aggregate Values	120
19	Real Values	126
20	Government Debt	132
21	The Record Interpreted	136
22	Money	141
23	The Creation of Money	145
24	Depression	153
25	The Economics of Keynes	158
26	Inflationary Economics	166
27	Interest and the Money Wealth	176
28	The Economics of Disaster	187
29	The Crux	191
30	Taxes	193
31	American Taxes	203
32	Government Expenditure: The National Dividend	215
33	Employment	224
34	Investment and Growth	235
35	Dogma	240

THE LAST ACTS
The American Prognosis

36	Act Two, Scene One: President Nixon Begins	253
37	Act Two, Scene Two: Price Controls and Other Follies	259
38	The Way Out	267
39	The Way Ahead	276
40	Democratics	286
41	Political Reorganization	293
42	Self Defense	298
43	Self Defense Continued: The Stock Market	306
44	A World of Nations	313
45	Interscript	323
	NOTES	329

Foreword

Most of us have at least a general idea of what we think inflation is. Inflation is the state of affairs in which prices go up. Inflation is an old, old story. Inflation is almost as ancient as money is, and money is almost as ancient as man himself.

It was probably not long after the earliest cave man of the Stone Age fashioned his first stone spearhead to kill boars with, perhaps thirty or forty thousand years ago, that he began to use boar's teeth or something of the sort as counters for trading spearheads and caves with neighboring clans. That was money. Anything like those boar's teeth that had an accepted symbolic value for trading which was greater than their intrinsic value for using was true money.

Inflation was the very next magic after money. Inflation is a disease of money. Before money, there could be no inflation. After money, there could not for long be no inflation. Those early cave men were perhaps already being vexed by the rising prices of spearheads and caves, in terms of boar's teeth, by the time they began to paint pictures of their boar hunts on their cave walls, and that would make inflation an older institution even than art. Some strong leader among them, gaining greater authority over the district by physical strength or superstition or other suasion, may have been the one who discovered that if he could decree what was money, he himself could issue the money and gain real wealth like spearheads and caves in exchange for it. The money might have been carved boar's teeth that only he was allowed to carve, or it might have been something else. Whatever it was, that was inflation. The more the leader issued his carved boar's teeth to buy up spearheads and caves, the more the prices of spearheads and caves in terms of boar's teeth rose. Thus inflation may have become the oldest form of government finance. It may also have been the oldest form of political confidence game used by leaders to exact tribute from constituents, older even than taxes, and inflation has kept those honored places in human affairs to this day.

Since those dim beginnings in the forests of the Stone Age, governments have been perpetually rediscovering first the splendors and later the woes of inflation. Each new government discoverer of the splendors seems to believe that no one has ever beheld such splendors before. Each new discoverer of the woes professes not to understand any connection with the earlier splendors. In the thousands of years of inflation's history, there has been nothing really new about inflation, and there still is not.

Around the year 300 A.D., the Roman Empire under the Emperor Diocletian experienced one of the most virulent inflations of all time. The government issued cheap coins called *"nummi,"* which were made of copper washed with silver. The supply of metals for this ingenious coinage was ample and cheap, and the supply of the coinage became ample and cheap too. The *nummi* prices of goods began to rise dizzily. Poor Emperor Diocletian became the author of one of the earliest recorded systems of price controls in an effort to remedy the woes without losing the joys of inflation, and he also became one of the earliest and most distinguished failures at that effort. The famous Edict of Diocletian in 301 decreed a complex set of ceiling prices along with death penalties for violators. Many death penalties were actually inflicted, but prices were not controlled. Goods simply could not be bought with *nummi*. Like every later effort to have the joys without the woes of inflation, the Edict of Diocletian failed totally.

So it has gone throughout the millennia of man's development. For at least the four thousand years of recorded history, man has known inflation. Babylon and Ancient China are known to have had inflations. The Athenian lawgiver Solon introduced devaluation of the *drachma*. The Roman Empire was plagued by inflation and, more rarely, deflation. Henry the Eighth of England was a proficient inflationist, as were the kings of France. The entire world underwent a severe inflation in the sixteenth and seventeenth centuries as a result of the Spanish discoveries of huge quantities of gold in the New World. "Continentals" in the American Revolution and the *assignats* in the French Revolution were precursors of the wild paper inflations of the twentieth century. Steadily rising prices have been the general rule and not the exception throughout man's history.

The twentieth century brought the institution of inflation to its ultimate perfection. When economic systems are so highly organized as they became in the twentieth century, so that people are completely dependent on money trading for the necessaries of life, there is no place to take shelter from inflation. Inflations in the twentieth century became like inflations in no other century. The two principal inflations that occurred in advanced industrial nations in the twentieth century will probably prove to have done more to influence the course of history itself than any other inflation. One of these was the German inflation that had its roots in World War I, grew to a giddy height and a precipitous fall in 1923, and contributed to the rise of Adolf Hitler and World War II. The other was the great American inflation that had its roots in World War II, grew in the decade of the 1960's toward an almost equally giddy height, and contributed to results which could not even be imagined at the time this book was written.

Foreword

This book is not a history of inflation, because most inflations of history hold only a passing interest. This book is written primarily about the great American inflation, and it was written at a time when that inflation was still in mid-career. No one then knew where it might end, but it seemed altogether possible that no inflation of history, not even the German, would appear in retrospect to have troubled the waters of time more deeply than the great American inflation.

Inflations may be of every conceivable variety of degree, from the mildly annoying to the volcanic. Inflations may be fast or slow, accelerating or decelerating, chronic or transitory. A merely annoying inflation usually causes no one very much real harm. A volcanic inflation, on the other hand, is the kind of catastrophe that confiscates wealth, withholds the means of life, breeds revolutions, and precipitates wars. Every volcanic inflation of history began as a mildly annoying inflation. The true nature of any inflation is not often visible on its surface. As with volcanoes, an annoying inflation that is about to subside and die out looks on its surface like one that is about to erupt. It is the disquieting nature of an inflation that no one knows with certainty what it will do next.

The era of the inflation in the United States was an era of many kinds of discomforts. The nation was fighting a small but dismal and unpopular war in distant Southeast Asia. Crime was rampant. Cities were degenerating. Negroes were in ferment, students in rebellion, and youth in general in a state of defection. The illness of inflation might have been lesser or greater than any of these. It might have had nothing to do with any other illness, or it might have lain near the root of them all. There were those who dismissed the inflation as the least of the panoply of American illnesses, but they were less numerous than formerly and might be still less numerous later.

Scarcely a person in America was untouched by inflation's handiwork. Every citizen, in his daily life and with his earthly fortune, danced to a tune he mostly could not hear, played for him by the government's inflation. It was up to every citizen to learn for himself what was happening and to look out for himself if anyone was going to, because no one else was looking out for him. The government certainly was not. The government was compelled by its other duties not to protect him but the opposite, to continue to steal from him by the inflation as long as it could. The forces at work were such that there was no practical possibility the inflation would end or abate. The only real question was whether or not it would continue to become steadily worse. A hundred million Americans or more, almost all of them serenely unwitting, lived their lives and made their homes on inflation's epicenter. They were on ground zero for inflation's shock waves. Only time would tell whether the tremors rumbling beneath their feet would pass off without a quake.

The past is prologue, it is said. No more instructive prologue to the American inflation, which was still unfinished, could be chosen than the German inflation, which was long since completed. Let us begin then by turning first to that inflation and taking our text for the day from the scripture of history.

PROLOGUE

The German Inflation of
1914-1923

I
The Ascent

In 1923 Germany's money, the Reichsmark, finally was strained beyond the bursting point, and it burst. Persistent inflation which had steadily eroded the mark since the beginning of World War I at last ran away. Germany's "disastrous prosperity" came to an end, and in its place the German people suffered a period of hardship and real starvation as well as a permanent obliteration of their life savings. When the débâcle was finally stopped, the old mark, which had once been worth a solid 23 cents, was written off at one trillion old marks to one new one of the same par value. The most spectacular part of that loss was lost in the mark's final dizzy skid; all the marks that existed in the world in the summer of 1922 (190 billion of them) were not worth enough, by November of 1923, to buy a single newspaper or a tram ticket. That was the spectacular part of the collapse, but most of the real loss in money wealth had been suffered much earlier. The first 90 percent of the Reichsmark's real value had already been lost before the middle of 1922.

The tragicomic dénouement of Germany's inflation—the workers hastening to the bake shops to spend quickly their day's pay bundled up in billions of paper marks and carried in wheelbarrows—is perhaps at least vaguely remembered nowadays. The more sinister and more permanent scars which the inflation left are less well known. Still less clearly remembered are the years before the mark blew, with their breakneck boom, spending, profits, speculation, riches, poverty, and all manner of excess. Throughout these years the structure was quietly building itself up for the blow. Germany's inflation cycle ran not for a year but for nine years, representing eight years of gestation and only one year of collapse.

The beginning was in the summer of 1914, a day or two before World War I opened, when Germany abandoned its gold standard and began to spend more than it had, run up debt, and expand its money supply. The end came on November 15, 1923, the day Germany shut off its money pump and balanced its budget. Over the nine years in between, Germany's inflation followed not a constant course but a characteristic ascent and descent, a ripening and a decay.

Germany started by not paying adequately for its war out of the sacrifices of its people—taxes—but covered its deficits with war loans and issues of new paper Reichsmarks. Scarcely an eighth of Germany's wartime expenses were covered by taxes. This was a failing common to all the combatants. France did even worse than Germany in financing the war, Britain not much better. Germany's bad financing was due in part to a firm belief that it would be able to collect the price of the war from its enemies, whom it expected to defeat; but to a greater degree it may have sprung from distrust that its people would support the war to the extent not only of fighting it but also of paying for it. Whatever the reason, Germany's bad war financing did not immediately demand its price. Inflation in the sense of rising prices was moderate. Domestic prices only a bit more than doubled to the end of the war in 1918, while the government's money supply had increased by more than nine

The Ascent

times. The government's debt increased still more. So long as the government in this way could spend money it did not have faster than its value could fall, Germany had both its war and life as usual at the same time, which was the same as having the war free of charge.

After the war, Germany and all the other combatants underwent price inflations which served as partial corrections for their wartime financing practices. The year 1919 was a year of violent inflation in every country, including the United States. By the spring of 1920, German prices had reached seventeen times their prewar level. From this point, however, the paths of Germany and the other nations diverged. The others, including the United States, stopped their deficit financing and began to take their accumulated economic medicine by way of an acute recession in 1920 and 1921. Their prices fell steeply from the 1920 level. Germany alone continued to inflate and to store up not only the price of the war but also the price of a new boom which it then commenced enjoying. Germany's remarkable prosperity was the envy of the other leading countries, including the victors, who were in serious economic difficulties at the time. Prices in Germany temporarily stabilized and remained rock-steady during fifteen months in 1920 and 1921, and there was therefore no surface inflation at all, but at the same time the government began again to pump out deficit expenditure, business credit, and money at a renewed rate. Germany's money supply doubled again during this period of stable prices. It was this time, when Germany was sublimely unconscious of the fiscal monsters in its closet, which was undoubtedly the turning of the tide toward the inflationary smash. The catastrophe of 1923 was begotten not in 1923 or at any time after the inflation began to mount, but in the relatively good times of 1920 and 1921.

The stimulation of the government's easy money spread through virtually all levels of the German economy. The life of the inflation in its ripening stage was a paradox which had its own unmistakable characteristics. One was the great wealth, at least of those favored by the boom. These were the "profiteers" of whom everyone spoke. Industry and business were going at fever pitch. Exports were thriving; that was one of the problems. Hordes of tourists came from abroad. Many great fortunes sprang up overnight. Berlin was one of the brightest capitals in the world in those days. Great mansions of the new rich grew like mushrooms in the suburbs. The cities, particularly in the eyes of the austere countryfolk, had an aimless and wanton youth and a cabaret life of an unprecedented splendor, dissolution, and unreality. Prodigality marked the affairs of both the government and the private citizen. When money was so easy to come by, one took less care to obtain real value for it, and frugality came to seem inconsequential. For this reason, Germans did not obtain so much real wealth as the growth of money alone would have indicated.

Side by side with the wealth were the pockets of poverty. Greater numbers of people remained on the outside of the easy money, looking in but not able to enter. The crime rate soared. Although unemployment became virtually nonexistent and many of the workers were able to keep up with the inflation through their unions, their bargaining, and their cost-of-living escalator clauses, other workers fell behind the rising cost of living into real poverty. Salaried and white-collar workers lost ground in the same way. Even while total production rose, each individual's own efforts faltered and showed a measurable decline, and the quality of production deteriorated. Accounts of the time tell of a progressive demoralization which crept over the common people, compounded of their weariness with the breakneck pace, to no visible purpose, and their fears from watching their own precarious positions slip while others grew so conspicuously rich. Feelings of disunity and dissent were epidemic among the Germans, and nationalism among them was never weaker. Regional separatism was so strong that it came close to breaking up Germany into fragments.

Along with the paradoxical wealth and poverty, other characteristics were masked by the boom and less easy to see

The Ascent

until after it had destroyed itself. One was the difference between mere feverish activity, which did certainly exist, and real prosperity which appeared, but only appeared, to be the same thing. There was no unemployment, but there was vast spurious employment—activity in unproductive or useless pursuits. The ratio of office and administrative workers to production workers rose out of all control. Paperwork and paperworkers proliferated. Government workers abounded, and heavy restraints against layoffs and discharges kept multitudes of redundant employees ostensibly employed. The incessant labor disputes and collective bargaining consumed great amounts of time and effort. Whole industries of fringe activities, chains of middlemen, and an undergrowth of general economic hangers-on sprang up. Almost any kind of business could make money. Business failures and bankruptcies became few. The boom suspended the normal processes of natural selection by which the nonessential and ineffective otherwise would have been culled out. Practically all of this vanished after the inflation blew itself out.

Speculation alone, while adding nothing to Germany's wealth, became one of its largest activities. The fever to join in turning a quick mark infected nearly all classes, and the effort expended in simply buying and selling the paper titles to wealth was enormous. Everyone from the elevator operator up was playing the market. The volumes of turnover in securities on the Berlin Bourse became so high that the financial industry could not keep up with the paperwork, even with greatly swollen staffs of back-office employees, and the Bourse was obliged to close several days a week to work off the backlog.

Another busy though not directly productive sector of activity was in capital goods and industrial construction. The boom's excessive emphasis on producing new means of production was striking. Travelers remarked the contrast between Germany's new, humming factories and the old, depressed ones of neighboring countries. Much of this indiscriminate growth in plant capacity made sense only in the bloated inflationary expansion, but not otherwise. After the inflation ended, much of Germany's brand new inflation-built plant was "rationalized," which often meant simply torn down again.

Concentration of wealth and business was still another characteristic trend. The merger, the tender offer, the takeover bid, and the proxy fight were in vogue. Bank mergers were all the rage, while at the same time new and untried banks sprouted. Great ramshackle conglomerates of all manner of unconnected businesses were collected together by merger and acquisition. Armies of lawyers, brokers, accountants, businessmen, and technicians who spent their time pasting together these paper empires bolstered the lists of the more or less employed. The most fabulous of the conglomerates was the empire of Hugo Stinnes, which comprised hundreds of companies at its peak in coal, iron, steel, shipping, transport, paper, chemicals, newspapers, oil, films, banks, hotels, and more. Stinnes was Mr. Everything who had also begun to colonize abroad and is supposed to have contemplated organizing all German industry into a single super-conglomerate. After the inflation ended, Stinnes' empire and many lesser ones were found to be functionally and financially unsound, and they disintegrated more or less messily. Stinnes died.

It was typically true that the Germans who grew the richest in the inflation were precisely those who, like the speculators, the operators, and the builders of paper empires, were least essential to German industry operating on any basis of stability or real value. With the end of the inflation they disappeared like apparitions in the dawn, and scarcely a one of the "kings of inflation" continued to be important in German industry afterward.

2
The Descent

That was how it was in the heyday of the boom, which was the ripening stage of the inflation. Inexorably the inflation began to stalk the boom. From having been steady during the fifteen months preceding July 1921, prices doubled in the next four months and increased by ten times in the year through the summer of 1922. Consumers put on pathetic buyers' strikes against the rising prices. Interest rates soared as lenders tried to anticipate the loss of value of their principal. Businessmen quoted prices to one another with gold or constant-value clauses, or they did business in foreign currency. The government's actual deficits were relatively innocuous. In fact, the government's budget was closer to balance at the brink of the crash in 1922 than at any time since 1914. But while the government's new deficits diminished, the inflation had become self-sustaining, feeding on the old ones. The government was unable to refinance its existing debts except by printing new money. The government's creation of paper wealth steadily fell behind the rising prices, and the inflation entered its catastrophic decaying stage.

The final convulsion when it began was at first bizarre and at last became sheer nightmare. Beginning in July 1922, prices rose tenfold in four months, two hundredfold in eleven months. Near the end in 1923, prices were at least quadrupling each week. Prices raced so far ahead of the money-printing plants that, in the end, the total real value of all the Reichsmarks in the world was smaller than it had ever been, a phenomenon which enabled the government's economists to argue that there was no true inflation at all, it was just numbers. This phenomenon also made money so scarce, even in the face of astronomical prices, that urban Germans could not find the price of their daily bread. The worker had to compute his pay in the trillions, carry it in bales, and spent it instantly lest he lose it. The forlorn buyers' strikes of earlier days against the mildly higher prices were no more; in their place the buyers were vying with one another to buy up any kind of goods at any price before their little money could evaporate. The seas of marks which had been stored up by Germans and especially by trusting foreigners flooded forth and fought to buy into other investments, foreign currencies, tangible goods, almost anything but marks. Legally "fair" interest rates reached as much as 22 percent *per day*. The price of a schnitzel dinner might rise 20 percent between giving the order and paying the check. Germany's money printing industry (another impressively large employer with 30 paper mills, 133 printing plants, workers in thousands) could not turn out enough trillions to keep up. States, towns, and companies got into the act by issuing their own "emergency money" (*Notgeld*). Barter became prevalent. Still money grew scarcer while prices continued to soar. The boom was long since over. Farmers, who were comfortable enough, would not sell their food to the townsmen for their worthless money. Starvation and abject poverty reigned. The middle class virtually disappeared as professors, doctors, lawyers, scientists and artists pawned their earthly goods and turned to field or factory to try to earn a little food. A former conductor of the Boston Symphony Orchestra earned a dollar's worth of trillions a week conducting an orchestra in North Germany. Every level of life above the barest existence was shed. Malnutrition and the diseases of malnutrition were rife. Production began to fall. As factories closed, the workers too became unemployed and joined the starving. The whole system ground to a halt. Food riots and Marxist terror broke out throughout Germany. Eighty-five persons died in a riot in Hamburg. The famous beer hall *Putsch* led by Adolf Hitler in Munich in November 1923, the last month of the inflation, was only one of the many and not the worst.

Once the old Reichsmark had been thoroughly obliterated, the return to a stable currency was so absurdly simple as to become known as the "miracle of the Rentenmark." The Rentenmark, or "investment mark," was the new interim currency. The government of industrialist Wilhelm Cuno, which had ruled during most of the worst of the inflation, finally fell in August of 1923. Gustav Stresemann, who was later foreign minister throughout the trying 1920's and has been described as by far the greatest German of the Weimar era, was promptly summoned as chancellor. In October, the Reichstag voted him dictatorial powers under the Weimar constitution. He in turn called upon Dr. Hjalmar Schacht, who was later Hitler's financial wizard and was tried (but acquitted) at Nuremberg, as the commissioner for the new Rentenmark. As Dr. Schacht relates, he accomplished the introduction of the Rentenmark with no staff but his secretary and no establishment but his dark back office and a telephone. The Rentenmark was placed in circulation beside the devalued Reichsmark and carried no real value of its own but the naked avowal that there would be only so many Rentenmarks and no more. The Germans miraculously believed it and, still more miraculously, it turned out to be true. The old Reichsmark was finally pegged at one trillion to one Rentenmark on November 15, 1923; simultaneously the German finance ministry under the estimable Dr. Hans Luther, who was to become chancellor of one of the later governments, balanced its budget, and that was the end of the inflation.

Stabilization through the Rentenmark was by no means painless. To convince the skeptical required first a series of severe bloodlettings administered by the resolute Dr. Schacht to foreign-exchange speculators, issuers of the *Notgeld,* and businesses which required credit, all of whom depended on the continued depreciation of the official currency. When the president of the Reichsbank throughout the war and the inflation, Rudolf Havenstein, died at the moment of the stabilization, Schacht was appointed to succeed him. Schacht's greatest achievement was not so much in the introduction of the Rentenmark but in making a new non-inflationary money policy stick. The granddaddy of all credit squeezes ensued from Dr. Schacht's order of April 7, 1924, which stopped all credit from the Reichsbank. New inflation, which had begun to stir again, was then abruptly and finally stopped. The intrenched interests in Germany, especially the industrialists like Stinnes, characteristically fought Schacht every inch of the way, although a few later acknowledged the rightness of his course.

Germany now took its stored-up dose of hard times. Germans who had been caught in the inflation were relieved of their worldly goods. Businesses which were based on nothing but the inflationary boom were swept away. Credit for business was practically impossible to come by. Unemployment temporarily skyrocketed. Government spending was slashed, government workers dismissed, taxes raised, working hours increased, and wages cut. Almost 400,000 government workers alone were discharged. The shock to the German people of the final inflation, the stabilization, and the unemployment was so great that in the elections of May 1924, six months after the close of the inflation, millions of voters flocked from the moderate center parties to either the Communists or the Nazis and Nationalists on the extremes. These parties gained dramatic strength in the "inflation Reichstag," as it was called.

Germany very quickly began to feel better economically,

The Descent

however, as the stabilization medicine did its work. New elections only seven months later, in December 1924, repudiated the Nazis and Communists and restored the strength of the middle-class parties and of the Social Democrats, the orthodox labor party. Only by the greatest efforts did Germany get itself going again in this way. Even so, because of the permanent shortage of credit Germany's revival was unhealthily based (against Schacht's warnings) on new foreign loans. The world depression which followed 1929 knocked debtor Germany flat again, and Hitler followed close behind.

3
The Gains and Losses

When the inflation was over, everyone who had owed marks suddenly and magically owed nothing. This came about because every contract or debt that called for payment in a fixed number of marks was paid off with that many marks, but they were worth next to nothing compared with what they had been worth when they had been borrowed or earned. Germany's total prewar mortgage indebtedness alone, for example, equal to 40 billion marks or one-sixth of the total German wealth, was worth less than one American cent after the inflation. On the other side, of course, everyone who had owned marks or mark wealth such as bank accounts, savings, insurance, bonds, notes, or any sort of contractual right to money suddenly and magically owned nothing.

The largest gainer by far, because it was the largest debtor, was the Reich government. The inflation relieved it of its entire crushing debt which represented the cost of the war, reconstruction, reparations, and its deficit-financed boom. Others who were debtors emerged like the government with large

Gains and Losses

winnings. Until the last moment of the inflation borrowers continued to make huge profits simply by borrowing money and buying assets, because lenders never stopped underestimating the inflation. The good fortune of the debtors demonstrated the prudence of following the government's lead: one must beware of being a creditor whenever the government was a huge debtor. Farmers in particular were the classic case of invulnerability to inflation, because they always had food, their farms were constant values, and the many who had mortgages on their farms were forgiven their debts outright.

The debtors' gain was the creditors' loss. Foreign holders of marks were huge losers. Germany was estimated to have made a profit of about 15 billion gold marks, or 40 percent of its annual national product, on sales of its paper marks to foreigners, even after deducting reparations payments. The wealthy in Germany suffered heavily but unevenly; the more nimble perceived early enough the need to invest in something other than mark wealth, while those who were not nimble lost everything. Trustees were forbidden by law until the very end to invest in anything but fixed obligations and consequently lost all the value of their trusts. The endowments of great charitable institutions, similarly invested, were wiped out. Financial institutions such as banks and insurance companies, which were both debtors and creditors in marks, were generally weakened though not destroyed in the inflation because of their inability to see clearly what was happening. Speculators tended to believe in their own game until too late and emerged as net losers. Sound business escaped weaker but intact; their debts were relieved but their boom business was gone. Inflation-born businesses disappeared.

Industrial stocks, the darling of the inflationary speculation, had a peculiar history. At the height of the boom, stock prices had been bid up to astronomical price-earnings ratios while dividends went out of style. Stock prices increased more than fourfold during the great boom from February 1920 to November 1921. Then, however, shortly after the first upturn of price inflation and long before the inflationary engine faltered and business began to weaken, a stock market crash occurred. This was the Black Thursday of December 1, 1921. Stock prices fell by about 25 percent in a short time and hovered for six months while all other prices were soaring. The real value of stocks declined steadily because their prices lagged far behind the prices of tangible goods, until for example the entire stock ownership of the great Mercedes-Benz automobile manufacturer was valued by the market at no more than 327 cars. Investors were extremely slow to grasp that stocks were poles apart from fixed obligations like bonds, quite wrongly thinking that if bonds were worthless stocks must be too. Nearer the end in 1923, relative prices of stocks skyrocketed again as investors returned to them for their underlying real value. Stocks in general were no very effective hedge against inflation at any given moment while inflation continued; but when it was all over, stocks of sound businesses turned out to have kept all but their peak boom values notably well. Stocks of inflation-born businesses, of course, were as worthless as bonds were.

The mass of the workers who lived mostly on their current wages, and who had no savings to lose, suffered only temporarily with privation and unemployment in the very last throes of the inflation; but these problems passed and left them where they had been or not much behind. To them, the agony of the inflation was largely someone else's, just as the boom had been.

At bottom, it was the unsuspecting middle class who were Germany's savers, pensioners, purchasers of life insurance, including everyone from workers who saved to the modestly well-off, who not only suffered the worst of the agony while the inflation lasted but also were left after it was over with the most staggering permanent loss in relation to their whole substance. This class paid the piper for all of Germany. Great numbers of pensioners were left totally impoverished and forced back into the work gang to end their days there. The encouragement to thrift, an old German weakness, turned out to have been a complete swindle. Instead of a levy on all the Germans to pay for

Gains and Losses

Germany's indulgences, a levy which might have been heavy but could have been fair, Germany left the levy to fall on those who were too innocent to evade it, and from them it took everything they owned. In any case, it was not the piper who went unpaid.

The effect was a confiscatory tax on these victims. John Maynard Keynes, who later rightly or wrongly was adopted as patron saint by inflationary governments, excoriated them on this occasion:

> "Lenin is said to have declared that the best way to destroy the capitalist system was to debauch the currency. By a continuing process of inflation, governments can confiscate, secretly and unobserved, an important part of the wealth of their citizens. By this method they can not only confiscate, but they confiscate *arbitrarily* . . ."

Adolf Hitler, whose economics were far more astute than those of the government's economists, shared roughly the same view of the inflationary government confiscators with Lord Keynes:

> ". . . once the printing presses stopped—and that is the prerequisite for the stabilization of the mark—the swindle would be at once brought to light . . . the State itself has become the biggest swindler and crook."

Despite the obliteration of the wealth of millions of individual Germans, the inflation was merely a transfer of their wealth, like any tax, and not in any sense a destruction of wealth. For every German's total loss, there was an equivalent gain to some other German debtor or to Germany as a whole, through the discharge of their debts.

4
The Roots

The expansion of Germany's Reichsmark circulation, that is to say its money supply, always led the way in the inflation. When it abated temporarily, the inflation abated temporarily. When it stopped permanently, the inflation stopped permanently. Nevertheless, the inflation was officially blamed on everything under the sun but the government's spending, its deficits, and its money issues. These, the government economists said, followed and did not lead the inflation. According to their theories, the money supply must increase to meet increasing needs (rising prices and expenditures) and not needs fit themselves into existing supply. The government finances could not be put right, they said, until the price increases and the fall of the mark stopped. These in turn were generally attributed to external factors such as war reparations, balance of payments deficits, the constantly declining foreign-exchange value of the mark, the profiteers who were raising prices, foreign and domestic speculators who were supposedly attacking the mark, and the upward spiral of wages and prices.

The Roots

As for the profiteers, Lord Keynes for one discredited the accusations:

"These 'profiteers' are, broadly speaking, the entrepreneur class of capitalists, that is to say, the active and constructive element in the whole capitalist society, who in a period of rapidly rising prices cannot help but get rich quick whether they wish it or desire it or not . . . By directing hatred against this class, therefore, the European Governments are carrying a step further the fatal process which the subtle mind of Lenin had consciously conceived. The profiteers are a consequence and not a cause of rising prices."

As for speculators, the most extraordinary feature of the Reichsmark's joyride was not any attack against it but quite the opposite, an incredible ("pathological," it was later called) willingness on the part of investors at home and abroad to take and hold the torrents of marks and give real value for them. Until 1922 and the very brink of the collapse, Germans and especially foreign investors were absorbing marks in huge quantities. Only the international reputation of the Reichsmark, the faith that an economic giant like Germany could not fail, made this possible. The storage factor caused by the investor's willingness to save marks kept the marks from being dumped immediately into the markets, and thereby for a long while held prices in check. The precise moment when the inflation turned upward toward the vertical climb was undoubtedly timed by no event but by the dawning psychological awareness of the German and foreign investor that Germany was not going to back its money. With that, the rush to get out of the mark was on. Like a dam bursting, the seas of marks flooded into the markets and drove prices beyond all bounds. The German government strove mightily to outflood the sea.

The balance of payments problem was similarly misinterpreted. It was true that Germany had one. More of its cheap money was going out than hard money was coming in, in spite of constantly rising exports and constantly falling imports. This payments deficit actually helped hold the inflation problem at bay, because it kept the pressure of Germany's cheapening Reichsmarks off its own markets and prices. The existence of the payments deficit was an accurate indicator that Germany, while sick, was not yet dying. The reversal of the payments deficit was a sure signal that the end was near. In the collapsing stages, Germany ran a huge payments surplus as all her worthless marks came home from abroad in search of something to buy. This reversal of the balance of payments toward surplus was therefore not an occasion for hope, but for deepest fear.

The chronic fall of the Reichsmark's foreign exchange rate against other world currencies was a striking phenomenon of the German inflation. At that time, unlike the era after World War II, there was a free and uncontrolled market in foreign exchange, and every nation's currency was free to rise or fall as sharply and as far as the forces of supply and demand in the marketplace might dictate. Under these circumstances, the German mark was almost always falling, and it almost always had a considerably lower foreign exchange value than its internal purchasing power within Germany. This merely meant that the foreign exchange rate was a much quicker and more sensitive indicator of the inflation of the mark than internal prices were. The undervaluation of the mark in foreign exchange as compared with internal prices had the effect of making German exports abnormally competitive. German exports increased and imports decreased continuously throughout the inflation. Other nations fitfully took steps to defend themselves from being flooded with cheap German exports. The effect of these unnaturally cheap exports on the German nation as a whole was simply to give away to other nations, without adequate return, a considerable portion of the fruits of the nation's effort. It has been estimated that Germany lost 10 billion gold marks, or 25 percent of a year's national product, on sales of underpriced exports in the inflation. The fall of the mark in foreign exchange preoccupied all the Germans, especially in view of Germany's dire need of foreign exchange to pay reparations. The Germans habitually said that the inflationary money issues could not be stopped until the mark stopped falling, but this of course was trying to stop the result before touching the cause.

The war's effects were unusually malignant forces in Germany after the war. First there was economic reconstruction, not as difficult a problem as after the ravages of World War II. After that came the reparations, something that the second war fortunately did not see repeated. The Treaty of Versailles and the demands made under it by the victorious allies, especially France, for reparations beclouded the entire postwar era. Lord Keynes in a famous 1920 polemic against the treaty proclaimed the insanity of the reparations policy. The allies' first firm bill for reparations, presented in May of 1921, amounted to the fantastic sum of 132 billion gold marks. This was about four times Germany's maximum annual national product and greater even than Germany's entire national wealth; it was like asking the United States in 1973 to pay more than *four trillion dollars* in gold over a period of years. There was much struggle over this preposterous demand during the succeeding year, until finally the French army occupied the German Ruhr in January of 1923 in an effort to enforce the demand. German passive resistance to the French occupation hampered Germany's economic machine for most of the remainder of 1923.

Germans liked to point to reparations jointly with the fall of the exchange as the cause of the inflation. Some outside observers also give credence to the proposition that the reparations demands drove down the foreign exchange and forced Germany to issue inflated money. But the fact is that Germany never paid in reparations anything like what the allies demanded. In the entire period from the end of the war until the end of the inflation, the Germans paid only a paltry 2.4 billion gold marks in reparations, which was about five percent of a year's national product and less than Germany later paid in a single year under the more benevolent Dawes Plan. Germany paid no reparations at all for more than a year from September 1922 to the end, while the inflation was at its worst. Foreigners actually lost six or seven times more on the billions of worthless marks they acquired than Germany paid in reparations, so that Germany had a goodly net profit from foreigners as a whole in the inflation. Germany unquestionably could have paid the trivial amount of its actual reparations without destroying its money. If reparations were any cause of inflation, they were perhaps a psychological but not an economic cause. Germans' resentment against the reparations may explain why they lacked the will, though not the power, to keep their money hard and pay their debts out of sacrifices. Germans may subconsciously have felt they had to bring their economy to utter collapse, irrelevant as that was, in order to dramatize their claim of inability to meet the allies' preposterous demands; if so, the economic slaughter of the innocents in Germany was a high price to pay for dramatization.

The upward spiral of wages and prices in pursuit of one another is another convenient scapegoat which the government seems to blame in every inflation, and the German inflation was no exception. Karl Helfferich, who as we shall see was the one man probably most responsible for the German inflation, best summarized the government's professions of helplessness before the wage-price spiral, even while freely admitting that stopping the money creation would automatically have stopped the inflation. His apologia will ring strangely familiar to anyone who has ever listened to any government explaining away any inflation:

> "But claims were put forward and effectively pressed to raise the standard of comfort and at the same time to reduce the intensity of labour. This could have but one result—a race between wages and prices such as we have witnessed in the last few years. The social and political position of labour was sufficiently strong to enforce higher wages notwithstanding the fact that less work was done. As the profits of capital had shrunk to a minimum, the higher wages could be paid only if higher prices were obtained for the products. But higher prices raised the cost of living and brought about fresh demands for higher wages, which in turn led to a further rise in prices. And what was the part played by money in this vicious circle? The

The Roots

race between wages and prices gave rise to a corresponding increase in the demand for money, both on the part of the people and on that of the financial administration of the State. *A monetary organisation which offered resistance to such an expansion of monetary demand would thereby have put a stop to the race between prices and wages. The acute shortage of money would have brought about a collapse of wages and prices, probably accompanied by crises and catastrophes.* The German monetary system, however, makes possible in practice an unlimited expansion of the circulation, and it offered no such resistance. The monetary machine and its working, therefore, aided in the development pursued by wages and prices, but only in a secondary and passive manner. The increase in the issue of paper money is, within this complex of phenomena, not the cause but the consequence of rising prices and wages. At the same time, *the fact that it was possible for paper money to be issued in unlimited quantities provided the necessary condition for unlimited increases in prices and wages."* (Italics added)

The government, confidently convinced of its claim that the inflation was being forced on it by external forces beyond its control, tried the usual array of palliatives to stanch the hemorrhages, such as import and export controls, exchange controls, and price controls. As always, these measures found no success. They did achieve some rather strange distortions within the economy. Rent control was a conspicuous example. Rent control was effective enough so that the real cost of housing virtually disappeared from German budgets, the property of landlords was *de facto* confiscated for the benefit of tenants, and the housing shortage predictably became extreme.

The government appealed to voluntary restraint and even to patriotism when the flight from the mark assumed the proportions of a panic. It characterized as practically traitorous those little citizens who, long after the smart money and far too late to save much, finally repented of their faith in the government and joined the stampede to get out of the mark.

The government also tried one or two measures which did work but could not be continued. One was to stop the money and credit. This was done in late 1921, and the mark began to harden instantly. But the resulting credit squeeze began to strangle the boom equally fast, and business screamed. The plain fact was that the boom could not live without the inflation, and the fearful pains of withdrawal from the inflation did not then appear necessary or inevitable. Easy money resumed and accelerated and never stopped again until the bitter end.

The government tried supporting the mark with the Reichsbank's gold reserve early in 1923. This too worked magically while it lasted, but as long as the government continued to pump out new money with the other hand it merely lost its gold. That likewise quickly came to an end.

5
The Great Prosperity of 1920–1921

It is impossible to overemphasize the importance to Germany's collapse of the period from about March of 1920 to the end of 1921, in which Germany was feeling quite healthy and prosperous while the rest of the world was enduring a severe recession. Prices in Germany were steady, and both business and the stock market were booming. The exchange rate of the mark against the dollar and other currencies actually rose for a time, and the mark was momentarily the strongest currency in the world. From the first moment of this prosperity, however, Germany had already embarked on a new monetary inflation which bought the boom. Germany's fate was thus already chosen at the moment when the boom began, and it was gradually sealed as the boom progressed.

The route to Germany's inflationary destiny may be traced out in the epic conflict between two men, Karl Helfferich and Matthias Erzberger. Helfferich must be identified as the chief architect of Germany's economic disaster. He was minister of finance and vice-chancellor during the war, and he was directly responsible for the war policy of not paying for the war but rather saving up the cost to be collected from Germany's defeated enemies. He also had great personal influence in later administrations that failed to deal with the inflation. Helfferich was neither a fool nor a political hack. To the contrary, he was a brilliant monetary theorist whose stature was compared, with some validity, to that of Lord Keynes. His ponderous treatise on money, *Das Geld,* translated, was still in print in the United States as late as 1973, and a reading of his book is convincing proof of Helfferich's intellectual capabilities. Ironically enough, after contributing the most to the destruction of the mark, Helfferich also made the principal theoretical contributions to the formation of the miraculous Rentenmark plan which ended the inflation. As his book demonstrates, Helfferich knew perfectly well the relationship between money creation and price inflation; but, he said in substance, under the circumstances in Germany nothing could be done about it. Germany had to create money because Germany needed money. Helfferich's abysmal failure in the German inflation represented more than anything else a tragedy of pure intellect, for he was constantly resorting to the most finely-reasoned theorization for answers that ignored simple observation of the facts. Helfferich illustrates the dangers of allowing pure intellect to rule practical government policy. Helfferich was described as cold, arrogant, pharisaical, moralistic, and intolerant, and he had the most supreme disdain for the mere politicians with whom he had to deal in the government. Helfferich also was a scion of the archreactionary Nationalist party which had been most warlike before and during the war, and was most irreconcilable to either democracy or cooperation with the victors after the war. The fatal sin of Helfferich and all the Nationalists was that they would not bow to anything, certainly not to mere reality; if their intransigence spelled the destruction of the Reichsmark and all the little Germans, so be it.

Matthias Erzberger was a bourgeois and a mere politician who sprang from the Catholic Center party. Like others (notably Gustav Stresemann) who later became the leading German moderates, he had been as enthusiastic an annexationist at the beginning of the war as the Nationalists. This merely reflected the monumental folly which infected all the belligerents, including France, Britain, and Russia along with Germany and Austria, all of whom marched gaily into that hell with hearts high and all flags flying. Men like Erzberger and Stresemann were capable of change, as others like Helfferich were not. Erzberger became a leader of the peace movement and a signatory of the Treaty of Versailles, for which reactionary Germany never forgave him. Erzberger was described as blunt, tactless, and impulsive. Erzberger and Helfferich were imbued with a mortal personal hatred of one another dating from long before the war.

Erzberger became minister of finance in June of 1919 in the first postwar government of Gustav Bauer. Erzberger confronted the German war debt of 153 billion marks, which was considerably greater than Germany's annual national product, and he resolved to try to make good on it. From then until early in 1920 he introduced a program of tax reforms and tremendously increased taxes, especially taxes on capital. Opposition from propertied interests was naturally enormous. Erzberger's principal opponents were Helfferich himself and Dr. Johannes Becker, a crony of Helfferich's who later as minister of economics was principally responsible for the miserable failure of the Cuno government to do anything effective about the collapsing inflation from 1922 through 1923.

Erzberger succeeded in forcing his taxes upon the nation, and as a result Germany's real tax yield in 1920 was the highest of any year from the beginning of the war to the end of the inflation. At the same time, the Reichsbank was induced to follow a tight money policy for an extended period in the latter part of 1919, the only time during the entire nine years in which the German money supply stopped rising for more than a month or so. Because of the skyrocketing price inflation during 1919, the money supply was increasing much less rapidly than prices throughout this time. By March of 1920, the enormous price increases of the preceding year had brought Germany's price level to about seventeen times the prices of 1914. As a result, the price level had increased by a factor roughly comparable to that of the money supply, and accordingly a temporary new equilibrium had been achieved and the inflation was stopped. For well over a year, the price inflation then remained stopped. The real burden of the war debt had been cut by five-sixths as a result of the price inflation of 1919. By the spring of 1920, therefore, Germany was in a position to build on a stabilized foundation.

Meanwhile, public verbal warfare between Erzberger and Helfferich rose to a crescendo. Erzberger quite accurately denounced Helfferich for being the man most responsible for the inflation and Germany's financial plight; he also quite accurately accused Germany's industrialists like Hugo Stinnes for being at the bottom of Germany's political inability to put financial matters to rights. Helfferich and the industrialists thundered back at Erzberger. Helfferich lured Erzberger into a libel suit against Helfferich. As usually happens in libel suits, it was quickly the plaintiff Erzberger who was on trial. The issues were mainly certain alleged improprieties and conflicts of interest in Erzberger's private dealings with businessmen while in office. On March 12, 1920, the court returned its judgment and said that Erzberger was guilty of some of the improprieties, imprudences, and carelessness that Helfferich had alleged, although without evident corruption or personal gain. Helfferich was also found to have libelled Erzberger and was levied a small fine, but he had won. Erzberger was ruined, and he immediately resigned from the government.

This very day of March 12, 1920, may be taken as Germany's turning point, for from this day her crusader for financial probity was gone. This was also the very month in which Germany's prices at last stopped rising, the very month in which Germany's inflation had finally been stabilized by the effective measures urged by Erzberger over the preceding year.

Prosperity of 1920–1921

This too was the month in which Germany's boom prosperity began, and it lasted for more than a year. Prices remained passive, the exchange value of the Reichsmark rose, and the German stock market in the same month of March began a long rise during which stock prices trebled before the crash of December 1921. Erzberger's exit, almost to the day, therefore marked the commencement of the great prosperity of 1920–1921 for which he had laid the foundation.

From the day the boom began, however, its end was already forming. The Reichsbank had already turned on the money pump again. That was what fueled the new boom. The German money supply doubled again during the era of steady prices. With Erzberger safely out of the way, taxes were reduced and deficits increased. By the summer of 1921, when price inflation at last began to rise again in pursuit of the money inflation, the die was assuredly cast.

As a postscript, we might record that the mere ruination of Erzberger did not complete reactionary Germany's retribution against him. An unsuccessful attempt to assassinate him had already been made during his trial. Something more than a year later, on August 26, 1921, as the inflationary end of the boom impended, Erzberger was successfully assassinated. The execution was administered by members of the terrorist gangs who multiplied among Helfferich's reactionary wing of Germany, although clearly Helfferich himself was not implicated in the murder plotting. The man Erzberger who had been intrepid or incautious enough to point a finger in the right direction was thus extinguished.

6
Politics

The political situation in Germany contributed greatly to its inability to deal with the inflation. Germany had suffered a Marxist insurrection before the end of the war which was not fully controlled until after bloody fighting in the early months of 1919. Even after that, governments were constantly forming and falling, extremist secret groups were busy, rebellions like the reactionary Kapp *Putsch* in 1920 were frequent, and the country remained in a state of perpetual political ferment.

Out of the war and to some degree the Marxist activity came enormously strengthened labor unions. A rash of liberal labor legislation such as the controversial eight-hour day was enacted. The unions raised wages and cut work. Employers liked to lay much of the blame for the inflation on this increase of labor's power, forgetting however that business and not labor profited the more from the inflation.

The Weimar republic's new constitution was a masterpiece of democratic theory, and in the best democratic tradition the government was hopelessly responsive to its sources of support.

A government so plainly a weathervane to the prevailing winds was ill suited to override the shortsighted self-interest of its power groups and deal sternly with hard realities. The chief supports of the republican government were the Social Democrats or SPD, who were the orthodox labor party, and the liberal intellectuals. Business and capital also had great influence through their economic strength. When the government tried to evolve adequate tax plans, labor blocked income or consumption taxes which would weigh upon workers, and business and property blocked taxes which would weigh upon capital. So, very simply, no one paid. The government's most incredible step of all was the tax reduction of 1920 in the midst of deficits, after the departure of Erzberger when the die for its fate was being cast.

The Social Democrats were the largest single party in Germany at all times, and for that reason if no other must bear some part of the responsibility for what happened politically. The republic's honored first president, Friedrich Ebert, was a Social Democrat, as were a few of its chancellors. The Social Democrats were undeniably a stalwart and steadfast party, indeed the unflinching backbone of Germany after the war. The Social Democrats spoke for the overwhelming majority of the German workers. It lies to the credit of the steadfastness of the German workers that the Marxist turmoil utterly failed after the war; the actual murders of the Marxist leaders, Rosa Luxemberg and Karl Liebknecht, though often compared with the Russian Mensheviks' failure to dispose of Lenin in similar circumstances, were quite superfluous because the German workers through the Social Democratic party had already shown that they wanted no part of Marxism. Later on, the Social Democrats were an unimaginative and sometimes block-headed party and furnished comparatively few important leaders in relation to their size. Their worst failing was a dim-sighted obstinacy against infringing on any of the newly won privileges of labor; as a result, they obstructed bold cures for Germany's ills, but they also were not actively responsible for the most harmful of Germany's policies. Occasionally, though rarely, they rose above themselves to support the sound policies of an enlightened leader from some other party, such as Stresemann, and this in the end made it possible for Germany to save itself.

Most of the political wisdom that was shown in Germany of the inflation came from individuals of the several middle-class parties, each of whom had relatively small political backing of his own. Erzberger, of the Center Party, was an example. Gustav Stresemann was pre-eminently an example; his People's party was generally far more rightist than he was, and included even such leading reactionaries as Hugo Stinnes and Johannes Becker. Any of these good leaders, in order to act, had to piece together a coalition ranging from the Social Democrats all the way to the semi-reactionary parties like the People's, stopping short only of the Communists on the left and the Nationalists and Nazis on the right.

By all odds the principal blame for the inflation must rest with the right-wing parties and with the industrialists and propertied interests who backed them. Helfferich of the Nationalists laid the groundwork with his mismanagement during the war. Magnates like Hugo Stinnes and Fritz Thyssen and the entire voice of big business obstructed every effective effort to put a stop to the inflation, because very simply the inflation was good business for them. When Germany at last turned to the prominent industrialist Wilhelm Cuno in November 1922, in the hope of finding succor in a government of businesslike soundness, his impotent administration from then until August 1923, with the inimitable Johannes Becker in charge of economics, presided inertly over the worst months of the inflation.

Even in November of 1923, the last ditch for the German nation, political paralysis was so pervasive that chancellor Stresemann's only way to shortcut the interminable parliamentary deliberation, which had brought Germany to this pass, and institute the miraculous Rentenmark, was to assume dictatorial power to rule by decree under the emergency provisions of the Weimar constitution. These same extraordinary powers under

Politics

the constitution were later accused of facilitating Hitler's usurpation of absolute power, which they did. Indeed, Stresemann's sweeping enabling act of October 1923 was strikingly similar to Hitler's infamous act of March 1933. Only Stresemann's wise and brief use of the Weimar powers in 1923, however, saved Germany from an immediate choice between Hitler and Communism. For his pains, Stresemann was turned out of office as chancellor less than ten days after the inflation had been finally halted by the Rentenmark, and scarcely three months after he had taken over the office. Stresemann thereafter served brilliantly as foreign minister through most of the remaining years of the Weimar republic, but he never again was chancellor.

7
The Lessons

Throughout the inflation, the characteristic of the Reichsmark which was most vitally important and at the same time most securely hidden was the unrealized depreciation in its value. This was the difference between the relatively small decline in its effective value, which had already been realized through rising prices, and the much larger fall in its intrinsic value which was caused by pouring out ever-increasing numbers of marks as diminishing shares of the more or less constant total value of Germany. The unrealized depreciation of the mark was almost always present and almost always worsening, but it was difficult to detect and practically impossible to measure.

The phenomenon of the unrealized depreciation explained the spectacularly beneficial effects of the ripening stages of inflation, when new marks could be turned out much faster than their value could fall and could thereby create real wealth out of thin air. Unrealized and unsuspected depreciation also ac-

The Lessons

counted for the remarkable complacency of Germans, who were prone to think they were always more or less square with their past fiscal sins. If they escaped from the war extravagance with endurable price increases, and from the even greater extravagances of the 1920–1921 boom with practically no price increases, they were able to feel safe. They were understandably bewildered when the inflation then burst over their heads in an unforeseen enormity and for no apparent reason. The unrealized depreciation of the mark measured precisely its capacity for an explosive and self-sustained inflation which was no longer affected by what the government might do.

The capacity to absorb unrealized depreciation was a bit of patient leniency on the part of the respected Reichsmark. It was always possible that the unrealized depreciation might never be realized, if the growth in the real value of Germany had ever been allowed to make good the spurious value of the mark. Some degree of unrealized depreciation also could have been carried by the mark indefinitely. The exact degree is so uncertain that, as Dr. Schacht said, a government finance minister must feel the danger line with his fingertips. Any degree of unrealized depreciation was of course less safe than none, and once used was no longer available as a reserve against economic reverses. To go still further and exploit the mark to the very limit of its flash point was risky at best, especially when the government ministers were totally unaware that anything like Schacht's fingertip sensitivity was needed.

The government's practical ability to make good on the mark, as distinct from its theoretical ability, was undoubtedly limited. Once begun, the inflation required ever more inflationary expansion just to support the old debts. Germany had to run faster and faster to stay ahead of the engulfing wave, until it simply could not run any faster. Stopping the inflation would have killed the boom, and that seemed excessively unpleasant. In this respect, peacetime inflation was far more insidious than wartime inflation, which produced only war goods to be expended and no boom for the people to become addicted to.

Hugo Stinnes in a much-noted speech declared that it was madness to think that a defeated Germany with all its huge burdens could spend more, have more, work less, carry an ascending prosperity, and do it all with mirrors. But Germany seemed quite willing to try.

It was theoretically possible for Germany to extricate itself at virtually any time it chose. If any of the inflated mark wealth was to be salvaged in the process, Lord Keynes and Dr. Schacht, two wizards of the black art of economics, both happened to agree that the way to do it was to stop the money and debt and to close the gaps with capital taxes designed to soak up some of the excess supplies of money. This incidentally was what Erzberger tried to do in a crude way. Capital taxes made sense, because the brimming coffers of capital were where the profits of the inflation gravitated; wage and salary earners were already laboring heavily under the inflation and had no more capacity to pay taxes. An impartial tax on all capital would clearly have been less destructive than the totally confiscatory tax which eventually fell on one part of capital—the savers and lenders. In any case, neither this nor any other means of dismounting from the inflationary wave was ever resolutely tried.

Though it was always possible to dismount, it was never possible to dismount painlessly. Every day that passed, appeasing the inflationary dragon with more inflation, increased the assured severity of the inevitable medicine. So long as the Siren-like lure of the easy wealth continued, it was impossible to persuade enough of the nation that titanic measures of austerity and self-denial were necessary. When the Siren's song stopped, the crash had already begun and it was too late.

In final analysis, there is more difference of expert opinion than one might expect about whether the inflation was good or bad. Its horrors while it lasted and the permanent harm to millions of individuals which it left in its wake might appear to speak for themselves. From a transoceanic distance, detached economists like the American Professor Frank Graham were able to weigh up the pluses and minuses and discover the cold-

The Lessons

blooded conclusion that the inflation may actually have been a good thing for Germany as a whole from a strictly material standpoint. Germany as a whole suffered no net loss in the inflation; no real wealth was destroyed; the economic machine was still intact, ready to go again rather quickly; for every loser there was a gainer. The great middle class and all the savers and lenders who lost all their wealth merely saw it transferred to debtors and to the government for the rest of the people, not destroyed. Production increased, employment increased. Conceivably the inflation may have helped Germany recover from the war and come out from under its load of liabilities more lightly than it could have done in other ways. It may even have been a net gain to the productivity of Germany in a material sense to wipe out all the pensioners and herd them back into the labor force, as Professor Graham notes. If so, the Germans who lost might be excused for finding no comfort in knowing all of this.

In the end, Germany perhaps did not get off altogether so lightly from the inflation, nor did the world. The later agony of Germany and the world, personified in Hitler, was deeply rooted in the inflationary crash. It was no mere coincidence that Hitler's first *Putsch* occurred in the last and worst month of the inflation, and that he was in total eclipse later when economic conditions in Germany improved. When still another economic crash struck Germany in the 1930's, Hitler rode into power not by coup but by election. His most solid supports at that later date were an implacable middle class, the same who had paid the piper for all of Germany in 1923 and who suffered grievously again when the Depression came. Middle class parties which had polled twelve million votes in 1920 had virtually disappeared into the Nazi column in 1932, and Hitler required only a plurality of fourteen million votes in that year to win. Writing in his generally astute analysis of the German inflation in 1930, barely two years before the onset of the Hitler nightmare, Professor Graham was able to make this marvel of miscalculation of the psychological scars of the inflation:

"With all these reservations taken into account, however, it cannot but be asserted that, considering only the material aspects of the matter, the Germans, *as a nation*, profited rather than lost through the collapse of their currency. *The adverse effects on the national psychology were no doubt of import, but they cannot be measured, and these effects will perhaps more quickly disappear than is ordinarily supposed.*" (Italics added)

It is of course impossible to prove just how much the millions of decisions by individual Germans to vote for a stronger government in the Hitler election of 1932 were influenced by lingering bitterness against the inflation's injustice. What is clear is that the inflation was less than ten years past, which is a short memory span for an extreme injustice compounded by even more recent woes. Misgoverning the country perpetually at the expense of its quietest and steadiest class cannot be disregarded as possibly the best explanation why the plurality of Germans at last turned to Hitler. The wages of economic charlatanry proved to be rather high and not merely economic.

ACT ONE

The Rise of the Great American Inflation

8
The War

For the time being, forget completely one obvious and important fact about the American inflation. That fact is that the American dollar lost only about 70 percent of its value from 1939 to 1973. Prices were not quite 3.5 times as high at the end of that time as at the beginning. In thirty-four years, that was a smaller loss than the Reichsmark suffered in a single year after the inflation steamroller began to roll, or in just two or three average days as the inflation approached its final crash. By comparison, a loss of only 70 percent of value in three decades was not too bad. The American inflation was therefore obviously much different from the German inflation. For now, forget that. Postpone until the end of the book deciding whether they were so fundamentally different that nothing could be learned from the German inflation. It is not necessary to decide now, and deciding now will only cloud your judgment.

The United States inflation welled up from much the same sort of original fountainhead as the German inflation, namely a war. In 1939 the preparations for World War II were already beginning, and the American economic experience of that war when it came was a standard wartime experience. As with the German experience of the first war, three aspects characterize it: accumulating war debt, money expansion, and comparatively mild price inflation.

In the seven years' titanic struggle of the second war, the Federal debt of the United States increased to the level of $269 billion, which was about one-fourth greater than the annual gross product of the nation at the time. The gross product of the nation had itself increased by about half from its prewar level. Monetary expansion in the same seven years was even more startling. The American money supply grew by 3.5 times before it topped out in 1947. The performance of prices during the war, on the other hand, was remarkably docile. In June of 1946, when the war had been over for almost a year, prices had increased by less than half from the beginning of 1939. For a seven-year period embracing the greatest war effort in history, that was fairly good. It was also fairly typical of big wars. German price inflation during actual hostilities in World War I had been almost equally mild.

There are several probable explanations for these low rates of price inflation during actual warfare. One is price controls; the United States had a rigorous and comprehensive system of price controls during World War II. Another is the absorption of money into the financing of war debt itself, rather than the purchase of goods. Still another is the tendency of people during big wars to hold money for safety's sake rather than to spend it on anything. This causes what is known as abnormally low money velocity, and it reduces the pressure on prices.

By war's end, however, a much larger inflation was already built and ready, waiting to happen. The latent depreciation of the dollar was much greater than the actual depreciation had yet been. Monetary expansion during the war had already established an equilibrium price level much higher than the actual level that prices had yet reached. As it turned out, the real value of the dollar was something like two-thirds of its apparent

The War

value at the end of the war. It was an absolute certainty that prices would proceed quickly upward toward the higher equilibrium as soon as the controls were released, even if the government did no more inflating. Under the circumstances, there was nothing for the government properly to do but to stop inflating, release the controls, let the inflation happen, and wait. To its great credit, that is exactly what the government did do. The inflation burst out, ran its course and, at the preordained level, stopped.

The government's excellent management after the war seems to have been more inadvertent than deliberate. It is truer to say that price controls fell apart than that they were removed. The Democratic administration fought manfully against removal of the controls they so dearly loved. Harry S. Truman, who was president at the time, pleaded with Congress to extend price controls for at least another year after June 30, 1946. Congress was bent on putting an end to the controls, however, and sent him a bill so weak that he vetoed it. In the single month of July, before another bill could be readied, wholesale prices rose by more than ten percent. Eventually another bill did provide for temporary continuation of controls, but they proved unworkable and finally broke down before the end of 1946. In the two years following the breach of the price control dam, prices increased by about as much as they had done during the entire war, although the government added no new debt or money. In the end, prices were twice as high as they had been in 1939, and at that level they stabilized.

The explosive growth of the money supply during the war began to decelerate as soon as hostilities ended. For two full years while prices galloped upward, the money supply increased by less than prices did. As long as this condition obtained, the nation could confidently wait for the result. In due time the inflation would stop and did stop. For three full years from 1947 to 1950, the money supply remained essentially static. This was the longest period of monetary stability in the United States after 1928. Prices too were steady as long as this condition prevailed. The nation underwent a recession in 1949 as a result of the monetary stringency, but fortunately the unfilled desires of the nation for civilian goods bolstered business reasonably well while the anti-inflation medicine was being taken.

President Truman's administration displayed little understanding of what was happening or of its own good management. In his June 1946 veto message pleading for stronger price controls for another year, President Truman was able to say unabashedly, "For the last five years we have proved that inflation can be prevented [by controls]." This of course was wholly wrong. At that point, the big inflation to come had already been built. Nothing that the government did after the war was responsible for the price inflation of the next two years, and nothing that the government could have done could permanently prevent it from happening.

By November of 1947, after a year's severe inflation, President Truman was back again with a panicky plea to a joint session of Congress for the whole array of new price controls, rent controls, credit controls, and rationing. Reviewing the disheartening course of the inflation since the preceding year, he asked querulously, "Where will it end?" Thanks to balanced budgets and the continued quiescence of the money supply, the inflation was in fact already within a few months of ending. Congress had become Republican in the previous autumn's elections and gave the president substantially none of his controls. The inflation nevertheless ended within a few months in early 1948, right on schedule.

The Federal Reserve System, which like the Reichsbank in Germany was the guardian of the money supply, seems to have been as uncomprehending as the Truman administration was. In 1947, it too was calling for new powers and controls. The remarkable stability of the money supply throughout these years occurred without the conscious volition of the Federal Reserve. In other words, it was pure luck. In those days, the monetary policy of the Federal Reserve was dominated by its duty to control interest rates on government obligations. If interest rates

The War

tended to rise, the Federal Reserve issued money to stop their rising, but not otherwise. It happened that interest rates did not tend to rise during the postwar years, partly because of budget surpluses and partly because of general fears of depression, and for this totally fortuitous reason the money supply remained steady and the price inflation was allowed to end.

The American experience of World War II had some similarities to Germany's of the previous war, and some differences. The war debt burdens were quite comparable in the two cases. The American war debt of $269 billion was about a quarter more than the annual national product; the German war debt of 153 billion marks was about a half more than the annual national product. Where Germany's performance was dismally worse was in its inflation of its money supply by 25 times, compared with the American monetary inflation of only 3.5 times. Germany's price inflation after the war was just that much worse than America's was. Germany's prices were multiplied by seventeen times by the time they stabilized; America's, by only two times. The ratios of price increase to money increase were virtually identical in the two cases, prices having increased by about 60 percent as much as money supply, even though the magnitudes of expansion of both kinds in the two cases were radically different.

The much more extreme price inflation in Germany had the perverse effect of leaving Germany somewhat better off after the war with respect to its war debt. As Lord Keynes observed at the time, nations are subject to a practical limit of how much debt their taxpayers will bear. Any nation's debt which exceeds the limit must somehow reduce the debt to come within the limit. The only three ways to reduce the debt are to repudiate it, to assess capital levies and pay it, or to inflate and dilute it. Inflation is the way which is invariably used. Germany's postwar inflation was so acute that the real burden of its 153 billion marks of war debt was cut by five-sixths to a mere 25 or 30 percent of its annual product. Even with the continuous addition of new government debt during the ensuing boom, the real value of Germany's national debt never again rose above about 40 percent of annual product.

By contrast, the postwar inflation of the United States was so much less acute that the value of its war debt was still fully 90 percent of annual product in 1950. As late as 1968, more than twenty years after the war, the war debt of the United States was still worth 30 percent of annual product, a level which Germany had reduced to within two years. Total Federal debt of the United States in 1968 approximated the 40 percent figure which appeared to be Germany's practical maximum.

The United States and Germany thus each reached a point of stability after the respective wars at which their wartime inflations had been effectively liquidated. The burdens of their past conduct were reduced to manageable proportions, and they could move in any direction they chose. The inadvertent success of the government in the United States compared with the good work of Matthias Erzberger in Germany. Germany's inflation was enough worse so that Germany was better off, but Germany also had many other problems like reconstruction, revolution, and reparation which the United States did not have. Germany's stability was therefore more frail and transitory.

The economic experience of the United States was a standard wartime experience; it was not the only way a war could be financed, but it was the way virtually all wars are financed. After the war, the economic system, the currency, and above all the enormous Federal debt and corresponding paper wealth of the United States were intact. This was fortunate in one way, unfortunate in another. A nation is in a stronger position to rebuild its life on a healthy base if all the overblown old money and credits have been written off, although this is hard on those who lose their values. A quick and clean inflation, which destroys paper wealth like an amputation, is often less vicious than a suppressed and protracted inflation. But bankruptcy reorganizations like this are what happen to losers of wars, not to winners.

9
Grappling with Stability

The United States became embroiled in another smaller war in Korea in 1950. This was a minor war by any standard and especially by comparison with World War II. The Federal budget did not even run a deficit fighting the Korean War. Nevertheless, the wartime inflation which need never occur was allowed to occur again. From the end of 1949 until the end of 1953, when stability was regained, the American money supply was permitted to expand by 16 percent. Prices dutifully increased likewise by about 13 percent.

The Korean War inflation was a most unusual sort of inflation. From the day in June 1950 when the North Koreans attacked the South Koreans to start the war, wholesale prices in the United States ascended smartly. Buyers and sellers, with the memory of World War II and its controls and inflation fresh in their minds, were quick to raise prices jointly. Within a mere eight months wholesale prices had risen 18.6 percent above 1949, while the money supply had not yet expanded by a third as much. This inflation was a psychological one, not a monetary one. The equilibrium level of prices was actually lower than actual prices were, so that there was an unrealized *appreciation* of the dollar. If the government had done nothing more, the trend of prices would have had to be constantly downward. The psychological expectations of inflation would have been disappointed, and prices would have subsided to near their original levels.

The trend of prices was in fact downward from the initial peak, but the government meanwhile inflated the money supply to catch up with the prices. This money expansion validated the price inflation and made good on the expectations. The effect was to stabilize prices at the higher level rather than to let them fall back. The administration, still Democratic under President Truman, also joyfully clapped on price controls again, but they were superfluous and accomplished nothing good or bad. Since there was no ready-built inflation, no unrealized depreciation of the dollar, literally nothing happened to prices when President Eisenhower unceremoniously terminated the controls a month after his inauguration.

The Federal Reserve's management of the money supply in this Korean phase was again rather insensitive, and luck was not so good as during the three years before the war. At the commencement of the war interest rates rose steeply for much the same reasons that prices did—psychological reasons—and this meant automatically that the Federal Reserve must inflate the money supply according to its duty to support the prices of government bonds. The resulting rate of money inflation was much less fast than that of prices, but it was nevertheless substantial. In short order, the Federal Reserve and the Treasury were forced to reach their momentous Accord of 1951, which relieved the Federal Reserve of the formal duty to support government bond prices. The Federal Reserve's inflation of the money supply did not quickly end, indeed it continued largely unabated for two more years, but at least one irrelevant criterion was theoretically removed from its policy making.

The month following the Accord of 1951 also brought to

Grappling with Stability

the Federal Reserve a new chairman, William McChesney Martin, who remained its helmsman and its spiritual patriarch for nineteen years through both the prickly stability of President Eisenhower and the orgiastic inflation of Presidents Kennedy and Johnson.

A change of political command now occurred. Dwight D. Eisenhower, formerly supreme commander of all the allied armed forces in Europe in World War II, won the presidential election in November of 1952. He was a Republican and his administration leaned toward conservative business principles, but the change from the Democrats of President Truman was not so great in the realm of economic management as might be supposed. The Truman administration, for example, had had no net budget deficit for its total span of years, leaving aside the fiscal year 1946 which wound up the big war expenditure. President Eisenhower was not quite as successful as President Truman in maintaining budget balance, mainly because of deficits incurred in fighting the recession of 1958, but his efforts were similar. President Eisenhower's financial administration picked up where President Truman had been forced to leave off at the outbreak of the Korean War, confronting problems of stability and prosperity which President Truman had then only begun to face.

The years of President Eisenhower were the least inflationary of any period of similar length in the United States since 1914. The money supply averaged an increase of only a bit over 1 percent per year, and prices did about the same. This policy persisted after President Eisenhower left office, so that the monetary stability embraced the nine years from 1953 to 1962. One of the results was an extraordinary period of seven years (1958 through 1964) in which wholesale prices never varied by as much as 1 percent above or below their mean.

The years of the Eisenhower administration and after were not years of uniform stability, however, nor of uniformly satisfactory prosperity. The same nine years of average stability saw serious and recurrent recessions. From the time when President

Eisenhower took office at the beginning of 1953, the nation's economic condition passed through a series of gradually worsening monetary oscillations, every one of them followed by alternating boom and recession. The government first tried a noninflationary money growth of less than 1 percent per year in 1953 and 1954. That was too tight and produced a recession. The government obligingly next tried a more liberal money expansion of 3.9 percent per year from 1954 through 1956, which produced a very pleasant boom followed by an inflation. After that the government expanded and contracted money with increasing vigor and on a shorter and shorter cycle; it contracted in 1957, inflated in 1958–59, contracted in 1959–60, inflated again in 1961, and contracted again in 1962. Every burst of monetary inflation was followed by a stock market rise and a boom prosperity; every contraction, by a stock market fall and a recession. Whenever the expansions and contractions were allowed to persist long enough, they were followed eventually by price inflation or stabilization, respectively. But prices were always slowest to follow, so that they stopped responding to the shorter cycles and remained steady after 1958. Stock market boom and bust, prosperity and recession, employment and unemployment, being more sensitive, never failed to follow the monetary lead. A recession and rising unemployment in late 1960, following the monetary contraction which had ended some months earlier, helped defeat Richard Nixon, Republican successor to President Eisenhower, in the presidential election of November 1960. At the time, a monetary expansion was already well under way, but the usual economic upturn did not develop until early the next year.

The Eisenhower years thus showed an average line of overall stability in both money and prices, but this stable line represented a median between fairly sharp swings upward and downward. These years also showed no more than partial success at grappling with the problems of stability. The booms were fairly good times, but no better than they ought to be. The recessions were worse than they should be. Price inflation followed mone-

Grappling with Stability

tary expansion and prosperity like a somewhat distant shadow, and the government consistently failed to maintain a reasonably satisfactory level of prosperity with a monetary policy tight enough to prevent inflation. The 3.9 percent rate of money growth of 1954 to 1956 which started it all, although low by standards of the next decade, was nevertheless enough to start the inflation of 1956 and therefore was obviously not tight enough. On the other hand, the monetary non-growth of 1953 and 1954 was enough to produce the recession of 1954 and therefore was obviously too tight. There seemed to be no golden mean between the two kinds of policy, which were themselves not at all extreme.

The Eisenhower administration was a time of mixed returns. Critics called it a time of stagnation. Champions called it a time of stability and a leaking off of inflationary pressures. Undoubtedly there was room for improvement at its close. A simple continuation of the policies of the Eisenhower administration into later years, as might possibly have followed if Richard Nixon had been elected in 1960, would not have been the very best possible course for the nation, but even that course would have been infinitely preferable to what actually did occur. The United States had consolidated its economic base and was stronger than at any time before or since, ready to move in any promising direction that a shrewd leader might have chosen.

10
The Great Prosperity of 1962–1968

The year 1960 marked the continental divide in the postwar economic history of the United States. If there turns out to have been a day of decision that corresponded to the fall of Matthias Erzberger in Germany on March 12, 1920, it must surely be November 8, 1960, which was the Election Day on which former senator John F. Kennedy was elected president of the United States. In both cases these days of judgment occurred even before the great booms of the two countries began.

John Kennedy was a Democrat who owed his extremely narrow victory in the election to economic problems of the previous administration. He was a very young man as presidents go, and he was vigorous and active as young men go. He gained office on the famous vow to "get the country moving again." He was a wealthy young heir who had neither compiled wealth of his own nor ever done any productive work, but had spent virtually his entire adult life serving in one or the other house of Congress. His own intellectual credentials were indifferent at best, in spite of a Harvard education, but he had an extraordinary weakness for intellectuals. He surrounded himself with academic theorists as advisers, especially economists, and he submitted to their guidance as no political government had submitted before. So armed, he addressed himself to getting the country moving again. And the prescription that his doctors ordered was two-hundred-proof inflation.

The band of academic economists who accompanied President Kennedy into power represented the final accession to the wheelhouse of what was commonly called the "New Economics." These economics had been germinating in the universities ever since the publication in 1936 of John Maynard Keynes' *General Theory*. They thus constituted Keynesian economics to a degree, but they transcended anything that Keynes himself had ever written. In brief and in part, they stood for a thriving economy and full employment to be achieved by actively sought government deficits, plentiful new money and credit at low interest rates, liberal government spending, and extreme emphasis on capital investment. The United States had made a polite gesture toward Lord Keynes by abstractly embracing the full employment principle in the Employment Act of 1946, but neither the Truman administration of that time nor the Eisenhower administration bore the faintest resemblance to the New Economics. The professors of the New Economics were left to simmer in their cloisters and to await their day. Their day came after the inauguration of President Kennedy in 1961.

The man who was chosen to serve as economic mastermind to the Kennedy administration was Walter W. Heller, an economics professor from Minnesota who became chairman of the Council of Economic Advisers. In fairness to President Kennedy, it has been observed that he did not respond with alacrity to the advice of his economic confessors, but it took Mr. Heller nearly two years to "educate" his somewhat backward pupil, the president. In fairness to Mr. Heller, it has also been observed that five out of any six American economists chosen at random would have advocated the same policies that he and his fellow advisers did. The American inflation had no towering personal figure to shape it as Helfferich had done in Germany; Professor Heller was but a spokesman for virtually the entire economic priesthood which must bear the blame if any blame there be.

The Kennedy administration was slow to make itself felt economically. Fully a year and a half passed, from the beginning of the administration in 1961 through most of 1962, during which time essentially the Eisenhower economics persisted complete with monetary expansion and contraction, stock market rises and falls, and less than satisfactory employment. Partly this delay was due to the need for Professor Heller to educate the president in modern economics, and partly it was due to President Kennedy's preoccupation with non-economic matters such as his saber-rattling over the construction of the Berlin wall by East Germany, his involvement with the Bay of Pigs invasion of Cuba, and his showdown with Russia over the Cuban missile crisis.

The commencement of both the great inflation and the great boom can be traced to the month of October of 1962. In that month began an unremitting monetary expansion which extended, with only brief interruptions, through the next eleven years with no end coming into view. It was the longest and steepest monetary inflation in the United States since World War II, almost twice as fast as that of the 1956 boom, considerably faster than and three times as protracted as that of the Korean War. The monetary inflation proceeded at the rate of 4.6 percent per year for the first 43 months (through April 1966) and 7.2 percent per year for 27 months more (January 1967 through April 1969). The total money inflation over the seven years was about 38 percent. Up to 1969, the inflation was interrupted only by the nine-month period of no expansion in 1966, which was accompanied by stock market collapse and economic recession but precious little effect on price inflation. At the close of this time, monetary inflation was proceeding faster than ever.

The commencement of the inflation in October of 1962

happened to coincide with the enactment in that month of the Revenue Act of 1962, one of the first solid accomplishments of the New Economics under President Kennedy. The principal feature of that tax law was the unfortunate investment credit, a tax subsidy to business equal to 7 percent of expenditures on new capital assets such as machine tools, computers, office desks, and airplanes. The philosophy behind this law was the orthodox Keynesian fixation on business investment as the determinant of economic prosperity. Several months earlier, the Treasury Department had greatly liberalized tax depreciation allowances to the same end. These measures led to the exaggerated investment boom of the 1960's decade.

Already in 1962 the economic advisers were in pursuit of bigger game. The big tax cut in the midst of deficits in 1964 which was to be the star in the diadem of the New Economics was already in gestation in 1962 thanks to the unflagging efforts of Professor Heller and his associates. This tax cut was of course the blood brother to the inexplicable German tax cut amid deficits in 1920.

President Kennedy was assassinated in November of 1963. He was succeeded by his personally chosen vice-president, former senator Lyndon Johnson, a lifelong politician from Texas. Mr. Johnson was in turn re-elected by a landslide in the following year against the challenge of a Republican conservative, Senator Barry Goldwater. President Johnson, who had long been majority leader of the Senate, was a top sergeant type who knew well how to do what was demanded, but apparently not how to decide what to demand. Antithetical though he was to President Kennedy in virtually every way, he nevertheless changed nothing upon his succession except to outdo his predecessor. He retained the Kennedy crowd and pursued the Kennedy ideas, for lack of any better ideas of his own. One of the better virtues of President Kennedy's administration had been its very inability to accomplish its own objectives; one of President Johnson's more serious flaws, his unfortunate ability to accomplish what was better not accomplished.

A boom gathered steam from 1962 onward. There can be

no denying that there was apparent prosperity; the excellent year of 1956 paled beside it. The government succeeded in deliberately increasing its budget deficits to the vicinity of $7 billion per year, surmounting even the growing tax revenues which the boom yielded. The big tax cut, when it came in 1964, eased the increasingly difficult task of expanding the budget deficits. The stock market had been dutifully soaring ever since the commencement of the monetary inflation in 1962. The exultant New Economists proclaimed that they could "fine tune" the prosperity like a television set, a claim which they later learned to rue.

The big tax cut and the intentional deficits of the Kennedy and Johnson administrations received most of the economic attention, but the less noticed behavior of the Federal Reserve Board was even more remarkable. The Federal Reserve inflated obligingly throughout the boom and long after. This was a Federal Reserve in which no dramatic changes of personality had occurred, a Federal Reserve which was still under the chairmanship of the estimable William McC. Martin who had been closely associated with the far more restrictive Eisenhower economics. It is true that President Kennedy made menacing omens when Chairman Martin dared to speak as if the Federal Reserve would not underwrite the deficits, but the fact is that the Federal Reserve accommodated itself to the economics of the government in power. This it should and must do. There cannot be two or more captains steering a ship, no matter how dubious the judgment of the chosen captain may be.

Prices displayed considerable inertia during the first several years of the boom, but at last they began to stir. Slowly at first and then faster, they ascended. The abortive period of tight money imposed by the Federal Reserve in 1966 sought to stop the price inflation. It throttled the boom for the moment but had little success with prices. The rate of price inflation continued to gain speed, until by 1969 it was approximating the average rate of monetary inflation (5 percent) over the seven years of its life to that date. Even while rising smartly, however, prices lagged ever farther behind the cumulative level of the monetary inflation. Wholesale prices, for example, were still only 11 percent higher in April 1969 than at the stability level of September 1962, while money supply was 38 percent larger and increasing faster. As we shall see later, the difference between these two percentages represented the unrealized inflation and was of the utmost importance to every aspect of the inflation.

This is where the story of the great prosperity leaves off. There was much more to it than this, of course. In 1965 President Johnson precipitated the nation into deep involvement in another war, which had been gradually begun by President Kennedy, this one in Viet Nam which was a remote and unimportant part of Southeast Asia. The war, an exceedingly unpopular one, threatened to tear the fabric of American society to tatters with its protests, its demonstrations, and its riots. The deepening involvement in this war happened to coincide with the time when prices began to rise in response to the inflationary boom, and for this reason the war was widely blamed, though unjustly, for the inflation. In the presidential election of November 1968, President Johnson did not even dare to run again. Richard Nixon, who had just missed gaining power over a stable situation in 1960, had the extreme misfortune of being elected to inherit this shambles. The year 1968 ushered out the great prosperity of the decade, leaving the price of it still mostly unpaid.

11
The Inflationary Syndrome

The immense outpouring of inflated money by the American government from 1962 through 1968 did apparently have its intended effect, which was to produce prosperity. The Democratic government did succeed in getting the country going again, in a way. The gross national product increased by an astounding $360 billion, or 7 percent per year, compared with only 4.8 percent per year in the difficult Eisenhower years from 1955 to 1960. Unemployment constantly decreased. The stock market was almost constantly rising for more than six years. It was apparent prosperity such as the nation had seldom seen.

The immense outpouring of German Reichsmarks in 1920 and 1921 had apparently succeeded in procuring prosperity too. Money inflation of these magnitudes almost never fails to achieve dazzling prosperities of this order *in the beginning.* That is what inflation has been all about for lo these thousands of years. Given the extraordinarily solid base of stability which had been painstakingly laid in the United States by President Eisenhower, or in Germany by the reforms of Matthias Erzberger, any simpleton could have made a prosperity by the ancient and honored elixir of inflation without any bad effects to show for years to come. This is what the government did. The great American prosperity of the 1960's was built on nothing but the money inflation.

Clearly the managers of the American inflation succeeded far better than the Germans did. They inflated far less rapidly and in a more controlled manner, and by so doing they sustained the inflationary cycle much longer near its delightful peak. A few percentage points of money inflation produced almost as great a prosperity but allowed the inevitable retribution to be much longer postponed and initially much less violent. That does not alter the basically identical shapes of the inflationary cycles.

Everyone loves an early inflation. The effects at the beginning of an inflation are all good. There is steepened money expansion, rising government spending, increased government budget deficits, booming stock markets, and spectacular general prosperity, all in the midst of temporarily stable prices. Everyone benefits, and no one pays. That is the early part of the cycle. In the later inflation, on the other hand, the effects are all bad. The government may steadily increase the money inflation in order to stave off the later effects, but the later effects patiently wait. In the terminal inflation, there is faltering prosperity, tightness of money, falling stock markets, rising taxes, still larger government deficits, and still roaring money expansion, now accompanied by soaring prices and ineffectiveness of all traditional remedies. Everyone pays and no one benefits. That is the full cycle of every inflation. The United States by 1968 had not yet seen anything but the upslope of the cycle.

On closer examination, that awesome apparent prosperity up to 1968 that was to be dearly paid for in later years begins to look as fundamentally illusory as the German prosperity had proved to be. An 11 percent growth was necessary just to keep up with population, and another 16 percent just to keep up with prices. The actual growth considerably exceeded those requirements, but if inflation is too much money, inflationary prosperity was too much prosperity. No amount of prosperity is truly too much if it is firmly founded, of course, but inflationary prosperity is not. Inflationary prosperity is a balloon rising on hot air, quickly cooling. It rests on the creation of paper wealth faster than its value can fall. Some citizens stand in the way of large shares of the paper flows, and they benefit. Larger numbers of citizens do not benefit, but they do later pay.

There were something like 27 million production workers in the United States who were doing all the basic productive work of the nation. These were the production workers in farming, mining, construction, manufacturing, transportation, communications, and utilities. Their total numbers were almost exactly the same in 1968 as they had been in 1960. They were a steadily diminishing 13 percent of the population in 1968, and substantially less than half the total work force, but they still produced most of what the entire nation lived on. As had been true in Germany, the inflationary binge was someone else's party and not the workers'. The gains in real earnings secured by production workers in private industry during the inflationary boom can only be described as paltry. From 1960 to 1968, the average hourly earnings of production workers, discounted for price inflation, increased by only 1.9 percent per year. That was scarcely half of the apparent growth, 3.7 percent per year, of overall personal income per capita, also expressed in constant dollars. In other words, production workers received far less than their proportional share of the inflationary pie, and this was true of every major category of production workers including even those in the construction industry, where wage increases were thought to be notoriously excessive. By contrast, the real earnings of production workers throughout the decade of the 1950's, and even in the difficult Eisenhower years from 1955 to 1960, improved substantially faster than overall national income and faster even than they did in the later inflationary boom. Their real earnings increased an average of 3.1 percent per year from 1950 to 1960 and 2.0 percent per year from

1955 to 1960. The times were not apparently as lush, but their shares were that much better. All of these comparisons worsened still further after 1968. These are surely the most damning of all the statistics of the inflationary false prosperity. There is something deeply amiss about any inflationary boom like this one which excludes the nation's most numerous and useful class from any share in its spoils. In this respect most inflationary booms are alike, and the German and American inflations were quite similar.

Strangely enough, while workers did poorly in the inflationary boom, capitalists in the most fundamentally useful industries fared no better. Profit margins were lower in 1968, a boom year, than in 1960, a recession year, in many of the largest and most basic industries including agriculture, mining, transportation, communications, utilities, steel and primary metals, automobiles, chemicals, petroleum, paper, and others. Profit margins, like workers' earnings, grew still worse after 1968. The rates of price inflation in these kinds of industries had also been very modest up to 1968 and thereafter, compared with much faster rates of inflation elsewhere in the economy. For example, the weighted average price inflation from 1960 to 1968 was only about 6 percent in the basically productive half of the economy consisting of farming, mining, manufacturing, transportation, communications, and utilities, while it was 27 percent in the other half of the economy. There was obviously a connection between the inability of these industries to share in the price inflation and the inability of their workers and industrialists to share in the spoils of the boom.

If all the production workers fared worse in the inflationary prosperity, and the most important of the industrialists also fared worse, where then did all the rich fruits of the inflation go? It is an obvious question. The answer must be: into the coffers of the speculators, the conglomerators, the fringe activities, and the distributees of the government's largesse. It was all very much the same as it had been in Germany.

Stock market speculation, which adds nothing to the wealth

of any nation, is the inflationary activity preeminent, and it was the craze of America in the 1960's as it had been of Germany in 1921. A buoyantly rising stock market marks the opening stages of every monetary inflation. A sharply rising stock market proves to be an unfailing indicator of monetary inflation happening now, price inflation coming later, and a cheap boom probably occurring in the meantime. The stock market boom like the prosperity is founded on nothing but the inflation, and it collapses whenever the inflation stops either temporarily or permanently. American investment in the 1960's, with its instant fortunes, its swamping volumes of turnover, and its absurdly high prices for incredibly useless ventures, underwent a species of insanity that was quite typical of inflationary booms. In 1968, the last year of full bloom of the inflationary prosperity, the volume of trading on registered stock exchanges alone was $200 billion, or more than four times what it had been in 1960. The income of the securities industry increased from $1.2 billion to $4 billion. The exchanges were compelled by the overwhelming volume of trading to close for part of the week, as the German Bourse had done in 1921. Capital gains of individuals reached $36 billion, more than three times the levels prior to 1962, and more than the income generated by the entire American gas and electric utility industry and agricultural industry combined.

John Maynard Keynes leveled the classic broadside at the American penchant for stock market speculation, even in normal times:

"In one of the greatest investment markets in the world, namely, New York, the influence of speculation . . . is enormous. Even outside the field of finance, Americans are apt to be unduly interested in discovering what average opinion believes average opinion to be; and this national weakness finds its nemesis in the stock market . . .

". . . speculators may do no harm as bubbles on a steady stream of enterprise. But the position is serious when enterprise becomes the bubble on a whirlpool of speculation."

Inflationary Syndrome 75

Chronic inflation by the government, which came in the train of Keynes himself, enormously amplified the speculative bubble he criticized.

Stock market speculation had its customary companions, such as the conglomeration of industries. Germany had Hugo Stinnes and his kind, and America had its own well-known names among the conglomerators. In the peak year of 1968, conglomerate mergers sucked up enterprises having $11 billion of assets, ten times the conglomerate mergers of 1960. New investment in stock market issues went into "hot stocks," which were often marginal activities that had little or no productive justification for being. Productive industries changed their names pell-mell to names which described nothing, perhaps to conceal the embarrassing fact that they produced anything. The nation's keenest business minds devoted themselves to dealing and disdained production, as they had similarly done in Germany:

> ". . . production is abandoned in favor of mere business activity, and such production as is carried on is conducted by entrepreneurs of less average ability than were profits are possible only through skilful management."

The managerial genius of the nation was channeled into paper empire building, and the empire builders who contributed nothing of their own literally bought and sold the creators and managers of real-life businesses. There was this statement of the inflationary lunacy, which might well serve as an epitaph to the great American boom:

> "Up to now the idea was to make money only with goods or machinery or something else. But more people are realizing that there is a way to make money with money and save the trip in between."

Legions of Americans—investors, conglomerators, brokers, advisers, lawyers, accountants, analysts, clerks, programmers, bureaucrats, and so forth—served the business of making money with money and creating absolutely nothing even as a byproduct. By 1970, after just a little curtailment of the money inflation, the stock market had collapsed, conglomerates and new issues and hot stocks were a thing of the past, and all the legions that had been caught up in the frenzy were a sick lot indeed.

Another peculiarly inflationary obsession is capital investment. Capital investment means the building of new means of production, such as factories and machines. Capital investment is the heart and soul of capitalist industry, so that it cannot be said that capital investment adds nothing to the wealth of the nation. Nevertheless, capital investment too suffers from a diseased and useless overgrowth in an inflation. The German passion for plowing back inflated profits into producing more means of production was so acute that every observer of the German inflation dwelt on it. One said,

> "In the acutest phase of the inflation Germany offered the grotesque, and at the same time tragic, spectacle of a people which, rather than produce food, clothes, shoes and milk for its own babies, was exhausting its energies in the manufacture of machines or the building of factories."

After the German inflation was over, much of the new investment was found to be useless and was demolished.

In America, the capital investment boom was scarcely less pronounced. As it happened, the New Economics of the government had a special love for indiscriminate investment and provided an investment tax credit to help exaggerate a tendency that would have been strong even without help. More than ten percent of the apparent growth of the American national product from 1960 to 1968, or $37 billion, represented an increased rate of production of industrial and commercial buildings and producers' equipment. On the other hand, the construction of housing for the people underwent an absolute decline throughout the apparent prosperity. The real value of residential construction in constant dollars had actually moved downward ever since 1955. Busying itself with building superfluous factories and office buildings, America could not house itself. The

Inflationary Syndrome

phenomenon was the same in the briefer German experience. The true character of America's investment boom, valuable or valueless, could not be clearly seen until after the inflation was over. What was clear, however, was that capital investment *can be* valueless, bad capital investment is total waste, and the strong tendency of capital investment in an inflation is to be misdirected and to exceed all valid requirements.

Still another pronounced tendency of an inflationary boom is to channel its growth into fringe activities, which means activities that constitute the overhead of society and do not directly generate any well-being for its members. Germany had this tendency acutely, and the United States did too. Inflation's most prominent characteristic is feverish hyperactivity, and generally it is indiscriminate activity at forced draft for its own sake and without any considered connection to a useful purpose. Inflation has no tendency to stimulate productive activity most, but quite the opposite.

In the United States from 1960 to 1968, even while the total number of productive workers in all the fundamentally useful industries remained constant at 27 million, 12 million more workers found some other kind of new place on the national payroll. There were over a million more nonproduction workers in the productive industries; a million more in military service; 3.5 million more government employees; 2.7 million more employees in wholesale and retail trade; and 3.9 million more in banking, securities trading, financial services, and other miscellaneous services. Paperwork and office workers proliferated, as they did in Germany. The Xerox machine and the IBM machine, both paperwork machines, were the twin monuments of the decade. Bank buildings and office buildings were the most conspicuous form of construction. The office equipment industry was the most glamorous of industries. A prodigious $131 billion of the nation's apparent growth from 1960 to 1968, or 36 percent of it, was found merely in increased government expenditure. Another $42 billion was found in the increased cost of wholesale and retail distribution, which compares with the thriving growth of "middlemen" in the German inflation. Still another $41 billion of apparent growth was found in auxiliary activities like financial services. Not only did fringe activities like these show the largest growth and the most new jobs, but they also showed the most price inflation which meant that they were generally more lucrative than productive work. As previously noted, the average price inflation in this half of the economy was 27 percent while that in the other half was only 6 percent.

Very little of all this activity added anything to the wellbeing of the citizen-consumer if he did not hold a job in these activities. The conclusion is inescapable that very much of the frenzied economic activity of the American boom must have been for all practical purposes useless. Nonproductive fringe activities, like the overhead of a business, are all useful to a degree, but only to the very limited extent that they help to increase the output of the productive activities *by more than the cost of the overhead.* Fringe activities in an inflationary boom do not do that. In inflation, the first faculty that becomes anesthetized is the ability to weigh up real gain against real cost, and consequently the fringe activities blossom and become positively parasitic. Useless activity serves as well as any kind of activity to support those employed in it, and that is admittedly important, but even while securing for them their shares of the national pool of well-being the activity adds little or nothing to that pool. The fact of the inflation was not true unemployment but rather the millions upon millions of jobs of spurious employment. A spurious job was one that the system could quite well have eliminated altogether, paying its holder the same large amounts for not doing anything at all, and no one would have noticed the difference. It goes without saying that if the system did not continue paying these citizens for doing effectively nothing but paid them the same for reapplying their efforts toward something useful, the total lot of all Americans could have been vastly improved. Stated another way, this means that Americans very probably could have worked as

Inflationary Syndrome

much as a day less a week *with no loss of either real output or income,* if they had simply dispensed with all the useless work and reassigned the productive work among themselves.

Determination of what activity is useful and what is not is properly not a question of any one man's judgment. It is not properly a matter of the government's judgment when it decides to stimulate this activity and not to stimulate that, and it most certainly is not a matter of my judgment. Determining what activity is useful is a matter for the sole decision of the person who pays for it, *using his own purchasing power to do so.* Useful activity is that which would exist in a free market if there were no artificial stimulations or distortions. But the essence of inflation is distortion. The invariable habit of inflation is to stimulate nonproductive activities at the expense of productive ones, which means that inflation is invariably a subsidy by the productive citizens to the nonproductive ones.

To say that millions of nonproductive jobs in the inflation were useless is not to say that their holders were useless. Exactly the opposite is true. Many of these jobs were among the system's better-paid jobs, and their holders tended to be among the nation's better men. People are not at fault in doing useless work. They merely go where the rewards are, and the government's inflationary forces are what place the rewards. It is a tragic fact that millions of the nation's best people were led by the government's stimuli to invest their lives in pursuits that perhaps should not have existed, and which might well not exist whenever the government's inflation either ended or fell apart.

There was no way to measure accurately just how much useless activity and therefore spurious growth the inflation had generated. In view of all the magnitudes that have been examined in this chapter, however, it is not at all difficult to surmise that the nation's real growth in individual well-being during the early inflation from 1960 to 1968 might well have been closer to zero than to that huge apparent increase in the gross national product. The real improvement in the individual's lot might well have been quite similar to the paltry and dwindling 1.9 percent per year that the real earnings of production workers grew, which was worse than at any time since World War II. No one could say exactly. The unnerving quality of an inflation is that no one knows anything for sure—how much his money is overvalued, how much of his prosperity is illusory, how much of his work is useless and would not even exist in conditions of stability. All standards are lost.

In the same way that inflation overstimulated useless activity and dampened true production, inflation had a way of turning all values upside down and all principles inside out. The least useful activities were the most rewarding, and vice versa. Skilled workers were steadily less well compensated in relation to unskilled workers, and there was therefore a chronic and worsening shortage of skilled workers. In the midst of vast spurious employment and considerable outright unemployment, fewer and fewer people could be found to do the useful work, while there were always plenty of applicants for the useless places. Humble economic activities which were nice to have available in their day were simply too humble for the era of the big money and could no longer be carried on in America. Every man can think of his own examples. Useless activities took their place.

On the other hand, there were different kinds of activities, likewise unqualifiedly good in their natural state, which did not disappear but became so overstimulated and overgrown in the inflationary distortion as to become a diseased growth of another sort. Education and law were two good examples in the American inflation.

One must tread softly before finding anything so priceless as education to be useless in any manifestation; and one may find himself forced back on the impersonal rule that what is useful is that which exists without any artificial stimulation. After the exercise of all due caution, one finds the hypertrophy of American education in the inflation still glaringly real. The government had decided that if education was good, more education must be that much better. Expenditure on education increased twofold by $30 billion from 1960 to 1968. Employment in education increased by 1.7 million jobs. Higher education alone increased by $14.4 billion, and the percentage of students among the age brackets from 18 to 34 increased by two-thirds, representing 3.4 million more students. But education appeared to represent more activity and less learning than ever before. Education provided occupation for millions of man-years of effort for which the system had no other immediate use, not only of students, faculty and staff but even of construction workers who built the dormitories and classrooms, but that was about all the educational activity seemed to do. The government and the educational system encouraged every young American of every race and every intellectual endowment, or lack of it, to think that higher education was for him. As a result, the educational system found itself flooded with unqualified, uninterested, and disaffected students who demanded relevance from an institution that had always been luxuriously free from any obligation to be relevant; who were insulated by education from ever discovering what the real sources of social wealth were; and many of whom were progressively incapacitated by education from ever filling a productive place, thus becoming transformed by education into the excess baggage of society. To the two old kinds of education, which were *enabling* education and purely *enlightening* education, America added a third kind which was *disabling* education. In the end, the overpriced, overpaid, and overexpanded educational system found itself in deep financial trouble which was held at bay only by the government's constantly continuing inflation.

The hypertrophy of law was somewhat similar. No nobler creation ever sprang from the mind of man than the institution of law, but law is still a social overhead. It creates no wealth directly, although it does lubricate the cogwheels of the economic and social system that does create wealth. Beyond doing that, law can become useless and even a hindrance, and that is what it became in the American inflation. The proliferation of laws, legislation, regulation, litigation, and legal calculation exceeded any imaginable assaying of its worth. Complexity alone in law is pure waste, and every new development in American law increased its complexity and decreased its utility. General litigiousness abounded. New rights of legal action sprang into existence daily. Judges and legislators felt themselves deifically capable of rectifying all unhappiness with some kind of legal right of one person against another. No grievance was too absurd to be heard, but the principal effect of hearing each new one was to call forth a thousand more. Every person can choose his own favorite examples of puerile legal contention, among them these: prayers in schools, constitutional rights of clothing and haircuts in schools, rules of conduct in schools, busing in schools, nonbusing in schools, constitutional rights not to be disciplined, graded, judged or restrained from any act, sex discrimination, age discrimination, discrimination against the poor, discrimination against the incompetent, every other imaginable kind of discrimination, obscenity as free speech, evasion of the civic duties of military service, electoral redistricting, labor disputes, rent strikes, freeing criminals for abstract mistakes in procedure, tort liabilities far in excess of any injury that money could make good, securities law liabilities redistributing losses and winnings among the players in the casino, antitrust prohibitions against routinely innocuous business practices, general harassment of the industrial system that supported us all, and so on. The American legal world was a weird one. It gave occupation and amusement to the participants, but not much more. Going so far afield, perhaps it really sought to improve the general sense of justice, but it was enough to prove that one man's justice is merely another man's injustice and that the pursuit of universal justice is pursuit of a chimera.

Possibly some of the strange frenzies of the American inflation could be justified as a form of entertainment—law and

Inflationary Syndrome

politics, for example, as a relatively harmless form of sweet aggression, or speculative finance as a *Monopoly* game for adults. True entertainment was one of the real values that had languished rather badly in the inflation, but if finance, law, education, and a few others were classified as part of the entertainment industry its growth would have seemed much more respectable.

There was much more to the inflationary syndrome than merely its effects, great and small, on economic activity. The tendrils of the syndrome insinuated themselves even into social, moral, and spiritual life. Surreality in economic life appeared to evoke a corresponding surreality in personal life. Liberation from all the plodding old rules of economic reality, such as the one that two plus two equals only a nonsynergistic four, corresponded to a casting off of all the formerly constant values of individual codes, such as reasonable industry, reasonable dignity, reasonable self-restraint and forbearance, and respect for reasonable authority. An omnipresence of money resulted in an omnipotence of money and therefore in the most extreme sort of materialism. There was hyperactivity in all that the nation did. Change followed upon change, solely for the sake of change, shock upon shock until there was no shock, whether in personal appearance, personal conduct, arts, obscenity, or escapist addictions. Disaffection followed, and general rebelliousness pervaded the nation. There was crime and civil disturbance and labor strife, and alienation and disunity ran deeper even than the noisy protests of the numerous few.

This was the syndrome. Germany too had seen it all. It was difficult to prove that anything so specialized as monetary inflation could be responsible for all this, and it was difficult even to argue that an inflation as moderate as the American could be compared in any way to the extremes of the German. The *tendencies,* at least, were identical. When the German inflation ended, all of this was swept away. When the American inflation ended, as it surely must someday, the nation would at last clearly see how much of its social, moral, and spiritual maladies it had owed solely to the inflation.

When that time came, it might well turn out that the nation had taken the long first steps on the downward path of outright decline under the smokescreen of the inflationary boom. When all the superficialities had been stripped away, it might become apparent how very far down that path the nation had already descended. In all its economic history the United States had never learned to cruise, but only to accelerate, careen, brake, and smash, and the inflationary episode was another of those mad careenings in a vehicle whose windows were as distorted as amusement park mirrors.

12
Culprits and Scapegoats

It is not difficult to understand why the United States plunged into this bog. The reasons were much the same as for each of the many other countries who had taken this road in all the course of history. Ever since ancient Babylon enjoyed its first inflation and its first balance of payments deficit, governments had been discovering and rediscovering the wonders of monetary inflation, and every time they did the wonders were all new and breathtaking. Monetary inflation always works like a magic elixir at the first dose. Continuing the doses, or stopping them, is the problem. Nations can always clearly see objectives they would like to reach, such as fighting wars or being prosperous, and they are often willing to spend whatever is necessary to reach them. They are not often so willing to pay up. Inflation lets them apparently have it both ways. Inflation is buy-now-pay-later, and the cost comes due enough later that the causal connection between the purchase and the price is unclear. Politically, any cost postponed may not come due until the other fellow's regime, and perhaps the opposition party can be left to take the blame. Inflation is a wonder drug which is extraordinarily difficult not to use in every age of mankind.

Unlike most inflations, the American inflation had a theoretical foundation as well as a political one. Even Karl Helfferich in Germany did not actively advocate inflation, but was diverted from his clear better judgment by what he thought was necessity. Most politicians of history, aching to be allowed to use the magic elixir, did so only in defiance of warnings that it was theoretically bad. They hoped, as politicians will, that it would not be *too* bad. Naturally, the politician would much rather hear that the magic elixir is not really bad but good, and this the New Economics told him in 1961. From the New Economics put into actual practice, a boom and then inflation followed as the night the day. Policies dedicated to promoting sheer indiscriminate activity without any critical appraisal of its value inevitably produced a rich harvest of sheer indiscriminate activity without any value. Learned economists and modern theory answer for much that in other inflations was ascribed to rash, ignorant, or simply powerless politicians.

Inflation tends to produce a remarkable confusion of culprits and scapegoats, and the confusion tends to be similar from one inflation to another. In Germany the scapegoats were reparations, speculation, the balance of payments, foreign exchange rates, prices, wages, business, and labor. In the United States the scapegoats were the Viet Nam war, speculation, the balance of payments, foreign exchange rates, prices, wages, business, and labor. The script read with a familiar ring.

The Viet Nam war was the most unpopular war in American history and was also the most popular scapegoat for the American inflation. It is true that inflations tend to occur in big wars, for the reason that the required level of government expenditure is so high that money inflation is the only sufficient source of finance. But the Viet Nam war was only a

Culprits and Scapegoats

little war and could easily fit into a normal defense budget. There were no shortages. Total national defense, including the war, cost no more as a percentage of gross national product at the peak of the war than in 1959, when there was no war. Not until 1967, well after the price inflation was rolling vigorously, did Viet Nam cost as much as the moon race did. One might as justly say that the moon race caused the inflation as that the Viet Nam war did. The truth is, neither did. Just as a war economy is not necessary to prosperity, so it is irrelevant to inflation. To be as prosperous after a war as during, America would have to substitute equal amounts of non-war economic activity and inflation financing. The chronological coincidence of the onset of price inflation that had been gathering since 1962 and the increased intensity of the Viet Nam war was purely accidental. As far as inflation was concerned, the Viet Nam war was an innocent scapegoat and the end of the war was a false hope.

Speculation is another common bogy of an inflation. We have already noticed that the preoccupation with buying and selling paper investments is characteristically the prime activity, the prime unproductive activity, and the prime source of rewards in an inflation. In Germany, speculators were also much castigated as a cause of inflation. In truth, speculation in paper investment serves not to cause but for the time being to help ameliorate price inflation. Stock market speculation is a principal relief valve concealing latent inflation pressure. Booming stock market prices are themselves a form of price inflation, normally the most inflated of all, but never thought of as such. The stock market in America harbored a large portion of the latent inflation but no one disliked it because they were thinking of paper profits rather than the prices of real values. Floods of money which were kept busy inflating the stock market were diverted from inflating other prices. The stock market therefore relieved pressure temporarily from inflation elsewhere. The government had artificial devices for locking money into investment, such as its growing supplies of government debt and the tax inducements drawing money (about a tenth of the national wealth) into pension funds, and these government dikes around investment markets stored up inflationary potential in great brimming reservoirs and out of harm's way.

The balance of international payments, the foreign exchange value of the dollar, and foreign competition with American industry were another fraternally related set of villains. For a decade, the deficit in the United States' balance of payments was considered to be *the* economic problem of the country. So it was in Germany. The Kennedy and Johnson administrations tried stern measures to treat the symptom by impeding foreign investment by Americans and free currency exchange, even though existing foreign investments from earlier days were a main bulwark of the nation's international position. Nothing worked. Payments deficits worsened continuously. That was because payments deficits were purely an effect of inflation. If there is excess money, it flows out, as between vats of differing levels of fullness which are interconnected by pipes. More than that, payments deficits were highly beneficial in minimizing the domestic effects of money inflation. Net export of money reduces the price inflation at home and distributes it instead abroad. If America's payments deficits were successfully blocked and its inflated money shut up at home, America's price inflation would be worse and foreign inflation less bad. If dollars held by foreigners from the accumulated old deficits should come back to the United States through a surplus of payments, price inflation in the United States would be still further worsened. Precisely this took place in Germany at about the middle of 1922, when Germany's balance of payments moved into surplus at the same time that its price inflation moved utterly out of control. Payments deficits while they last are in reality no problem at all but quite delightful for the deficit country, allowing it to enjoy a flow of pleasant things like foreign goods and foreign vacations with its constantly cheapening money. Like a fall from a high building, it is not a payments deficit that hurts but the sudden stop.

The problems of foreign competition and the foreign exchange value of the dollar were precisely the reverse of those which beset the German inflation. At the time of the German inflation, foreign exchange rates were set by a free market, and as a result of the constant inflation the plummeting foreign exchange value of the Reichsmark fell even lower than its purchasing power. The mark became grossly *undervalued* by the inflation. In the American case, fixed and not free exchange rates operated, at least until 1973, and the fixed rates held the international value of the dollar constant in spite of the continuous dilution of its intrinsic value by the government. The dollar became grossly *overvalued* by the inflation. This situation enabled Americans to buy up foreign industry and import foreign goods unnaturally cheaply with their plentiful dollars. Like the balance of payments deficit itself, this was delightfully pleasant for some Americans. On the other hand, foreign competitors were also given an unnatural advantage over that part of American industry which was sensitive to foreign competition. The overvalued dollar and competitive disadvantage placed a heavy lid on the prices of all foreign-sensitive products, and this in turn helped enormously to hold the inherent price inflation in check in the United States. Low rates of price inflation, poor profits, and sluggish wages all correlated closely with foreign-sensitive industries—farm products, raw materials, steel, automobiles, shoes, chemicals, petroleum, and most other forms of manufactures. Vicious rates of price inflation, soaring profits, and rich incomes correlated with industries in which foreign competition was impossible—building construction, medical care, property ownership and rental, and all forms of services. Simply to compare the roughly 100 percent rise in construction costs in America in a decade with the price increases neighboring 10 percent in steel and automobiles is to see the point.

By 1973, the clamor against unfair foreign competition and unfair foreign exchange rates reached a bedlam, and the foreign exchange system broke down. It was quite rightly demanded that the overvaluation of the dollar be removed and that the nation's competitive disadvantage be removed. It was little noticed, however, that any effective step toward these ends, whether by decreasing the exchange value of the dollar or imposing import surcharges or quotas, would release the restraints on prices in the foreign-sensitive industries and allow them to enjoy inherent price inflation like that of construction, rents, and services. Precisely this kind of upsurge of price inflation did follow hard upon the breakdown of exchange rates into a free market in 1973. A nation which maintains an overvalued currency through inflation, as the United States did, grants an artificial subsidy to service industries at the expense of export industries and other foreign-sensitive industries. (A nation which maintains an undervalued currency, as Germany was doing at the same time, likewise grants the reverse artificial subsidy to export industries at the expense of the rest of the nation.) No real equilibrium could be regained until the inherent inflation was allowed to equalize itself and the natural balance of prices among industries to be restored.

It follows from what has been said that heaping blame for inflation on either business or labor, on either prices or wages, is wrong and unjust. The wage-price spiral is always a familiar whipping-boy for inflation, and a variant of it that was fashionable in the United States was the charge that monopoly power enabled big business and big labor unions to raise wages and prices higher than they naturally should have been. This charge is easily refuted by the plain facts that all production workers in all industries, including these, fared so poorly in the inflation; that profits in the largest and most powerful industries became poorer than ever; and that price increases in these same most powerful industries were the most innocuous in the entire national price spectrum. These industries strove mightily under tremendous handicaps to

Culprits and Scapegoats

mechanize, to automate, to compete, and to stay alive. It is an apt measure of the distortion of the nation's values that it lay popular obloquy at the door of those very elements, productive industry and industrial workers, who contributed most liberally to the nation in exchange for the relatively poorest returns. As Lord Keynes observed in a similar context with respect to Germany, industry and labor were "the active and constructive element in the whole capitalist society," and by directing blame against those elements the government was "carrying a step further the fatal process which the subtle mind of Lenin had consciously conceived." Prudence, justice, and prosperity lay not in loading fresh abuse and more onerous shackles on these industries or their workers, but in letting them up off the floor and readmitting them to their former and rightful shares of the national prosperity.

At bottom there is always politics, whether in Germany or in the United States or elsewhere. The eternal conflict, eternally short-sighted, proceeded between one productive class and another, especially between labor and industry. The instrument of their pursuit of self-interest was political power, and the principal casualties of that pursuit were they themselves. Labor habitually thought that good business profits came at labor's expense, industry that good wages came at industry's expense. Both are wrong. Wages and profits accompany and do not exclude one another. Good profits depend on the well-being of labor, and good wages on the well-being of business. Constantly seeking their separate advantage, however, both industry and labor were chronically found in the camp of inflationary politicians who managed the remarkable feat of offering everyone more and leaving everyone with less.

The position of labor in all this was particularly ironic. Admittedly, industrial workers were the good horse on which everyone else was riding. Workers' wages did not cause the inflation, and workers shared poorly in the inflationary riches. But labor had the votes, the Democratic Party was the party of labor, and labor elected the Democratic government that caused the inflation. Workers at the bargaining table do not cause inflation, but workers at the polling booths can and largely do. The same strange political alliance between stolid labor and mercurial liberals ruled in the United States as it did in Weimar. Liberals, being normally unsullied by acquaintance with real economic work, nevertheless affected a paternal interest in workers. Workers' chosen union leaders endorsed them, and workers dutifully followed. The only possible way of satisfying, even apparently, labor's constant demand for "More!" was to inflate, but inflation whose ostensible purpose was to improve employment and prosperity of workers benefited everyone else more than it did them. Not only were productive workers left out of the inflationary gains in income, but as we shall see later the principal targets of the inflationary theft were workers' normal kinds of savings such as pension rights, savings accounts, and insurance. Inflation was, as it always is, a fraud on workers, and workers were the perfect dupes of their chosen leaders. Seeing none of this, workers grew constantly more militant and less tractable in much the same way as Germany's rebellious labor of the 1922 era.

As the numbers and relative importance of productive workers declined, like those of farmers before them, the time might come when all the productive contributors of society combined—farmers, workers, managers, entrepreneurs, and investors—might be less numerous than the free riders of society. That time seemed not so far off when it was considered that the 27 million productive workers in the United States were already fewer than half of all the ostensibly employed Americans. If that time should come, it would no longer lie within the political reach of the producers to act for their mutual benefit and that of the nation. The closer that time approached, the more urgently the nation needed a timely ability of all of them to see mutuality rather than conflict among their interests, and to see that the road to greater abundance for all lay in the direction of demanding less grasping shares for any.

13
The Open Questions

We arrive at this point in the history of the American inflation, after the bloom had passed and the fruit had fallen but before the efforts of the Nixon administration to contain the inflation had begun, and still we essentially do not know where this point was. If there is any lesson to be learned from a study of inflations, it is that one never knows where he is in the midst of it, but he certainly is not where he appears to be. All reference points for navigating or fixing position have become beclouded. The apparent prosperity proves in time to have been illusory, but no one knows until then how illusory. Rewards and values prove in time to have become inverted, but no one knows until then how inverted. The currency proves in time to have been worth less even than it appeared to be, but no one knows until then how much less. The questions raised earlier in this part of the book—whether the degree of the inflationary trouble had any direct relationship to the German débâcle, and whether the later processes of that débâcle taught anything directly useful for the earlier stages of our own—cannot be conclusively answered. The questions remain open.

What should be clear beyond peradventure, as we shall presently proceed to examine analytically, is that the direct cause of the inflationary plight was the great Kennedy-Johnson orgy of the 1960's. The inflation was not intended, to be sure, but the deliberate acts of the government were the cause of the inflation as surely as they were of the earlier easy prosperity. The inflation was the simple price of the boom. As good as the boom apparently was, so bad or worse must the inflation actually be. The great prosperity had been too easy, was largely false, and in any case was past. Its price in inflation would be all too real and was mostly yet to come. As always, the inflation which came later was blamed on every sort of extraneous event that happened to coincide in time with the later emergence of the hidden inflation. It was reminiscent of the difficulty primitive peoples are said to have perceiving the causal connection between last night's ecstasy and next year's childbirth.

Notwithstanding the evidence, the difficulty persisted. Never yet was a New Economist heard audibly to recant. Never yet was it openly acknowledged that the deliberate economics of the government from 1962 to 1968 were a failure; not a little miscalculation here or an unfine tuning there, but in their deepest fundamentals an unmitigated failure. The nation still struggled to cope with its troubles using essentially the same economics, tinkered with a bit but not superseded. So long as this was true, the nation could be assured of having learned nothing from its ordeal and of making no progress out of it. So long as this was true, even if the nation's inflationary plight was not yet so grave as it had been in other lands at other times, in the fullness of time it would be.

INTERLUDE

The General Theory of Inflation

14
Welcome to Economic Theory

The chapters which follow in this part, dealing with the theoretical basis of inflation and kindred subjects, are unfortunately difficult. Controversy over these subjects has survived for millenniums, and absolution seems no nearer to us than it was to Junius Paulus in the third century A.D. It appears that we must endure controversy a while longer.

If I may borrow and paraphrase from Lord Keynes' preface to his *General Theory:* this book is addressed chiefly to my fellow citizens who are not economists; I hope that it may be intelligible to economists as well. I have labored as mightily as I could to make what follows both sound and clear. Notwithstanding that, economists may find these chapters too simple, and disdain them; readers who are not economists may find them too difficult, or too dull, or both, and skip them. That would be doubly unfortunate.

As for economists, I believe that there are numbers of thoughts in these pages which are worth their considering and which are not found elsewhere. But they may do as they wish.

As for persons who are not economists, my plea is to persevere. If these chapters in their fullness are too heavy going, try browsing in them more briefly to pick up principal ideas. Every citizen, meaning the machinist fresh from his lathe and the farmer from his tractor as well as everyone else, finds himself burdened with the duty to master this subject for his own sake if for no other reason. When economic management becomes a matter of popular vote, as it had become in the United States, then the very salvation of the nation depends on each citizen's assuming personal responsibility for enforcing healthful economic policies on his elected leaders. Political leaders can be found who will sell absolutely anything the people will buy. Economic experts can be found to do the same. If experts do not lead, people must lead. The responsibility stops nowhere short of machinists and farmers and all the rest of us. And if it is a sobering challenge that ordinary people must guide expertly where experts have lost their way, it is more sobering still to reflect that it is ordinary people, and not leaders or experts, who bear the consequences and pay the price if the way should remain lost.

15
Prices

Inflation has two different aspects. One aspect is rising money prices of things that people buy. If inflation is thought of as a bad thing, then it is this aspect of inflation which is meant. And clearly this kind of price inflation which is a bad thing is an effect, a result, of something else or a collection of other things. We sense that it does not happen of its own volition, without some systematic cause. If the cause of the evil of price inflation can be traced back to some localized and controllable source, then the evil of price inflation can be shut off by shutting off the source, provided that shutting off that particular source does not have some other effect which is just as evil as the price inflation or more so.

The other aspect of the generic term inflation is monetary inflation, which is nothing more than the voluntary act of the government to allow the existing amount of money to increase. If price inflation is an effect whose causes are uncertain, money inflation is a cause whose effects are uncertain. And if price inflation by itself is bad, monetary inflation by itself is neither good nor bad. Simply increasing the amount of money alone bothers no one. Only if a clear link can be established between monetary inflation as a cause and price inflation, a bad thing, as a result, can monetary inflation be convicted as itself a bad thing.

Further, we must distinguish between increasing prices of *some* things, which is not necessarily price inflation, and an increasing general price level of *all* things as an aggregate, which alone is price inflation. To take the most painful examples: if prices rise drastically in things like food or medical care, the least avoidable of all necessities, there is still no true price inflation if prices of other things have declined by a compensating amount, even though people as a whole do not care as much about the things which now cost less as about the food and medical care which now cost more. The farmers and food industry, or the nurses and doctors and medical industry, have simply succeeded in outcompeting the other industries. This they are entitled to do. If this changing balance of prices grows extreme, it may require economic remedies of one sort or another, but it is not inflation and does not require anti-inflationary remedies. When we speak of inflation we must always have in mind whether we mean price inflation (a bad thing, an effect) or monetary inflation (a neutral thing, a cause); and when we speak of price inflation, we must speak only of true price inflation of all things and not merely of rising prices of some particularly necessary thing.

What then causes true price inflation? More fundamentally than that, what determines prices of all things as an aggregate? The most obvious answer would be that prices of things are set by the people who sell them, or at most that prices are set jointly by the people who sell and the people who buy. Since all sales involve only two parties, buyers and sellers, who by mutual agreement fix the price which is acceptable to both of them, it would appear that between them they have absolute power to set prices as high or as low as they please. It is this sense of the joint autonomy of buyers and sellers over prices

Prices

which leads to the feeling that prices are set by their whim and are subject to no reliable laws. It leads further to the feeling that price inflation may be spontaneous and aimless like a self-governing sacred cow in the streets of India which rises, wanders about, and subsides entirely as it pleases.

The quaint notion that buyers and sellers determine prices as their voluntary act is largely false. The genuine feeling of each buyer and seller that he is free to do as he wishes when he agrees on a price, and therefore could do something else if he wished, is largely an illusion. Buyers and sellers of any one kind of thing, such as food or medical care, do have some freedom to increase the prices of that one kind of thing; but every dollar more that a buyer spends for food or medical care is a dollar less that he can spend for something else, and every increased price of one thing must come out of a decreased price of something else, unless someone provides some more dollars so as to allow for an aggregate price inflation. Buyers and sellers of any one thing therefore have some freedom to set their prices but not as much as they think they do. Buyers and sellers of all things together have mathematically no power whatever to increase prices beyond what are determined for them by external forces. Prices are no self-governing sacred cow blundering aimlessly through our garden party and subject to no law or restraint.

Prices as an aggregate are mathematically determined by the total amount of money which is available for spending in a given period of time, in relation to the total supply of all values which are available for purchase with money in that period of time. There are many vitally important refinements still to come, but the law of prices is basically as simple as that. To illustrate, suppose that we have a simple economy which has only one generalized thing of value available per day, a total money supply of $10, and a normal preference by the holders of the money to turn over (or *spend*) the money supply once per day. It is mathematically impossible for the price level of that economy's one thing of value to be anything but $10 per unit. In this illustration, the aggregate supply of values is one unit per day, and aggregate demand is $10 per day. The aggregate price level must equal aggregate money demand per day ($10) divided by the aggregate supply of values per day (1 unit), or $10 per unit.

This is nothing more than a routine application of economics' basic law of supply and demand. That law says that for a given supply and a given demand, only one equilibrium price is possible. If supply rises, price falls. If demand rises, price also rises. When this law of supply and demand is applied to individual kinds of goods, such as beef and pork, or steel and aluminum, demand is not a mathematical quantity but is subject to many psychological choices between alternative purchases, such as beef and pork. But when the law is applied to a comprehensive supply of all values, in which all alternative choices have been included and therefore eliminated, aggregate demand is nothing but money per unit time. Covetous eyes peering in at a shop window, but with empty pockets, may be psychological desire but they are *not* demand; money in hand and ready to spend, however jaded or indifferent, *is* demand.

The quantity of money is both definite and determinable. The Federal Reserve System in the United States publishes it every Thursday. The correct definition of "money" is somewhat arguable, but to work properly in this hypothesis it must mean that which people use to buy things of value with, but is not a thing of value itself. That in turn includes all dollar bills and coins and all checking account deposits, and nothing else. This money supply in the latter part of 1973 was moving upward through the vicinity of $260 billion in the United States.

One psychological factor still remains in the price equation, and that relates to the rate of use of money. Money quantity alone does not determine demand or prices; money available *per unit time* does, and that in turn depends on how fast the holders of the money supply choose to make it avail-

Prices

able for purchases. By taking the total supply of all values for sale into our accounting, we have eliminated all psychological choices between one possible purchase and another, but we have not eliminated the psychological choice between spending and not spending at all, that is to say between purchasing from the supply of values and holding the money itself. This factor can be thought of in different ways. Lord Keynes called it *liquidity preference,* looking to the cash balance relative to purchases which the average holder of money liked to keep on hand. The reverse of this is called the *velocity* of money, looking to the volume of purchases relative to the supply of money. In our illustration, we assumed that the holder of our money supply had a liquidity preference for a cash balance equal to one day's purchases, so that the resulting rate of turnover or velocity was 1.0 per day. No external force dictated this liquidity preference to the holder of the money supply, however, and we had no way of knowing it until we had statistical evidence after the fact. Of velocity and liquidity preference we shall have more to say later.

Notwithstanding the interposition of the velocity of money, which is a troublesome factor because it is variable, psychological, and not readily determinable, we have a law of what determines an aggregate price level. It may be restated as a simple equation (the only mathematical equation which this book contains):

$$\text{Price level} = \frac{\text{Money quantity} \times \text{Money velocity}}{\text{Supply of all real values}}$$

Price level moves in *direct* proportion to the quantity of money and to the velocity of money; price level moves in *inverse* proportion to the aggregate supply of real values. If money velocity is habitual and remains more or less constant, and if the supply of all real values is given and remains more or less constant, price level depends on the quantity of money. Prices are not matters of self-governing caprice.

Concrete numbers can be attached to these concepts. If

the money supply in the United States in 1973 was about $260 billion, and at a conservative estimate every dollar was spent an average of 50 times per year, then the prevailing aggregate money demand had to be the product of the two multiplied together, or *$13 trillion* per year. This was the total amount of purchasing power available for all the uses of money, including not only gross national product or final sales (only about $1.2 trillion per year) but also intermediate sales, buying and selling of stocks and debt and all other property, paying taxes, and making other non-sales transfers of money. The aggregate of the price tags attached to all these transactions either must rise high enough to absorb exactly the total available purchasing power, or be held low enough to fit within it. They are in equilibrium when, and only when, they match.

What we have stated to explain prices is a form of the quantity theory of money. This theory is as old and persistent as economics itself, dating from at least the sixteenth century and French royal philosopher Jean Bodin. Its fundamental validity went largely unquestioned through most of the history of economics. Most of the great figures of economics, including such men as Locke, Hume, Mill, and Ricardo, worked with and improved upon it. The great economists Irving Fisher and A. C. Pigou, American and English respectively, advanced its progress in the first quarter of the twentieth century. Before Lord Keynes set all of the New Economists flying off on a tangent in 1936, the quantity theory was a basic part of the equipment of every important economist. After that time, it fell into general disuse. Most orthodox modern economists denied the quantity theory. Professor Milton Friedman made himself an evangelist of innovation preaching what had been gospel for millenniums. But Lord Keynes himself was one of the clearest of all expositors of the quantity theory of money. Writing in 1924 in *A Tract on Monetary Reform,* he endorsed the theory and said that it was foolish to deny it. Karl Helfferich in Germany was also an excellent expositor of the quantity theory. He caused the German inflation by failing to apply his own precepts.

The issue of the quantity theory comes to this: the progressive economics of the thirty years after Keynes repealed all previous economic wisdom on this point, including that of Keynes. If the accumulated learning of the centuries was right at all, modern economics were wrong, and vice versa. To repeal history in this way may sometimes be right, however drastic, but the extremity of the act counsels caution.

16
Inflation

If quantity theory explains prices, then an application of it also explains price inflation. If what has been said is correct, then the sole root cause of price inflation is monetary inflation. In its simplest form, this is to say that if the money supply increases by 10 percent while the supply of values and velocity of money remain constant, the general price level must rise by 10 percent.

It is far too simple, however, to define monetary inflation as merely an increase in the supply of money. There are three variables at work on prices, not one; they are not only money supply but also money velocity and the supply of real values. An increase of 10 percent in the money supply is not inflationary if there is also a 10 percent increase in the supply of real values, or if there is a 10 percent *decrease* in velocity. By the same token, no increase at all in the money supply would still be inflationary if there has been a 10 percent *increase* in the velocity of money but no increase in the supply of real values. Any one of the three variables can move prices in either direction, but only one of the three—money supply—is subject to the control of the government. To prevent inflation and achieve price stability, this one controllable variable must be changed to offset changes in either of the other two. Monetary inflation can be defined as allowing to exist any money supply which is greater than the quantity which exactly does this. An inflated money supply might actually be a money supply which is decreased, but not decreased enough. Monetary inflation defined in this way is in fact the sole root cause of price inflation.

Monetary inflation is the cause of price inflation, but the response of effect to cause is far from instantaneous. If there is a sudden monetary inflation of 10 percent, experience tells us that prices do not immediately rise by 10 percent, nor in fact may they rise at all for a considerable time. The price equation as we have stated it does not appear to allow for this, and if it can be in error on this point perhaps it is wrong altogether.

The difficulty is only apparent. The price equation in the simple form only operates in *equilibrium* conditions. In disequilibrium, such as immediately after a monetary inflation has occurred, the formula can only state what prices *will be* when a new equilibrium is restored, and not what actual prices are at any time in between.

Consider how a monetary inflation actually works. In our earlier example, a money supply of $10 was turning over once per day so as to price an output of one unit per day at $10 per unit. Conditions were stable. Any seller who wished to raise his price would have forced some other seller to receive a smaller price, or the buyer to spend faster than he desired. More likely, the price-increasing seller would have lost his sale, so he refrained from raising his price and prices remained constant. This is the essence of equilibrium. If at this point the government should double the money supply to $20, it would appear *a priori* that equilibrium will remain undisturbed if, but only if, the government also prevails on buyers and sellers to double all prices to $20 per unit. But this is not what happens when there is monetary inflation. No one changes prices automatically, and in fact the government strives to restrain them from doing so; no one announces that there has been monetary inflation, and in fact it remains difficult to detect. In these circumstances, the equilibrium level which prices must eventually find will still be $20 per unit as a result of the doubling of the money supply, but for the moment actual prices will remain at $10 per unit.

The purchaser who holds the enlarged money supply of $20 has been accustomed to paying only $10 for a day's supply of values, and he has no real desire to pay $20 for the same thing without being forced to do so. He has a choice of either doing that or holding his $20 money supply for two days instead of one. He will always prefer to do the latter. He is apparently twice as wealthy as he was previously. The value of his money in terms of actual prices has not declined, but he has twice as much of it. He can spend his customary $10 per day for output, which was previously all the money he had, but now he has another $10 left. The velocity of his money will fall in half, aggregate money demand (quantity multiplied by velocity) will remain the same, and prices will not change. The only unstable factor so far as the buyer is concerned is that he is holding twice as large a money balance as he really wants.

On the opposite side, the seller in our economy has been charging $10 for a day's output of values, exactly meeting demand, and he hesitates to raise his price for fear of losing sales. He is not informed that the equilibrium price for his output is now $20. Only gradually will he sense that there is more money demand around than he is laying claim to, less reluctance to pay his price than there was at the $10 equilibrium level. He will gradually begin to feel out this new demand by raising his prices, and the buyer holding surplus balances will gradually begin to pay them. Actual prices gradually make good the equilibrium level which the $20 money supply

Inflation

dictated, and the price inflation becomes realized. The original increase of the money supply was what caused the inflation, and the buyers and sellers merely served as agents to put it into effect.

Modern conventional economics classifies causes of inflation as "cost-push" or "demand-pull" forces. This distinction is purely descriptive and not analytical. It merely states which of the two parties to an inflation, sellers or buyers, is pushing or pulling the harder to get their mutual prices up to their preordained equilibrium. If sellers are the more eager to claim the full prices which aggregate available money would justify, the inflation will be "cost-push"; if buyers are the more eager to reduce their cash balances and bid up the prices of available output, the inflation will be "demand-pull." As a means of analyzing the basic causes of inflation, the distinction is utterly useless.

The original increase of the money supply, temporarily masked by a reduction of money velocity, was what set the equilibrium level of prices higher than their actual level and thus created the inflationary bias. The difference between the actual price level at any time and the higher equilibrium price level is the *unrealized depreciation* of a currency, and the living process of working upward from the lower to the higher is the process of living an inflation. No meter anywhere has yet been devised to read out the unrealized depreciation of a currency, but if it were this meter would inform us surely where an inflation is going. The direction of the equilibrium level and the breadth of the gap indicates which way prices must move and how far at a maximum, but not necessarily when or how fast. Price inflation would tend to be more rapid and more immediate, the more extreme is the unrealized depreciation, but this is only a tendency. It depends on the minds of buyers and sellers. Price inertia is very strong, difficult to get moving and difficult to stop. If sellers are sufficiently unaggressive about raising prices and buyers sufficiently willing to hold their excess money rather than bid up prices with it, prices may remain steady even with a large inherent depreciation in the currency. Equilibrium may be not at all quick to emerge. To the contrary, an implicit disequilibrium may be persistent and even quite stable. Nevertheless it is the underlying money demand available which dictates to buyers and sellers which way their prices must go and where they must arrive, leaving it to them to decide when and at what speed they will accompany one another to that point. This much autonomy and no more do buyers and sellers have when the makings of a price inflation have been presented tc them by their government.

This analysis corresponds with the evidence of every important inflation of history, including the German inflation and the American inflation. Money supply increases, money velocity falls behind, and prices remain steady. Later money velocity recovers, prices begin to rise, and equilibrium eventually returns at the level fixed by the original money supply inflation. Transitory phases like the Korean War inflation may occur on psychological velocity alone, without a money supply basis, but they do not detract from the validity of the analysis.

As Professor Milton Friedman observed whenever anyone would listen, as well as whenever no one would listen, inflation is always and everywhere a monetary phenomenon. No one can cause an inflation but the government, and neither more nor less is required to stop an inflation than that the government stop causing it. This has been true since the earliest origins of inflation in the forests of the Stone Age. It was true of Germany. It was true of America.

Professor Friedman's solitary struggle to regain acceptance for the obvious surely attests to the lonely estate of being even partly right. A whole generation of modern economists was trained up to positions of respect and influence making no use of quantity theory as it developed over the centuries. Economists of the Keynesian school would fight to the death against the implications of quantity theory: to wit, that the fantastic German inflation of 1923 was caused by inflation of the money supply, or that the operative agent of their own sophisticated Keynesian techniques was also monetary inflation. Alas, what is oldest, most obvious, and most firmly accepted in the past is not always wrong, and fighting to the death against the obvious is sometimes fatal.

17
Velocity

Money has a well-known dual function. One function is to serve as a medium of exchange to help match up the sellers and buyers of various kinds of values without the need for exchange in kind, or barter. The other function is to serve as a store of value in itself. The first function is money in motion, the second is money standing still. The only truly legitimate function of money is the first, the exchange function. Without the need for a medium of exchange, there would be no need for money. As stores of value, other kinds of property are just as good or better. Money is not properly a store of value because it has no intrinsic value of its own. It has no utility except in exchange. Money which is being used as a store of value is money which is *hors de combat* for the time being. Nevertheless, the use of money as a store of value is traditional and can easily be tolerated, provided that it is adjusted for.

If it were not for the demand for money as a store of

value, the money supply would be nothing more than the average "float" between transactions, that is, a momentary balance on hand between a receipt of money income and a money expenditure. In this case, the average holding period for money would be very low, much lower than it actually is, and velocity would be high. At the extreme, if the efficiency of use of money in making transactions were increased to perfection, so that all exchanges were instantly matched up and liquidated, and if there were no demand whatever for money as a store of value, the velocity of money would be infinite and the only non-inflationary money supply would be zero. Conversely, if the money supply did not turn over at all, meaning that every citizen had a complete preference to use his money as a store of value and refused to use any of it in transactions, the velocity of money would be zero and the proper quantity of it infinite. In practice, normal liquidity preference represents a combination of a normal float between transactions and a normal amount of money held as a store of value.

Much learning has been expended on trying to determine what factors govern liquidity preference. Keynes, for example, after close analysis, found these factors to be basically the "income motive" (the float between receipts and expenditures), the "business motive" (working capital), the "precautionary motive" (reserves against reverses), and the "speculative motive" (anticipation of changes in the value of money). Others have expanded on this study. Indeed, the principal reason why Keynesian economists have abandoned the quantity theory is their belief that the behavior of liquidity preference and velocity is so unruly as to make the whole investigation futile. Evidence does not support this belief. The reasons why people change their liquidity preference make an engrossing academic study but not a reliably predictable force. Fortunately, it is not necessary to predict or control liquidity preference finely. It is sufficient to know that it can change, to keep a weather eye on its changes, to measure the changes, and to compensate for those changes that appear to be permanent.

Inflation can be a purely velocity inflation as easily as a quantity inflation. The initial Korean War inflation was an example of this, and the later stages of the German inflation were also based mainly on a skyrocketing velocity. If for any psychological reason the people's liquidity preference should fall by half and velocity double, equilibrium prices must surely double even though money supply remains unchanged. The reverse is true if people's preference shifts drastically toward holding money and not spending it. Prices must fall.

A purely velocity inflation is usually quite volatile. If velocity rises sharply for some psychological and spontaneous reason, unaccompanied by money quantity inflation, velocity will usually return to its norm about as quickly as it departed from it. This would have happened in the Korean War inflation if money quantity had not advanced to meet velocity. Sharp velocity inflations left to themselves are almost never permanent. This truth is precisely the opposite of quantity inflation, for a price rise based on money quantity is as irrecoverable as money quantity itself.

Unlike money quantity, money velocity cannot be measured even moderately well. One crude indicator of velocity is called "income velocity" and is the ratio of national product to money supply. In the United States in 1973 this number showed about 4.9 times turnover of money per year. This measure compares only one part of a nation's values, its gross national product, with a total money supply used for many other purchases, and for that reason it is a hybrid and completely invalid concept. Another measure is called "transactions velocity" and is the ratio of the total dollar volume of all payments made by checking accounts to total checking account balances. This number was of the order of 50 to 90 in 1973, depending on whether or not higher-velocity accounts in financial cities were disregarded. This measure is somewhat closer to the true idea of velocity, although it ignores the use of dollar bills and includes many kinds of check transactions that are not sales, and for these reasons it too fails to show velocity pure and true. Nevertheless, transactions velocity is probably the best measure of velocity available.

In spite of these serious defects of measurement, there is something that we can learn about velocity. It happens that both indicators, income velocity and transactions velocity, were in rough agreement on the *rate of change* of velocity, which was considerably more important than its absolute speed. Moreover, indications are that velocity and liquidity preference do not change nearly as erratically as they theoretically could. Trends in velocity are reasonably constant. According to both measures, velocity in the United States increased steadily from a low point in 1946, just after the war, through 1973. Transactions velocity increased by at least 279 percent, or a compounded rate of 4.8 percent per year, and this rate of increase was fairly constant throughout those 27 years.

Our price equation informs us that if the total supply of real values increased after the war no faster than the same 279 percent as money velocity, velocity alone would have supplied all the additional money demand that was needed, and money quantity could not have increased at all without causing inflation. In fact, however, the supply of real values in gross national product, at least, grew considerably more slowly than that rate, and money supply also increased by 141 percent during the same 27 years. Aggregate money demand (quantity multiplied by velocity) was thus more than nine times as great in 1973 as in 1946, and if the total supply of real values in the United States did not grow by this much there must inevitably be inflation.

Money quantity and velocity theoretically could move independently of one another, but in practice they do not. Quantity leads, and velocity follows. At the beginning of an inflationary cycle, velocity declines while money quantity increases, thereby offsetting one another and masking the true inflationary potential. This happened during the wars in both Germany and America. It happened also in Germany's prosperous expansion of 1920. We saw why this happened in our simple example, because money holders were temporarily willing to hold their excess money, slowing down velocity and leaving prices unchanged. Later, in the mid-course of an inflationary cycle, money quantity and velocity both increase, thereby compounding the inflationary effects of one another. After overcoming its initial inertia, velocity does not merely return to its former rate but may accelerate past it. People naturally wish to hold money less and to spend it faster when they see its value falling. At the end of an inflationary cycle, velocity rises faster than money quantity, though only for a limited time after the quantity inflation stops.

All of these relationships can be traced out in reverse in a deflationary cycle. Monetary contraction began in 1928 in the United States, but velocity rose for a time to compensate for it and the deflationary effects were masked. Deflation took hold in 1929 and both money quantity and velocity began to fall together. Prices and prosperity fell with them and much more steeply than quantity alone. At the depth of the Depression, long after money had stopped contracting, the hoarding of money—simple low velocity—persisted and frustrated all effective recovery.

The role of money velocity in the German inflation was extremely important, but it dovetails with all these general principles. Velocity decreased during both the war and the 1920 boom, hiding the quantity inflation which was forging ahead at both times. Velocity started to rise with moderate vigor in the summer of 1921, when Germans began to smell a governmental rat, and that signaled the gradual emergence of the latent price inflation. Velocity took an almost right-angle turn upward in the summer of 1922, and that signaled the beginning of the end. An explosive rise in velocity thus accurately marks the point of obliteration of an inflated currency, but it does not cause itself. People cause velocity, and they only cause hypervelocity after prolonged abuse of their trust. The German mark had been undergoing massive dilution for over two years, and the people only at last realized it when they turned on the velocity. At the end in 1923, the velocity of German money began to approach infinity, because paper bills could easily change hands hourly or faster and practically did.

In money velocity, what goes up must come down but only when the cause is removed. Whenever quantity inflation should stop, velocity must eventually fall to normal. In Germany, that would have been a problem in itself, because prices would have to fall by the same factor that velocity did unless money quantity should be increased again (i.e., inflated) to compensate. An interesting dilemma, that, but one that is neatly avoided if the people are not driven at last into desperation velocity.

High velocity was the cause in Germany of the remarkable coexistence of soaring prices and a low and falling *real value* of money supply. This in turn caused the government's bemused thinkers to say that there was no inflation. The government's erroneous response was to try to maintain real balances by increasing money supply. The government gave chase to velocity with quantity, but, like a contrary mule, velocity defies chasing. If chased, it runs away faster, and the top speed of this particular mule nears infinity. On the other hand, if the government just turns around and walks the other way, this mule comes galloping back and licks its hand. The fact that the collapsing German inflation rested mainly on velocity, a volatile and psychological phenomenon, is not reassuring and does not mean that the inflation was unique to its own circumstances. It is a warning never to inflate even distantly near the point of stampeding the people, and if they do stampede *do not follow.*

Money velocity is thus much the more sluggish, in the beginning of an inflation, of the two partners in aggregate demand, quantity and velocity. Later on, it is much the more prone to explosion. But velocity presents us with still another obstacle to gauging inflationary potential accurately. The problem is that it is not really *actual* velocity at all that we would like to know for our price equation, but *equilibrium* velocity. Actual velocity is no more than a rate of flow that happens to be occurring at the present moment. The price equation using actual velocity has often been criticized, and quite properly, as a tautology which discloses nothing about inflationary potential. The mathematical relationships are so inviolable that the equation using current velocity must balance out at the current price level, telling nothing about where the price level is bound. On the other hand, people's underlying liquidity preference is an equilibrium cash balance that people would like to arrive at, not what they have succeeded in arriving at to date. Equilibrium velocity is to actual velocity as a pressure is to a flow, or as voltage is to amperage in electricity. The rate of flow is always moving toward where the pressure is now. If we could know and substitute equilibrium velocity for prevailing velocity in our equation, we would have no tautology at all but an infallible calculation of equilibrium prices and inflationary potential.

All of these effects were apparent in our earlier example. When the money supply doubled, actual money velocity halved, and the price level remained unchanged. If we had inferred from this that buyers' underlying liquidity preference had doubled, we would have concluded that there was no inflationary potential but we would have been wrong. In all likelihood equilibrium velocity, which is based on buyers' inherent liquidity preference, remained as high as actual velocity had been previously, and if so equilibrium prices were twice as high as actual prices were.

Unfortunately, if actual velocity is difficult to measure, equilibrium velocity is impossible. The best we can hope to do is to deduce equilibrium velocity from surrounding circumstances including the behavior of actual velocity. The usual

Velocity

relationships between money quantity and money velocity will also help considerably. Velocity is always a follower. As long as quantity inflation is continuous, moneyholders continuously hold more money than they want, however little that may be, and actual velocity is continuously lower than equilibrium velocity. No matter how high or rapidly velocity may have risen, so long as monetary inflation continues it is always lower than it is going to be and therefore always understates inherent inflationary potential.

18
Aggregate Values

The third great determinant of prices, after money quantity which is determinable and money velocity which is not so determinable, is the aggregate supply of real values available for money in a given period of time. In short, the larger an economy is, the more money it needs to do its work. A large money supply is not absolutely inflationary. It is relative. Prices are inversely proportional to the supply of values, money quantity and velocity remaining the same. If the supply of values increases but money does not, prices must decline; this happened in the United States in the last quarter of the nineteenth century and was the source of the money pains of that era. If the supply of values increases, money may and should also, without inflationary potential.

Traditionally, in the evaluation of this relationship, the supply of values is equated to the gross national product, which is the economy's entire output of current goods and services in a given time. This is a mistake and a serious one. Gross national product is obviously important, but it is by no

Aggregate Values

means the entire supply of real values available for money purchase. To assume so is to disregard all of the existing capital wealth of the nation.

A man who has money in hand and has decided to spend it has two principal kinds of things he can spend it on. One kind of things, but only one, consists of current goods and services, the national product. The second kind of things consists of all existing property, including land and buildings, used goods, productive plant and equipment, and all sorts of paper property such as stocks, bonds, mortgages, savings accounts, insurance, and commercial paper. This second category of values lies entirely outside the national product and corresponds to the national wealth. Purchases in this category also correspond to what a layman is likely to mean by "investment." When an economist speaks of investment, he means the formation of new capital assets like construction of factories or equipment, but that is a part of national product. When a layman speaks of investment, he probably means the purchase of an existing capital asset like stock or a bond.

The purchase and sale of capital assets obviously requires the same quantity of money to serve as its medium of exchange as the sale of an equal volume of national product. As a result, at any given time some part of the total money supply is employed in national product transactions and another part is employed in capital transactions. There are at all times two distinct money supplies and two distinct velocities of money, one each in the market for national product and the market for national wealth. The comparison between the total supply of money and the gross national product alone, as is made in computing the so-called "income velocity" of money, is meaningless.

Each of the two separate markets must abide separately by the law of prices. The aggregate price level in each market must be higher as the quantity or velocity of money in that market rises, and lower as the supply of values in that market rises. But there is no dam between the markets other than the habits of the people, and these may change. The distribution of money demand between the two markets is not fixed. Any man may move his personal money supply from the stock market to automobiles and back again. So too may the people as a whole. Consequently the two markets must comply with the law of prices not only separately but also as an aggregate. As net money demand moves from one market to the other, prices must go down in the first and up in the second.

The exact division of money supply between national product and capital markets is extremely difficult to estimate, but the share employed in capital markets in the United States was not small. Stock sales on exchanges alone in the one year of 1968 required cash transfers of almost $200 billion, which was 23 percent as great as the annual national product and about equal to the total money supply. Of far greater importance was the aggregate American debt structure which amounted to $3.2 *trillion* in money claims by 1971. Even if the average maturity of this debt structure were as long as two years, the constant refinancing of this debt structure would require cash transfers of $1.6 trillion every year, which would be half again larger than the annual national product and almost seven times the total money supply. It is true that the need for cash in capital markets is diminished by the extremely high velocity of money in financial centers; transactions velocity in New York, for example, averaged almost one complete turnover every business day, which was more than four times as high as the velocity of money in non-financial centers. Nevertheless, it is not at all difficult to suppose that the money supply required for capital markets in the United States might be fully equal to the money supply engaged in selling national product.

The significance of all this is that the use of money in capital markets is a principal repository of inflationary potential. Monetary inflation invariably makes itself felt first in capital markets, most conspicuously as a stock market boom. Prices of national product remain temporarily steady while stock prices rise and interest rates fall. This happened at the commencement of the German inflationary boom of 1920, and it happened again at the commencement of the American inflationary boom from 1962 to 1966. Indeed, every monetary expansion in the United States since World War II was followed by a stock market rise, every cessation of monetary expansion by a stock market fall. Conversely, every stock market rise was preceded and accompanied by money inflation. Bull markets rest on nothing but inflation. The market fall following tight money merely brings the market back to its real-value level.

It is not difficult to understand why this is true. Virtually all, and not merely a proportionate part, of the excess money demand created by a monetary inflation goes temporarily into the capital markets. In our earlier example, the holder of excess money could either force up the prices of national product (price inflation) or hold the excess money longer than usual (low velocity), neither of which he had any wish to do. What he is actually most likely to do with the excess money is to buy himself some stocks, bonds, or savings accounts, in other words to "invest" the money or put it into the capital markets. This must force up the prices of real values in capital markets, to be sure, and this in turn is one form of simple price inflation, but no one thinks of it as such because no one is thinking of real values. One man's price inflation is another man's capital gain, and even the first man does not mind it if he is getting his capital gains too. The excess money which is happily at play in the capital markets is money which is not yet distressing the prices of national product, where it might hurt.

Notice what has happened in mathematical terms. In our original example, there was a partial money supply occupied with purchasing national product equal to $10. Velocity was one transaction per day, output was one unit per day, and resulting prices were $10 per unit. Suppose now more complexly that there is another separate money supply of $10 occupied with trading capital assets, making a total money supply of $20. Now if the money supply is doubled to $40 and all of the extra $20 goes into the purchase of investments, the money supply in the capital market will have trebled, not doubled, and prices there will at least treble too, perhaps more because of speculative high velocity. Money quantity and velocity and therefore prices in national product will remain temporarily unchanged.

In due time, there being no dam between the markets, a leakage of excess money demand back from capital markets into national product will occur. There will always be that spoilsport in the capital casino who will take his winnings and buy national product with them. There will always be that footslogger selling national product who senses that there is surplus money demand over yonder among the capitalists and demand some of it by raising prices. It is inevitable. Excess money which starts out in the capital markets winds up back in national product. If luck is good, the excess money will merely redistribute itself proportionately between the two markets. In the example, national product prices will double while capital prices fall back from three times their original level to merely twice their original level. By coincidence, these are precisely the relationships that held good in the German boom of 1920-21; the money supply doubled, the stock market at first trebled but then skidded to double as the prices of national product began to rise. If luck is bad and people lose faith in all kinds of capital investments, there may be a general exodus of money from capital markets which will make the price inflation in national product much worse than the money inflation would seem to justify. This too happened as the initial acceleration of the German inflation gathered speed.

What is clear is this: national product and national wealth are roughly equal partners in competition for aggregate demand; national product is by no means predominant; the two are inseparably connected as if by conduits, so that rising

Aggregate Values

prices in one must be compensated by falling prices in the other, or else there is inflation; the distribution of money demand between the markets is neither fixed nor reliably stable; and the entire amount of an inflation in the capital market represents inflationary potential which must be realized at least proportionately in national product before the potential can be considered liquidated. A boom in capital prices which exceeds the growth of real capital values and is not accompanied by falling prices in national product is an inflationary danger signal of the first order. The custom of ignoring capital markets and looking solely at national product in relation to total money demand is theoretically unfounded, may be dangerously tranquilizing, and in inflationary conditions will always lead to underestimating the magnitude of inflationary potential.

19
Real Values

Prices depend on the total supply of values in a country compared with its money demand, but real values are not the same thing as ostensible values. Gross national product and sales of capital assets tend to be taken into account at their face values, but this is highly misleading. The relative prices of one thing and another which prevail in one set of conditions, such as inflation, are not the same as would prevail between the same two things in another set of conditions, such as stability. Something which commands a high price and has a high apparent value in inflation may not command any price and may have no value in stability. If ostensible values are higher than real values, the difference represents spurious values. Spurious values have the effect of dampening inflation and understating inflationary potential, because they make the supply of values look larger and price equilibrium look nearer than they actually are. Money occupied in buying spurious values is money which is not forcing up the prices of real values as high as they should be. In an inflation, every nook and cranny of the value supply has its cache of spurious values which help to disguise and conceal the inflation.

National product itself is chronically overstated in an inflation. Earlier, we discoursed at length on the vast volume of useless but superficially economic activity which inflation engenders. Most of the growth in an inflation is shown in these activities. The most inflated relative prices become attached to goods and services of the most marginal real value, so that attaching face value to national product becomes doubly deceptive. It is possible that real values in the United States did not grow at all even while apparently growing by one-third. Whenever non-inflationary conditions should supervene, prices and demand for spurious values collapse like bubbles, shrinking the apparent supply of *saleable* values, worsening the inflation in real values, and placing price equilibrium farther away than it apparently was. Spurious values thus operated as a hidden storage tank for inflationary potential.

Surplus labor is a special case of overstated value. Whenever productivity rises so that less labor is required for the same output, the total supply of real values increases even though actual production may stay the same. The reason is that the total value of output is the same as before, but now we also have an additional supply of surplus labor which has been released from producing it. Surplus labor has a real value, of that there is no doubt. The more there is, the more valuable is the nation. But the correct valuation of this surplus labor is another matter. If surplus labor demands a higher and higher price for doing less and less, which is precisely what happens in inflationary boom, gross national product according to face value appears to go up and up but the supply of real values according to value offered per dollar actually goes down.

Education works like surplus productivity. If education of producers results in greater capacity to do useful work, the supply of real values increases more than population does; but if overeducation results in a decreasing willingness to do useful work, the supply of real values declines. The people as a part of the supply of values are worth less than they were before. In this way, both education and improved productivity may increase the supply of real values up to a point, but after that point they may often actually diminish it.

Capital values are equally overstated in an inflation. For every spurious activity in national product there is a spurious investment value available in capital markets. The most marginal of all investment values are those whose ostensible values rise highest. Capital values inherently cannot grow as buoyantly as national product can. One-sixth of national wealth is land, whose quantity is fixed and whose real value is virtually incapable of increasing. Another large part of national wealth consists of buildings and durable goods which depreciate in value constantly through use. Still another part of capital values consists of natural resources which are subject to permanent depletion. As the end of any nation's supply of a valuable resource such as iron or oil comes into sight, a permanent reduction of that nation's total supply of real values is inevitable. The real values of capital wealth are much more prone to fall and much more difficult to lift than the values of national product. The total supply of all values, which includes capital values, inherently cannot grow as quickly as national product alone can grow.

The fraction of all capital values which is available at any given time fluctuates. Only a small part of the national wealth is for sale at any one time, but it is that small part that enters into the total supply of values at that time. In stable economic conditions, the proportion of the total wealth available for sale at any time would probably be reasonably constant. In inflation, the turnover of capital assets increases. The total supply of real values is swollen by a disproportionately large segment of the capital wealth. This effect serves to understate the inflationary potential which would emerge if the momentary supply of capital values should fall back to normal.

Real Values

By any standard, the profusion of paper wealth constitutes the most enormous single reservoir of inflationary potential. Paper wealth is of several kinds but what we mean here is money wealth, which means debt. Paper property fixed in terms of money amounted to $3.2 trillion in 1971 and was increasing steadily. This was more than three times the gross national product and not far short of the total real national wealth of the United States. The number is fantastic.

Paper wealth is not real wealth in any degree. Real wealth consists exclusively of land, resources, productive plant, durable goods, and people. One class of paper property, such as titles to real estate, common stock ownership of corporation assets, warehouse receipts for tangible goods, and the like, represents direct ownership of real wealth and therefore is functionally equivalent to real wealth. The paper property facilitates trading in the real assets, and no spurious increase in the apparent supply of capital values is possible.

Money wealth works differently. Money wealth is debt, and debt includes all forms of money contracts such as bonds, mortgages, debentures, notes, loans, deposits, life insurance, and pension obligations. Debt does not represent the direct ownership of any real assets, but it does represent a subdivision of interests in real assets with the direct owners of the assets. The superstructure of paper wealth is capable of subdividing the ownership of one set of underlying real assets into many layers of ownership of paper assets.

For example, every man is a part of the real wealth but every man is sole owner of himself. Men as capital assets are not bought and sold, and no part of the money supply in capital markets is employed for this purpose. So long as a man thus remains sole owner of all his own productive output, he is not a part of the total supply of real capital assets purchaseable for money. If he borrows money, however, he subdivides the ownership of his future productive power with his lender, and they have created a paper asset which can be bought and sold. The borrower has subdivided ownership of himself, and he has added himself to the supply of capital assets. If he borrowed his money from a bank, and the bank borrowed its money from a depositor, still another layer of paper assets is based on the same fraction of one man's output. Subdivision and stratification of paper wealth proceeds to much greater lengths in the case of corporations through level after level of debt intermediation. Even government debt constitutes another layer of subdivision of the ownership of all of us by placing a lien on part of the productivity of all the citizens. Through this subdivision and stratification, the apparent supply of paper wealth can be increased to many times the real wealth.

Obviously, the real wealth of a nation is not increased merely because the paper wealth is multiplied, *but a moderation of inflation occurs just as if it were.* Paper wealth acts just as if it were real wealth. A nation's economy would have the same underlying real value with a small paper superstructure as with a large one, but the apparent supply of capital assets would be smaller and the permissible money supply must also be smaller. Conversely, a large paper superstructure gives employment to money supply in buying, selling, refunding, and reinvesting the paper assets fully as well as a supply of real assets would do. The apparent supply of capital assets is larger and the permissible money supply may also be larger. This immobilization of a monetary inflation with an expansion of paper wealth may proceed to almost any extreme so long as the paper wealth retains its credibility. So long as people do not doubt the paper wealth, all is well. If people should doubt the paper wealth and decide to desert it, all becomes suddenly not well. If the money wealth is repudiated, the total supply of *saleable* real values drops by the amount of the money wealth, and prices of real values must rise correspondingly.

As a practical matter, every advanced economic organization requires a considerable degree of complication of paper investment in order to function smoothly. In conditions of reasonable stability, the ratio of paper investment to real values would probably find a minimum level of best efficiency and remain there. Inflation, on the other hand, invariably stimulates a tremendous expansion of paper wealth in relation to real wealth. Government debt grows excessively, and private debt grows even more excessively. This colossal expansion of paper wealth is the most powerful single influence for absorbing, moderating, and containing inflationary force. On the other hand, the existence of this overexpanded paper wealth supplies the principal compulsion upon the government to inflate anew so as to erode the real value of the paper wealth continuously to manageable levels. A man who watches for inflationary storms must keep a weather eye on the paper wealth.

At every turn we have found pools, tanks, and reservoirs where the accumulated inflation of the decades has been stored away without harm. Lagging money velocity has helped; price appreciation in capital markets has helped; spurious values in product and property have lent their aid. The most mammoth reservoir of all, the size of an ocean, is the unnatural and artificial growth of the money wealth, and this is a factor which must remain in our minds throughout the remainder of our study.

20
Government Debt

Government debt does not differ in any respect from private debt or any other kind of money wealth. But since government debt and the budget deficits which create government debt are constantly debated as having special importance to inflation and economic well-being, they deserve some brief separate consideration. The principal conclusion to be drawn from that consideration is that they do not have such importance.

The government budget deficit was a bogy to orthodox conservatives and a magic talisman to Keynesian liberals for decades. In reality, it was as harmless but also as powerless as a pet cat. In the absence of its usual strong-armed accomplice, monetary inflation, government deficit invariably failed to work any magic. Monetary inflation was always what did the job. Still the fiscal liberals clung undaunted to their beloved budget deficits.

The truth is that government debt, of itself, is not inflationary. The creation of government debt through budget

Government Debt

deficit, of itself, is not inflationary. To the contrary, all of these, standing alone, are actually *deflationary*. By "standing alone," we mean deficits and debt which are not accompanied by an increase of the money supply.

The basis for these strange allegations is that the issuance of government debt, like any increase in the paper wealth, increases the total supply of ostensible values available for purchase even though there is no increase in the underlying real values of the economy. So long as the paper wealth retains its credibility, an increase in the supply of paper values, just like real values, must reduce the equilibrium level of all prices. This is deflationary. It may be that the only prices which will be deflated are prices in the debt market, which is to say an increase of interest rates, but this is in every sense an overall price deflation if no other prices go up to compensate.

Open market operations of the Federal Reserve System work in precisely the same way. In order to exert a tightening influence on money and a deflating influence on prices, the Federal Reserve sells government debt into the market. So too when the Treasury does it, and that is all there really is to a government deficit. The government is free to incur any deficit and issue any amount of debt it may wish, so long as it is willing to draw purchasing power away from other borrowers and to tolerate the rise in interest rates which will result. The debt will create no inflation.

Government deficits and government debt thus are not inflationary if they stand alone, but they never stand alone. The creation of government debt is practically always accompanied by an increase of money. Competing against private borrowers for a static supply of credit capital, a large government debt issue would drive interest rates upward, and high interest rates are anathema to a government. A large government debt issue simply could not be marketed without a large increase in the money supply. Therefore the government creates not only the debt but also the money with which to buy it. In addition, large government deficit expenditure tends to accelerate the velocity of money because the government spends its money more rapidly than caufious private spenders do. This combination of increased quantity and velocity of money, not the deficits, does the job, both for economic stimulation and for monetary inflation.

The combination of money quantity and velocity which practically always accompanies government debt is inflationary, but less inflationary than the money inflation alone, without the debt, would be. The presence of the new government debt as an addition to the supply of values has a mitigating and therefore beneficial effect. If the monetary inflation were small enough to balance the new government debt just right (it seldom is), the net inflationary effect could be zero. The same amount of money expansion without the new government debt would have been inflationary. There was a good deal of specious validity to the argument made during World War II that huge budget deficits and new government debt were positively necessary in order to soak up the inflated money and purchasing power that the government was spewing out, assuming that the government really had to spew out all that inflated money.

The converse of this is that a government budget surplus, standing alone, is *inflationary*. If the proceeds of a government surplus are used to reduce the total amount of government debt outstanding, the supply of values is reduced, the former holders of the debt still have the same purchasing power to use elsewhere, and the equilibrium level of prices must rise. In the same way, when the Federal Reserve System wishes to provide easy money and inflationary conditions, it buys government debt in the open market and substitutes money for part of the supply of values. So too when the Treasury does it. Of course, if the government should not use its surplus to reduce its debt but instead should simply hold the money immobilized, effective money supply would be reduced and the surplus would not be inflationary. To avoid the inherently inflationary

Government Debt

effects of a surplus, the government must do this, but it seldom does. Any reduction of government debt which is not accompanied by a reduction of money quantity or velocity is inflationary. Any resort to a government surplus to fight inflation is worse than futile, it produces the opposite of its intended result.

The only limit to the inflation-absorptive effect of government debt, like any money wealth, is the credibility of the debt. As long as the government can sell its debt, it can use debt to restrain the inflationary effects of its high-velocity spending and its money creation. Only if all trust in money wealth is lost through inflation is the restraining capacity of government debt lost. At that point, and only then, does government debt shift from a dampener to a fuel of inflation. Existing money which has been employed in debt markets leaves them for other markets, inflating prices there, and the government debt itself represents an obligation of the government to issue additional money in its place at maturity. Government debt which holds down inflation while the debt is credible amplifies and re-amplifies inflation when its credibility fails. That failure is the sole inflationary potential of government debt and the sole risk of running government deficits. Short of that, government debt does good work.

21
The Record Interpreted

Holding our freshly calibrated inflation tape measure in hand, we can now clamber over the historical record which inflation has left us in America and Germany and elsewhere and take some measurements for our edification.

This tape measure is unfortunately not yet a magic monitor for inflation. Even with its aid we have difficulty estimating *future* inflation. The reason is that two of the three variables which enter into our measurements, money velocity and the supply of values, are quite difficult to determine. Velocity is bad enough but the supply of values, as explored in the preceding chapters, is so complex as to be impossible. The tape measure works, but as to any current state of affairs our ability to isolate the components to be measured remains rudimentary.

With respect to *past* inflation, the difficulty is not so great. If there was inflation, *we know that the quantity of money was too great, and also how much too great.* From that knowledge and knowledge of what the quantity of money actually was

Record Interpreted

doing, we can deduce what the other variables must have been doing. From this analysis of the past, we can form some useful hypotheses about what is happening in the present.

From stability in 1939 to stability in 1948, prices in the United States increased enormously but only about 60 percent as much as money supply did. The same relationship existed in Germany of World War I, although the actual magnitudes of increase of both prices and money supply were much larger. The only possible explanations of why prices did not increase even more than they did, correlating more closely with the money supply, are that velocity decreased or the supply of values increased. Probably there was a little of the former and a great deal of the latter. Velocity in the United States declined steeply during the war and turned upward after the war, but by 1948 still was not as high as before the war. A moderate decrease of velocity therefore helped somewhat to abate the money inflation. A rise in the supply of values, absorbing the remainder of the gap between money increases and price increases, can only be inferred but is easily reconciled with the facts we do know. The wartime increase of American productive capacity, even after eliminating purely military production, was large. The increase of government debt as a new addition to the supply of values was even larger. Because of all these factors, the inflationary potential at the end of the war was not as great as the money quantity inflation alone. Any person who at the end of the war thought that inflation had been safely contained was wrong, but any person who thought that equilibrium prices were as much higher as money supply had already ascended was equally wrong. The unrealized depreciation of the dollar was something less than the money supply alone seemed to dictate.

By contrast, the salient feature of the record after the stabilization of 1948 was the much closer correspondence of prices and money supply at points of equilibrium. The principal points of equilibrium, which means the points at which money supply and prices were stable and in equilibrium with each other, may be taken to be late 1949, late 1953, and late 1962. The absence at these points of either upward or downward tendency of money or prices was the mark of stability. From each of these points of stability to the next, the percentage rise in prices was in a constant relationship to the percentage rise in money supply: *price inflation from stability to stability matched the money inflation, to the fraction of a percentage point, to the extent that money expansion exceeded something like seven-tenths of one percent per year.* Whenever prices and money were out of that relation to each other, there was disequilibrium and either upward or downward pressure on prices until they were forced back into that relation.

The quantity theory of money in its simplest form would suggest that prices might move in direct proportion to money supply in this way. We know that the theory in this form is too simple and not always true, because velocity and the supply of values are as important to prices as money quantity, but it happened that the simple direct relationship between equilibrium prices and money supply very nearly held good in the United States for fifteen years. This must have meant that the increase in the supply of real values during that time was approximately equal to the increase in the velocity of money, and that the two thus cancelled each other out. This is not implausible. The imperfect evidence that we have seems to indicate an average increase of velocity of at least 4.8 percent per year during this time, while the average annual growth in gross national product in constant dollars was something less than 4 percent per year.

If equilibrium prices were indeed in this constant relationship with money supply, the only money supply which could have avoided all inflation would have been a money supply that increased at a rate of no more than 0.7 percent per year. Furthermore, so long as this parity held good the unrealized depreciation of the dollar could be estimated between points of stability while an inflationary episode was in progress. The amount of latent inflation yet to be endured to the next point of stability could be estimated with some degree of confidence. The Index of Latent Inflation at any given time was the further percentage rise of prices which was necessary to put prices back in equilibrium with the expansion of money that had already occurred since the last point of stability. This kind of estimation would have proved itself precisely correct at any moment during the years from 1948 to 1962.

If this index would have correctly estimated latent inflation at all times before 1962, perhaps it might also do so after 1962, and nothing that had occurred through 1973 indicated that equilibrium prices and money quantity were in other than the same relationship. As applied to the great inflationary upsurge that began in 1962, the Index of Latent Inflation showed an almost constant increase from zero at its base point of stability, in September 1962, to more than 18 percent by the close of President Johnson's administration in 1968. It exceeded 22 percent by the end of 1972 under President Nixon. Never since the end of World War II had the assured but hidden depreciation of the dollar been permitted to grow so large. If the experience of those decades still applied, equilibrium would return and the inflation be ended when and only when price inflation was allowed to race ahead to catch past money inflation, without any new money inflation and also without any of the concomitant pleasures of money inflation.

These relationships cannot be taken as immutable, nor these temporarily accurate laws as holy writ. Guessing the unrealized depreciation of the dollar and the equilibrium level of prices was still as chancy as it had been at the end of World War II. If the apparent supply of values really contained much false value that would be sloughed off upon a return of stability, equilibrium prices might be considerably higher than the index would predict. On the other hand, a return of stability might very well halt the rise of velocity or even lower it, and in that event equilibrium prices might not rise as high as predicted. Until some better evidence offered itself, however, the Index of Latent Inflation based on the relative increases of money supply and prices since stability in 1962 seemed the best guess anyone could make.

It should be reassuring, if anything, to understand that inflation is not interminable and inflationary potential is not infinite. A further inflation of 20 percent or so was not, after all, unthinkable. It was much less than the 50 percent latent inflation that existed at the close of World War II, although it was also much more than the peak latent inflation of only about 4.5 percent at the worst of the 1956 inflation. Knowing the finitude of inflationary potential can go a long way toward removing its terrors. One of the interesting comparisons between the German inflation and other inflations, however, was not how large was the unrealized depreciation of the Reichsmark in that worst of all inflations but exactly the opposite, how really close to equilibrium even Germany was at all times while it destroyed itself. At the very peak in 1921, money supply had only about doubled while prices had not yet risen. The latent inflation of the mark was therefore probably never above 100 percent after the 1920 stability. If Germany had merely accepted another doubling of its prices and stopped inflating its money, it could undoubtedly have ended the inflation with no more pain than it ultimately had to suffer in 1923 and 1924. A worse inflationary potential than this had been cleanly liquidated immediately after the war by Erzberger's financial policies of 1919. But Germany in 1922 was incapable of submitting voluntarily to any pain whatever, so that instead of ending the inflation it gave chase to it. That was what spelled the difference.

22
Money

Let us pause for a brief digression or two on some conceptual matters that have importance to comprehending the economic riddle. The first digression is the proper conception of the thing called money.

Earlier we said that money's proper use was as a medium of exchange, that money doing its duty was money in motion. Later we saw that money combined with its rate of velocity was the opposite side of a balanced equation from the total supply of real values of all kinds. Money was the counterweight to all things of value, money was the opposite of value. Money's value is purely derivative; money has no value of its own. Money is a reflector of the economy it serves. The entire economy is the backing of the currency; more properly it is the "fronting" of the currency, because money and all things of value confront one another, they do not stand behind one another confronting something else. A unit of money is like a share in the entire economy it serves, and inflating the money is like diluting the shares.

No partial supply of gold or any other thing of intrinsic value is the true backing of a currency or has anything to do with the value of currency. Types of money like gold, which do have an inherent value other than as a medium of exchange, cannot do otherwise than obstruct the proper management of money. Gold was always best as money for the very reason that it came closest, after valueless paper, to having no non-monetary value, while at the same time being limited in quantity and scarce. Gold did therefore have a certain disciplinary quality, but the correlation between the actual supply of gold and the proper supply of money at any time, if there was any correlation, was always purely coincidental. A properly managed fiat currency, frankly having no inherent value even imaginary, is infinitely superior as money to gold or any other commodity having a conflicting real value.

One of Karl Helfferich's more striking exercises in scholasticism, reminiscent of how many angels can dance on the head of a pin, was his extended theorization of whether money was a thing of value in itself. His arguments were ingenious, persuasive, and wrong. He said that it did. It does not.

Money, being derivative of value, reflective of value, a reciprocal to everything else of value, is a kind of anti-value. The more vigorously people seek to use money, the more it should disappear. If they use money with perfect efficiency, there should be no money. Where then did the value go? When a money supply does exist, implicitly because of a degree of inefficiency in the use of money, that money supply is a quantity having no inherent value. Money may appear to be, and is, something of value to any one member of an economy because it represents a valid general claim by him against all the other members; but to the economy as a whole all of these claims against one another are cancelled out leaving money an absolute cipher in the real value of the economy.

This is not an exercise in scholasticism equal though opposite to Helfferich's. Because of the rigorously vacuous nature of money, we do well to look through the money level of all economic flows, as through a window, and see instead the underlying flows of real values among the members of an economy. If we succeed in doing this, we go far toward shedding the misconceptions of economic management which a preoccupation with money may cause. For example, if I buy a car with money which I earned by operating a machine, I am really trading some of my machine-operating services to the man who sold me the car. If he did not happen to want any of my services, I gave him a negotiable receipt—money —from another man who did. Money is but a unit of notation among three parties—myself, the man I sell my values to, and the man I buy my needs from. Barter trading involves only two parties and money trading involves three, but in either case the true subject matter of the trading is the flow of real values among the parties and not the paper receipts.

To the economic system as a whole, money is even more militantly neutral. The real value of an economy is its people, land, capital assets and natural resources. Real value is the same whether the system has only a simple paper superstructure consisting of little money and few debts, or a huge superstructure of much money and many levels of paper investment. Neither form of organization is richer than the other, except for the waste implicit in any organization which is unnecessarily complex for its purposes. Increases of real wealth can only be achieved by luckily discovering new natural resources, or by strokes of genius resulting in technological discovery, or by working harder, in no other way, and most certainly not by creating money.

All of this is relatively obvious and relatively elementary, but it is not always remembered. Economists, politicians, and plain people are constantly harping on money as if the money itself mattered. A person is spoken of as "having money" when he does not really have large cash balances at all, but non-monetary real assets which can be converted into money and then into some other real assets more or less at will. A government is spoken of as "finding the money" for some national objective, such as housing, instead of another, such as war, when it really seeks to divert resources out of one activity, choking off that activity and destroying investment and employment in it, and reapplying them to another. Money means nothing to any of this. Money is merely the hypodermic instrument by which the lifeblood is drained out of one economic body and injected into another. "Having money" or "finding money" is metaphorical, but its metaphorical nature seems constantly to be forgotten, deluding people in the subtlest of ways into thinking that money is the problem.

Money is a monumental nothingness. Creating money cannot create real value, and destroying money cannot destroy real value. Real wealth does not rise if the money world booms, nor does it diminish if the money world falls apart. The real world is too real and the money world too evanescent. To use money as a positive instrument for real well-being is to use a vapor for a hammer. All that money manipulation can do is to alter the direction of flow of real values and to alter the distribution of real values among the members of the economy. Money manipulation is of course not the only way to redistribute wealth, but redistribution of wealth is the only way that money manipulation can work. If money manipulation increases wealth anywhere, real assets must be taken from somewhere else. What we seek to do is to look through the money flows and to see where the real wealth we have apparently gained actually came from.

23

The Creation of Money

The second digression is on the subject of the creation of money. Since money quantity is the controllable variable, creation or destruction of money is the mechanism for managing a currency to exclude inflation. Some rather strange goings-on happen in the dark little room of the economic house where money is created or destroyed.

Money management consists of creating money to match exactly any increase of the supply of values, and to offset exactly any decrease of money velocity. Monetary inflation consists of allowing any greater quantity of money than this to exist, and monetary deflation any smaller quantity. In principle, it should be possible to set up a computer readout on the desk of the Chairman of the Federal Reserve Board to indicate the intrinsic value of the dollar from minute to minute, and his organization could then add or subtract money to hold the indicator steady. In practice, the raw statistical data for the computer are so fragmentary that this is not possible. Money management is less a matter of information conversion than of instinct.

The government's tools of economic management divide into two parts, monetary policy and fiscal policy. Monetary policy means manipulating the money, and the Federal Reserve System has charge of this. Fiscal policy means manipulating the taxes and expenditures of the government, and the Treasury Department has charge of this. The government's economic responsibility is a deeply divided responsibility. In this chapter we are speaking of monetary policy and the Federal Reserve System.

If money has the principal function of a medium of exchange and the incidental functions of a store of value and a standard of value, then money also has the principal duty of having a *constant* value. The proper business of the Federal Reserve as guardian of the money is to provide it a constant value. The United States would take a long stride forward if the Federal Reserve would do no more than figuratively to set up that computer readout on the desk of its chairman and bend all its efforts to holding the indicator steady. Professor Milton Friedman, chief critic of the Federal Reserve, made this point repeatedly, and it is difficult to add much to his arguments. Never in its entire history had the Federal Reserve taken as its sole duty the stabilization of the value of the dollar. Instead it meddled with controlling interest rates, financing the government, producing economic growth, providing jobs, dampening booms, and reversing recessions. All of these may well be the business of the government, but not of the money guardians. On the other hand we sometimes found the Treasury Department trying to stop inflation, which is not its business either. If the Federal Reserve would narrow its focus to achieving constant prices and thereby remove all the purely monetary causes of economic ill health, like inflation, it would do all that was required of it and far more good than monetary policy had ever achieved before.

This task, while definable, was not easy. The Federal

Creation of Money

Reserve knew reasonably well what the money supply was, but that was all that it knew reasonably well. Its information about velocity, about the relative use of money in capital and product markets, and about the supplies of real values in all markets were all poor. Monetary policy, in short, needed much greater familiarity with its own job and much less concern with other jurisdictions of economic management. In the end, the task might turn out to be a little easier than it seemed. In stable conditions, if they should ever be established, all the variable factors might maintain a fairly constant relationship to one another. If so, the Federal Reserve would not need so desperately to know each of the component variables. The better monetary policy did its proper job, if it ever did, the easier it might be to continue doing it.

Once the monetary authority were persuaded to confine itself to controlling the money, it would find that its control of the money was none too firm either. This was principally because of that remarkable feature of the money system known as fractional-reserve banking. Most of the money in the United States, as in other countries, was not created by the government at all but by private banks. Only about one-third of all money was government money the way a dollar bill is.

All money consists of currency, like dollar bills and coins, and checking account deposits with commercial banks. The quantity of checking account deposits in the United States was almost four times as large as the quantity of dollar bills and coins. All of the dollar bills and coins were issued by the government, and they were government money. In addition, the commercial banks had reserve deposits with the Federal Reserve, and these reserve deposits too were obligations of the government and therefore government money. The rest of the checking-account money was not. The total of all the dollar bills and all the Federal Reserve deposits, constituting all the government money in the country, was only one-third as large as the total money supply. The reason for this was that the banks' reserve deposits with the Federal Reserve equalled only a small fraction of the deposit money which the banks created. The reserve requirement was set by the Federal Reserve Board and was mostly around 17 percent in the 1960's. The result of this extraordinary system was that two-thirds of the money supply was no more true money, like a dollar bill, than the promissory note of your friendly banker, or, for that matter, of your corner druggist. If everyone demanded this part of his "money" in dollar bills or other government money, he could not get it because it did not exist. It functioned like money but it was not money.

The economic effects of this kind of system were astounding. The most breathtaking was the awesome gift which it made to bankers. The power to create money was obviously a lucrative one. Whenever the Federal Reserve increased the money supply, it created only the reserve portion and the banks created the larger remainder. For every dollar of new reserves issued by the government, banks were permitted to create four or five additional dollars out of thin air and lend them out at interest. This subsidy to banks is especially spectacular in inflationary times when money is being voluminously created. Lord Keynes exclaimed his incredulity of the phenomenon in Germany, by which the Reichsbank did not even reserve a monopoly of money inflation but let the private banks share. In the United States, in the single twelve-month period from June 1972 to June 1973, the banks were allowed to create over *thirteen billion dollars* more than the government did. By giving away this much of the money creation privilege, the government gave away to the banks more than twice the entire expensive farm subsidy programs, about half its extremely large budget deficit, and more than one-fourth the entire growth of the real national product for the same one-year period. Farming out the government's money creation rights to commercial banks had many of the characteristics of the infamous tax-farming systems of history, by which the tax farmers made fortunes and the governments

Creation of Money 149

realized precious little revenue. It goes without saying that this system contributed mightily to the overflowing profits of the commercial banks during the money inflation of the 1960's and helped explain why plush new skyscraping bank buildings were one of the more conspicuous forms of growth of that period.

Fractional-reserve money has other even more destructive effects. The government's control of the money supply is weakened by it. Bankers and people in general can cause the money supply to increase or decrease in direct opposition to the Federal Reserve's efforts to manage it. If the Federal Reserve increases reserves, still no increase in the money supply will occur if the banks will not create the money and lend it out. This may cause what is known as a "liquidity trap." Conversely, if the Federal Reserve tightens reserves the banks may still increase the money supply by borrowing reserves from the central bank. If people for no conscious reason shift one net dollar from paper money into checking accounts, four or five more dollars of checking accounts may spring into existence because of the reserve multiplier without any desire by the Federal Reserve that money expand. Conversely, for every net withdrawal of one dollar from checking accounts into paper money, the bankers must destroy four or five more dollars of checking accounts regardless of the will of the Federal Reserve. Precisely this wholesale destruction of money in the 1930's, caused by a flight into paper money compounded by the reserve multiplier, underlay the banking crises of those years and the great depression itself.

The fractional-reserve system potentially can contribute fully as much mischief to disastrous inflation as it did to the great depression. If government debt should lose its credibility so that the government was compelled to substitute money for debt, the ultimate inflation of the money supply would not merely equal the replaced debt but might actually be four or five times greater because of the banks' powers to create additional money on the new reserves. Milton Friedman attributed the nation's severe inflation of World War II directly to the fractional-reserve system, hampering the Federal Reserve's control of money supply, and not to any basic defect in the nation's overall strategy for financing the war.

Any intelligent novice, first introduced to the workings of the money system, must find the pyramiding of money on the fractional-reserve base incredible. A few of the nation's foremost economists, led by Henry C. Simons and Irving Fisher, were of the same mind at the depth of the depression when they urgently advocated abolishing the system. The idea was simply to require 100 percent reserves for all checking account deposits, so that all true money was government money. Instituting that system would have been little more than a bookkeeping entry, but after it was done all the evils of the fractional-reserve system would disappear. The idea was called the only fundamentally creative idea to come out of the depression. But the idea passed into limbo. The best economic minds were in favor of it, but the commercial bankers could be counted on to resist to the bitter end the loss of their money machine, and the people and the legislators probably did not understand what it was all about. Little was heard of the idea in later decades except occasional, and rather inaudible, reminders by a few economists. This complacency would no doubt persist until still another series of disasters came to pass with the substantial aid and comfort of the fractional-reserve system.

If all money is to be true money, no one can be permitted to create or destroy money except the government. Each citizen who thinks he owns a dollar of real money should own 100 cents of claim on the government and not 15 or 20 cents. The government, when it wishes to expand or contract money, should simply add or subtract that many dollars and not have to add or subtract only a fraction as many as reserves, waiting for banks and people to do the rest. Above all, no one should enjoy the incidental benefits of money creation but the government, using these benefits for its public purposes.

Creation of Money

As these things stood in the United States, when money was to expand, the Federal Reserve must buy up debt obligations (supporting that market) to create reserves, and banks multiplied the reserves into money. If the government needed the money, it must go into the same markets to borrow it *and pay interest for its own money*. There was a wall between the Federal Reserve and the Treasury. Conversely, when money was to tighten, the Federal Reserve must sell debt obligations (depressing that market) to destroy reserves and banks must call in loans to destroy additional money, further depressing the credit market. Meanwhile the Treasury taxed and spent, blithely unconcerned with what the Federal Reserve was trying to do. Again there was a wall between Federal Reserve and Treasury.

There was a reason for the wall, to be sure, and the reason was a good one. The reason was nothing less than a frank, healthy, and fundamental distrust of political governments. The Federal Reserve was independent in the hope of avoiding the inflation which, it was thought, would inevitably follow if the insatiable exchequer had access to the money machine. But the independence was a fiction, and the hope was either futile or superfluous. Whether or not there was unification in form, the Federal Reserve and the Treasury must know how to speak to one another and to act like a right hand and a left of the same government. And they did. The Federal Reserve inflated when the government wished to inflate, as in the Kennedy-Johnson years; and held back when the government wished not to inflate, as in the Eisenhower years. The arrangement was no more inflationary than if the Federal Reserve were truly independent, and no less inflationary than if it were unified with the government. The form did not matter, only the substance.

This being so, money should be placed at the disposal of the government and vice versa. Whenever sound money management calls for new money—and normally it will call for *a small amount* of new money continuously in a stable, growing economy—the money should simply be issued to the government, interest-free, for spending on its public purposes. The first use should always be the government's and without any connection to credit markets. By the same token, whenever sound money management calls for an actual contraction of money—it seldom will—the huge taxing powers of the government should be at the service of money management. So much of tax revenue should simply be taken, immobilized, and not spent, again without any connection to the credit market. Bankers and private holders of debt should be neither benefited nor harmed when the government expands or contracts money.

These ideals of money management are many leagues away from the way money management worked in the American inflation. Change comes slowly; there was no perceptible improvement in these affairs in the entire twentieth century. Real progress usually is borne only of crisis at best, disaster at worst, and the opportunity to wring real progress out of the depression disaster was missed. It could only be hoped that there might still come either timely change or a superhuman ability of money management to overcome its own self-imposed disabilities.

24
Depression

We have now thoroughly mastered the problem of inflation. This may come as something of a surprise, but it is true. Properly understood, inflation is not really much of a problem at all. The problem of inflation is not widely understood properly, either, but that too is only one of the miscellaneous problems. Unfortunately, however, inflation is not the only major problem nor even the paramount one. Having mastered that one, we have still scarcely begun the battle.

The other side of the problem is depression. The problem of depression goes under many names and can be thought of in many ways—recession, the business cycle, the boom and bust of capitalism, secular stagnation, and above all unemployment—but all boil down to the same thing, which is depression. For a precisely imprecise description of this problem, we might call it a *chronically insufficient prosperity* for the people as a whole.

How much prosperity is sufficient, and how little is insufficient, is a nice question. There can never be so much prosperity that there could not be more, or so little that there could not be less. Mankind can always bring himself to accept more prosperity and usually could put up with less. For an answer to how much prosperity is "sufficient," we might adapt Lord Keynes' excellent definition of involuntary unemployment: sufficient prosperity exists when the people would not be interested in obtaining any more prosperity at the cost that would entail in harder work or greater expenditure of resources. Insufficient prosperity exists when the people would be interested in more prosperity, even at the expense of harder work, but are held back by some artificial restraint from doing what they are willing to do. Sufficient prosperity is not an absolute, related to quantity of production, but relative, deriving from the people's inclinations. Sufficient prosperity is a natural level at which people are freed to have just as much as they care to work for. According to this definition, prosperity which is lower than the theoretical maximum may still be "sufficient" by the lights of the people. Nevertheless, I accept the premise of activist economics that insufficient prosperity was a chronic problem of the United States in recent decades.

It has been a reversal of the usual order of precedence for us to study inflation before depression and to place price stability before prosperity. Economists have habitually been more deeply concerned with depression and unemployment than with price inflation. With this priority too, we must agree. Adequate prosperity is more important than an absence of inflation. If there is a necessary conflict between stability of prices and a reasonably fruitful economy, stability of prices must yield. The proposition of this book is that there is no such conflict. Even accepting the priority of prosperity over price stability, we were right to address the lesser matter of price stability first. If the requirements for price stability are set up first, not last, then the means to prosperity can be found and tested which do not violate these requirements. If on the other hand prosperity alone is set up as a goal and

Depression

prices are left to lodge where they may, as all modern economics did, the result is a fatalistic acquiescence in inflation. Economists offer the easy but false apology that inflation is the inevitable price of prosperity. Admittedly, demanding not only sufficient prosperity but also price stability makes the task of economic management more difficult than demanding prosperity alone. Economists would prefer to have the easier task. This is why it is perilous to let economists prescribe the specifications for their own performance.

Professor Milton Friedman of the University of Chicago was the leader of a school of economics, popularly called "monetarists" or the "Chicago school," which averred that regulation of the quantity of money controlled not only inflation but also the sufficiency of prosperity. Professor Friedman's epic work produced with Mrs. Anna Schwartz, *A Monetary History of the United States,* traced in minute detail from the Civil War to 1960 the correlation of money supply changes with the boom/depression cycle as well as with price inflations and deflations. The evidence was exhaustive and irrefutable. Monetary constriction preceded every major or minor depression, recession, rolling readjustment, pause, or other popular name for insufficient prosperity. Every monetary expansion preceded a boom and an inflation. Extreme monetary contraction as the cause of the extreme severity of the Great Depression was especially striking. Similar principles operated on the economic course of the United States after World War II, when each money expansion was followed in order by stock market boom, rising business and employment, and price inflation; and each money nonexpansion by stock market fall, insufficient prosperity and unemployment, and price stabilization.

Professor Friedman concluded from all this convincing evidence that expansion and contraction of money had been a principal contributing cause to economic instability. Efforts by monetary policy to offset the economic cycles worsened the cycles. To avoid that, Professor Friedman proposed that money expansions and contractions be stopped and replaced by a steady rate of money growth. Any rate of change, if steady, said he, would be less damaging than expansions and contractions were. Beyond that, Professor Friedman's ultimate conclusion was that if money policy simply stopped changing, stopped upsetting the economy, and adopted a steady, noninflationary growth rate, sufficient prosperity would take care of itself. In the truth or falsity of this proposition lay the acid test of the straight monetarist economics.

This book's extremely high regard for Professor Friedman's economics in general must have become obvious before now. Most of the sense that was uttered in English-speaking economics after Lord Keynes was uttered by Milton Friedman or that small coterie he represented. Professor Friedman was one of the few true prophets around, a more minor one than Keynes himself perhaps but at least a true one. Professor Friedman was no more totally immune from error than Keynes himself, but he carried a rich freight of validity in most that he said. He was right that money causes inflations, that money causes depressions, and that money cycles cause instability that a steady trend would avoid. But when he reached the ultimate conclusion that sufficient prosperity would take care of itself without inflation if money growth were only steadied, I fear he was wrong. The evidence, though less abundant, was to the contrary.

Professor Friedman's original proposal was for a money growth of 3 to 5 percent per year. Unfortunately this was the proposal that became lodged in the heads of the uncomprehending and was bandied about in pseudo-monetarist thinking of the 1969–1973 stage of inflation. By all the evidence since World War II, this amount of money growth would also establish a steady rate of price inflation of about 3 to 5 percent per year. The best example is the money growth that began in 1954 and produced the inflation of 1956 and was somewhat less than 4 percent per year. Later and much less noticed, Professor Friedman changed his mind

Depression

and said that the right money growth to avoid inflation should be only 1 or 2 percent per year. This was closer to the truth. Unfortunately, however, every postwar period in which money grew by no more than 1 percent per year, notably 1954 itself, still produced clearcut recession, insufficient prosperity, and unemployment.

With regret we must admit that Doctor Friedman's prescription, though entirely correct, would not be entirely effective. Monetarism alone would not do the job. Stabilization of money alone would not solve all the problems. It remained possible to have both sufficient prosperity and an absence of inflation, but it was not possible without other structural adjustments to the economic organization besides sound money.

25
The Economics of Keynes

The English economist John Maynard Keynes single-handedly built the twentieth century's economic milestone in 1936 when he published his work, *The General Theory of Employment, Interest, and Money*. It is if anything an understatement to describe the effect of this work as a Keynesian revolution. It is impossible to speak of matters economic after the appearance of this work without dealing primarily with Keynes. Its influence on apostles and skeptics alike was so profound that it was truly said, as Milton Friedman did say: we are all Keynesians today.

Keynesian economics were at the bottom of all the economic problems that scourged the United States and the world as the 1970's began, but nothing in this book is intended as a general attack on either Keynes or his *General Theory*. Quite the contrary. Keynes is an acknowledged master, or at least this book acknowledges him as master. If Milton Friedman was a true prophet, Keynes was not only a true one but the major prophet of the century in economics. This book is in-

Economics of Keynes

deed Keynesian in the deepest sense, what might be called proto-Keynesian rather than neo-Keynesian. The work of Keynes himself is to be clearly distinguished from that of his disciples; that is why this chapter is entitled "The Economics of Keynes" and not "Keynesian Economics." The latter name might better be applied to the next chapter, which is otherwise called "Inflationary Economics." Almost every true prophet's teaching tends to be perverted by his disciples, and blessed is he that has no disciples. Keynesians earned an undeservedly bad name for Keynes himself. Modern Keynesian economics were scarcely more true to Keynes than the Spanish Inquisition was truly Christian.

Keynes wrote many books, not just the *General Theory*. A number of them are quoted at various places in this book. Reading Keynes' work conveys more of the sense of a profound intellect at large, testing the circumstances with real understanding, than the work of any successor. To learn from Keynes, one does best to skip the Keynesians and go to Keynes himself. Keynes was not free from error; he was superior but not superhuman. Most of what he said was valid when he said it, and some of his most revolutionary thoughts were also valid for all times. The modern problem is to select and build upon the more timeless of Keynes' building blocks and not, as Keynesians did, on foundation blocks which were sound only in special circumstances like the Great Depression. One of Keynes' most interesting and flexible traits was his habit of changing his mind from one book to the next. He began each later book by discarding some of the basic ideas of the preceding one. He also was a great one for confronting present problems presently and putting to one side problems that did not yet exist though they might exist later. Specifically that was how he freed himself from concern about inflation during the depression when the *General Theory* emerged. A decade earlier, when inflation raged through Europe, he had been an equally incisive student and critic of inflationary economics. Keynes died just after World War II, and in his last conversations with friends was already reacting against the Keynesians. One entertains no doubt whatever that his *General Theory* would have undergone wholesale alteration in his later books if there had been any, just as his earlier works had done. The *General Theory* was simply Keynes' last word when the bell rang.

The *General Theory*, despite its title, was preeminently a product of its time, which is to say a product of the worldwide Great Depression of the 1930's. Keynes spoke from a time when great numbers of people who wanted to work could not find work to do, when productive plants were idle for lack of buyers of their products while the potential buyers also were in want of the products, when money had been allowed to disappear and the people would not spend what little money there was. There was excessive saving, underconsumption, underinvestment, and underemployment of people and capital. There was acutely insufficient prosperity. To Keynes or to any economist or layman, this situation made no sense at all. To any reasonably keen instinct it was plain that all the makings of economic prosperity were present. In terms of real potential nothing had changed from the 1920's, and therefore miraculous reimprovement of economic health could be wrought if someone could only find the key to make things start turning over again. All of this instinct was absolutely sound.

Keynes applied himself to this problem with a typical readiness to innovate. He cast aside the orthodox economic learning which had accumulated over past centuries, and he built a structure of thought from the ground up which incorporated some audacious new conclusions:

(1) the state must intervene; sufficient prosperity would not take care of itself if *laissez faire* economics left it alone;

(2) the body economic must be forced to consume more, thereby spending itself rich, and not try to save so much;

(3) consumption is stimulated by jobs, jobs by new capital investment, and investment by the state's creating artificially low interest rates on capital rather than high rates as the classical economics said;

(4) where necessary, the state should deliberately spend more than it taxes in order to stimulate investment, business activity, and consumption.

This reasoning contained the germs of all that later became the Keynesian economics: government management, full employment, low interest and cheap money, deliberate government deficits, investment, consumption, economic activity, and growth.

In the circumstances of the depression, Keynes placed prosperity before price stability in importance with a vengeance. His treatment of prices and inflation in the *General Theory* came last and weakly. His pragmatic strategy was to solve the depression first and worry about inflation later if it should become a problem later. In the abnormal circumstances of the depression, his trust in the work of his predecessors and himself in the quantity theory of money grew faint. He was content to say that as long as resources of people and capital were idle—in other words, as long as there was a depression—economic stimulation according to his suggestions should not cause inflation. When that was no longer true, he said, there might be a problem. There might indeed.

Keynes' propositions amounted to nothing more or less than a prescription of simple monetary inflation. This point might be disputed, but it is essential to following Keynes' policies to their sources. Keynes was a monetarist at heart. Through all of his intricate technical reasoning, a single precept shone forth: monetary inflation has marvelously stimulative short-term effects. Governments have been rediscovering this with delight throughout the ages by instinct, but Keynes clothed it in an aura of the recondite that made it seem wonderfully new and magical. It was still the faithful old home remedy of monetary inflation. Low interest rates and abundantly available money, which were a part of Keynes' prescription, were obviously a function of expanded money quantity. Less obvious but still true, government budget deficits also operated through accompanying monetary expansion, either by increasing the supply of money or by accelerating the velocity of existing money. As we have seen, without money inflation government deficits would cause nothing but higher interest rates and deflation. Monetary expansion was therefore Keynes' fundamental operative agent.

To say that Keynes' prescription was monetary inflation is not to say that it was an invalid prescription. Monetary inflation is a legitimate tool of economic management. It has some good effects and some bad ones. Instead of being taken as a matter of emotion, monetary inflation should be evaluated dispassionately like any medicine for its good effects and bad effects in particular circumstances. This medicine is proper when its good effects will do more good than its bad ones harm, or when its bad effects will be no worse than the existing state of affairs. Like a dose of cocaine, one calls for inflation when the situation demands, but not usually for a mild tummyache.

Keynes' years of the Great Depression were as apt a time for a prescription of monetary inflation as there ever was. To begin with, this depression was caused by an extreme monetary deflation. Money quantity and velocity each contracted by one-third by 1932, which meant that aggregate money demand as the product of the two was less than half its original level. Some of this contraction showed up in lowered prices, but the remainder showed up in reduced business activity and supply of values. Both effects were unqualifiedly vicious. If at any time the government had effectively counteracted these contracting trends, the depression could have been stopped from worsening. Massive monetary expansion by any of the Keynesian devices could have done this without inflation. Issuing and spending sufficient money to keep the quantity of money from decreasing is an obvious one. If the people's hoarding of

Economics of Keynes 163

money causes a one-third reduction of velocity, the government can issue and spend 50 percent more money quantity without inflation. If banks have lots of money supply to lend, but people refuse to borrow causing low velocity and low interest rates, the government can step in and borrow the money to spend by means of budget deficits without causing either excessive interest rates or price inflation. All of these propositions of Keynes were sound propositions in the Great Depression, and within the limits of the price equation none would have caused price inflation. In reality they would have constituted only monetary stabilization and not monetary inflation at all.

The true test of Keynes' *General Theory* comes later, after the deterioration of the depression has been halted. By 1936 when his book was published, the contraction had been over for several years and a new equilibrium had been reached, but the equilibrium was one of plainly insufficient prosperity. Money quantity and velocity were no longer decreasing or increasing, and there was no deflation or inflation. But velocity stayed low, interest rates stayed low, everyone lived more frugally than he formerly did, buying less and saving more and watching his money, and as a consequence many people and factories could not get as much work to do as they formerly did and would like to do again. This abnormally low consumption was mostly a psychological scar left over from the buffeting of the earlier contraction, and not a chronic condition of capitalist economy, but still it existed and called for remedy.

Here too, confronted by this acid test, it is possible that Keynes' prescription of monetary inflation might work without price inflation. Monetary inflation always has short-term stimulative effects, and in these depressed conditions the stimulus might very well cause the supply of saleable values to increase by fully as much as the monetary inflation. If so, there would be no price inflation. Remember that price inflation is by far the slowest of all the effects of monetary inflation. Economic stimulation comes first. In one of his earlier books Keynes made the famous quip, "In the long run we are all dead," by way of admitting that price inflation follows money inflation *but not right away*. In the meantime, other things may happen to forestall the price inflation. Fundamentally, what may happen is an increase of the supply of values.

Throughout the 1930's, the supply of real values available for sale and which could be sold was much lower than it had been in the 1920's. The supply could easily be increased, but the increased supply could not be sold. This was because of underconsumption; some people were unemployed and had nothing to buy with, and others who had some money saved it. If monetary stimulation by the government could put people back to work and give them the means to buy, the saleable supply of values would grow to meet these new means and put still more factories and people back to work. In the light of the proved ability of the nation to produce and consume as much as in the 1920's, all of this, magical as it seems, was quite possible in the special circumstances of the depression. If the growth of values fully equaled the monetary inflation before the price inflation could take hold, there would be no price inflation. Inflationary potential is thus not necessarily limited by the supply of values which the nation is actually buying at any moment, but by the possibly larger supply which it is potentially capable of producing and consuming. This is all that Keynes meant when he said that his monetary inflation was justified whenever an economy was producing below its capacity, and in that case would have no corresponding inflationary effect on prices.

Before leaping to the conclusion that creating money would have created wealth and prosperity, notice that it was not the money that would do it but the improved utilization of people and plant. People and factories were being held back by unnatural psychological restraints, and money might free them. Money could create no real values, but it might free the people to create them.

The theory was that in grossly depressed economic circumstances monetary inflation might have all of its usual good effects and none of its usual bad ones. The theory was not unsound, and the medicine might be right. In practice, the results were likely to be more mixed, but they might still be quite favorable. In any event, the Great Depression in which the prescription might be correct was a special case and not the general case. The circumstances of that depression had never existed before in the industrial era and never again existed afterward. The attempt to prescribe the same medicine in another era such as the thirty-year American inflation was quite another story.

26
Inflationary Economics

Keynes made a great point of the generality of his *General Theory*, from the very first sentence ("placing the emphasis on the prefix *general*") throughout. His was to be a theory for all seasons, not just a depression, or so he thought. If his followers erred in applying the theory to different circumstances, Keynes was not without fault in pointing the way. But Keynes' sin was only the sin of overreaching, not of being wrong. He sought to make a universal out of a good thing when he could not. His general theory was only a special case, and Keynes himself would have discovered that much sooner than his followers did.

Deep depression was peculiar to the 1930's, but insufficient prosperity was not. One of Keynes' most vital departures from the classical economics was to state that a developed economy might very well settle to an equilibrium level which represented less than full employment. In other words, unemployment might be chronic. According to Keynes, the classical economics had said that production creates its own demand, and economic equilibrium has a natural tendency to provide as much work as people want.

The probability of chronic underemployment in a developed economy cannot be refuted. The evidence supports Keynes. This is the same point that was made earlier in noting that insufficient prosperity, recession, and unemployment resulted in postwar America whenever money was restrained enough to prevent inflation. It is the same as saying that stabilized money policy alone would not solve the problem of prosperity. The reasons for chronic underemployment are not difficult to find. The more technologically developed an economy becomes, the fewer workers the economy will need to produce its output, but the more people will need work and the means to acquire the output. At the extreme, an economy might be so perfectly automated that it needed no workers whatever to produce all the needs of all the people, but for lack of work the people could not buy any of their needs. As far as America had yet progressed, the gap between need for workers and workers' needs was much less wide than this, but in modern industrial societies it could only become wider. Keynes himself alluded to this problem perceptively in an earlier (1930) article entitled *Economic Possibilities for Our Grandchildren.*

If underemployment and insufficient prosperity were to be chronic, Keynesian economists proposed to deal with them by slavishly using the same prescription as Keynes proposed in the Depression. In short, they proposed a continuous monetary inflation. The same possibility of increasing the saleable supply of values by employing unused resources should improve prosperity and avoid inflation, or so the theory went. The theory was wrong. The premise might be sound, but the conclusion did not follow. It is precisely by the application of this faulty syllogism that the entire line of descent of Keynesian economists went so far astray.

The hope that the real growth in the saleable supply of values may be at least as much as the monetary inflation, thereby avoiding price inflation, is illusory. The amount of production that the people can be induced to consume is finite, more so than the number of people needing work. In the depression, a rate of production and consumption at least as good as in the 1920's had already been proved possible, and therefore a growth back to that level was a reasonably good possibility. In a developed economy operating at reasonably normal vigor, as the United States was doing at all times after World War II, the possibility of achieving that kind of real growth is slight. This is true even though there may be unemployment. More workers are not needed. Most people already have most of what they want, and if more is crammed down their throats it is through artificially induced wants which are as wasteful and disturbing as unemployment is. The unemployed persons themselves often do not have qualifications that the system can use; if the machine is driven ever harder the unemployed mostly remain unemployed while the machine threatens to burst. In the extreme situation in which an automated economy produces everything, monetary inflation to stimulate employment could not correct the insufficient prosperity at all. Stimulate as one might, this economy still could not use any workers, and the totally unemployed workers still could not buy any production. As economic development advances, therefore, unemployment may become increasingly chronic, but monetary inflation does nothing to help. Monetary inflation does not produce more growth than itself, nor even as much. Through the economic waste of fostering spurious activity at the expense of useful activity, it may indeed produce a net loss.

This is not to say that monetary inflation does not work at all. It does. Monetary inflation has just as marvelously stimulative short-term effects in relatively normal times as it does in depression. It is a potent medicine at any time, its efficacy is almost perfect, it always works in the beginning. It is in the longer term that its threat of harm lies. In a depression, monetary inflation might do no harm even in the long term. At

Inflationary Economics

any other time, its long-term harm is greater than its short-term good. Keynes set the tone for his followers by his quip about all being dead in the long run. Monetary inflationists love to make the short run their own and leave the long run to someone else, but those of us who may be condemned to live the longer run might well give heed to both.

Since monetary inflation does work, it is worth knowing why it works. If we know that, perhaps we can find something else that might work just as well.

Assume an economy which is in a state of insufficient prosperity. It is not depressed, unemployment is not rampant, but still it is not sufficiently prosperous. Business is not booming, well-being is not rising fast, and people have difficulty getting jobs as good or pay as high as they would like. There is some involuntary unemployment. At this point the government indulges in a monetary inflation. This is done either by putting a dose of cheapened money into circulation or by borrowing and spending more than its taxes, or both. At the opening instant, the inflation only makes the original recipients of the money feel richer in the static sense of money in hand. Almost immediately the money begins to flow and stimulates business activity throughout the economy. Who the first beneficiaries are depends on how the government chooses to distribute the inflated money, but is not of lasting importance. The stimulus reaches almost everyone. If the government buys space rockets or military goods, first the contractors and workers in those industries will feel the prosperity, and later all the other industries that sell to them. If the government lifts social benefits, first the payees and then the consumer industries will benefit. If the government makes general credit cheap, first the bankers and then the capital goods industries will prosper, and then the other industries they buy from. Profits rise, wages rise, workers are in demand, a few unemployed will be employed, insufficient prosperity is rectified, and there is a boom.

Where did all that spending power come from? The initial inflation was only a few billion dollars worth of new money or new debt, and anyway we know that money or paper debt creates no real value. The spending power was real value, however, and it must have come from somewhere. And so it did. At the opening instant, the equilibrium value of money decreased by exactly the amount of the monetary inflation. More than that, the real value of all the money wealth in the nation decreased in the same proportion. These effects were still latent, actual prices had not changed, the apparent values of money and money wealth had not changed, and therefore the recipients of the inflated money were richer by the amount of the inflation while no one else was as yet apparently poorer by any amount. Nevertheless, the transfers of value had occurred at the opening instant when the equilibrium values of money and wealth were reset. Real value equal to the inflation had moved from the holders of money to the government or the bankers and borrowers. Real value proportional to the inflation had moved from the holders of money wealth to their debtors. The underlying flow of real values was exactly the same as if the government had taxed away the same amount of real value from its holders and spent it.

Price inflation is slow to follow, but it does follow. The price inflation is the cost of the original prosperity. Price inflation is the collection from the money wealth of the tax which had already been levied and spent on the prosperity at the opening moment. If no real gain in values was produced by the inflation, as it seldom is, the cost is exactly equal to the value of the original prosperity. If we look through the layer of paper deficits and paper wealth, which do not mean anything, to the flows of real values, which do, we see that none are created and none destroyed but only redistributed.

The tax on money wealth is of course not necessarily collected from the original holder. If he is clever enough to dispose of money property before the price inflation comes,

Inflationary Economics

he escapes the tax. The tax is paid by the incautious person who is caught holding the wealth when the price inflation does come. Money inflation thus works no magic but only a simple, massive, and surreptitious tax on money wealth, and the payers of the tax select themselves to be taxed by their own dullwittedness in holding the taxed property. The inflationary tax is the easiest of all taxes to levy, indeed so easy that it is more difficult not to levy it, and in the beginning at least is also the richest of all possible taxes. Other than that, it holds no magic. No real wealth is created, only seized. The government's accounts always balance, notwithstanding deficits on paper. It is impossible for the government to run a deficit in real terms, for whatever the government spends automatically pays for itself by exacting its cost from someone.

To understand the magnitude of the inflationary tax, consider the situation that existed when the great inflation began in October of 1962. Beginning then, the government inflated the money supply in the next twelve months by about $6 billion, or 4 percent. That amount was about the same size as the Federal budget deficits of those years, but the budget deficit was not important. Inflating by 4 percent, the government also laid a 3 percent tax on the entire body of money wealth that existed in the United States at that time. Money wealth is equivalent to total debt, and total debt was then about $1.8 trillion, so that a 3 percent tax on money wealth would have yielded about $54 billion per year. The nation could obviously buy itself quite a prosperity with $54 billion of real values to distribute to various citizens, considering that the entire Federal budget at that time was only about $111 billion. Notice the enormous leverage that was obtained from a small money inflation by the presence of a large money wealth. Only $5 billion was taxed away from the holders of the money supply proper, a comparatively small amount, but more than ten times that amount of real value was taxed away from the holders of the remainder of the money wealth. This was where the prosperity came from.

Inflation as a tax is not unknown to economics in spite of being obvious, although there is a tendency to think of the tax as falling only on the money supply proper and to overlook the much larger tax on the remainder of the money wealth. Once again, the outstanding exposition of the inflationary tax was given by none other than John Maynard Keynes at a time (1922) when inflation was the world's problem. His article, *Inflation as a Method of Taxation*, expressed the following thoughts among others:

> "A Government can pay its way . . . by printing paper money. That is to say, it can by this means secure the command of real resources—resources just as real as those obtained by taxation. The method is reprobated, but its efficiency cannot be disputed. A Government can live by this means when it can live by no other. This is the form of taxing the people which it is most difficult to evade and which even the weakest Government can enforce when it can enforce nothing else.
>
> * * *
>
> "On whom has the tax fallen? Clearly on the holders of the original notes . . . The burden of the tax is well spread, cannot be evaded, costs nothing to collect, and falls, in a rough sort of way, in proportion to the wealth of the victim. No wonder its superficial advantages have attracted Ministers of Finance.
>
> * * *
>
> "Experience shows that the public generally is very slow to grasp the situation and embrace the remedy. . . . But sooner or later the second phase sets in. The public discover, in effect, that it is the holders of notes who suffer taxation and defray the expenses of government, and they begin to change their habits and economise in the holding of notes . . . The public try to protect themselves in this way when they have convinced by experience that their money is always falling in value and that every holder of it loses.
>
> * * *
>
> "It is common to speak as though, when a Government pays its way by inflation, the people of the country avoid taxation. That is not so. . . . The same arguments which I have here applied to the note issue can be extended, with a few modifications, to all the forms of internal Government debt . . . *What*

a Government spends, the public pay for. There is no such thing as an uncovered deficit." (Italics added)

These words echo strangely from the man who was later claimed as mentor by the champions of the government deficit. Keynes' article was revised somewhat and reprinted as part of a remarkable book called *A Tract on Monetary Reform* in 1924, a book which every putative Keynesian economist might well be required to recite by heart and to harmonize with Keynes' other work before being allowed to practice Keynesian economics. What was extremely true of the extreme inflations of that day is proportionately true of the less extreme inflations of a later day.

We come now to the single most important law of inflation. It is so tremendously important that we must at least capitalize its name, thus: The Law of the Exponential Inflation; or perhaps italicize it, thus: *The Law of the Exponential Inflation.* We may also think of it as a law of geometric progression, and it is simply this: every inflation must compound itself at a geometrically increasing rate in order to continue to have the same beneficial effects as in the beginning. It means, in practical effect, that *every inflation, once begun, must become continuously worse.*

As little as a 4 percent rate of monetary inflation, starting from stability, produces a thoroughly marvelous prosperity. We know that from the American experience. The billions upon billions of dollars of real value which a tax of this small size slyly collects from the money wealth provide unexampled well-being for everyone standing in the way of receiving some. But this is only true until price inflation presents the bill. Once prices too have settled down to a steady rate of increase of perhaps 3 percent, a continuing 4 percent monetary inflation has no beneficial effects at all. The tax no longer collects any yield. The state of prosperity, sufficient or insufficient, will be exactly the same as before the inflation started, but now with steadily rising prices instead of steadily stable prices. To make everyone as well off as the 4 percent money inflation originally did, the government must now inflate every year to 104 percent of 104 percent, or a compound annual increase of 8.2 percent. And so on. That is the Law of the Exponential Inflation.

The proof of this likewise is readily found in the American experience. A rate of money inflation of less than 4 percent per year produced an excellent boom in 1955, and the same rate another excellent boom in 1963, in both cases starting from stability, but by 1970 the very same rate of money inflation was good only for a recession and a financial crisis. A 6.5 percent annual rate of monetary inflation could fuel the most fantastic of all booms in 1967 and 1968, but by 1973 it too was beginning to look like a recessionary rate. The government in 1973 was well trapped by the Law of the Exponential Inflation.

If it be asked how a few percentage points per year of increased money supply can make so much difference, consider this: every one percentage point of increase may amount to only $2.6 billion more of money quantity in, say, 1973 (when the money supply was $260 billion), but if every dollar is used fifty times a year that comes to more than $130 billion of new purchasing power poured into the system for each percentage point. At the 6.5 percent annual rate of money expansion which was actually prevailing in 1973, purchasing power was being increased each year by no less than *$845 billion,* which was two-thirds of the entire gross national product. Let no one seriously question the tremendous leverage exerted by mere percentage points of money inflation.

The Law of the Exponential Inflation refutes the Keynesian economists' comfortable proposition that a modern economy must and can have a little steady inflation in order to have a sufficient prosperity. It was true enough that the United States could not seem to obtain sufficient prosperity without at least a little inflationary money expansion. But if the nation could not do without a little inflation, it certainly could not stop with only a little inflation. Once any rate of inflation had been stabilized, it would no longer do

Inflationary Economics

any good and more would be required. The only difference between a little inflation and a lot of inflation is time. Low rates do not compound themselves as rapidly as high rates, but by the Law of the Exponential Inflation they still do compound themselves to equally high ultimate rates in a somewhat longer time.

Whenever a government remedies insufficient prosperity with monetary inflation, the price falls due and payable later in price inflation. Rather than pay the price, the government normally will indulge in additional monetary inflation. The ill effects otherwise would be so ill, the prosperity again so insufficient, that the government will inflate more rapidly as necessary rather than suffer them. This can go on as long as the government has the courage or lack of courage to keep increasing the inflation, and the public the obtuseness to tolerate it. If the inflation stops increasing, the government will have the same insufficient prosperity as in the beginning but with steadily rising prices. A return to stable prices is practically out of the question, because a return from steady inflation to stability would cause the same deep depression in prosperity as an outright deflation would have had in the beginning.

Since we are all Keynesians today, we are all monetary inflationists today. Admittedly or not, all Keynesian economists are monetarists. There were no other kinds of economists extant in the American inflation. Monetary inflation progressed from a radical economic tool for the Great Depression to literally the only management tool in the economic tool chest. Conservatives and liberals alike, Republicans and Democrats, offered nothing else. A conservative was one who advocated a more sparing use of inflation, and he showed frequent stagnation and creeping inflation for his caution. A liberal was one who advocated a more exuberant use, and he showed more truly magnificent binges and stemwinding hangovers for his enthusiasm. Neither of them had one single alternative to offer, and both left us all equally well checkmated by the universal Law of the Exponential Inflation.

27
Interest and the Money Wealth

Money wealth is the key to inflationary prosperity. Money wealth is the rich lode from which the government mines prosperity by the process of inflation. Inflation depends for its effectiveness on a large body of money wealth to be taxed, and inflation succeeded colossally well in the United States because of its colossally large body of money wealth. Money wealth is debt. It is paper property and not real wealth, but it is a claim of part interest in someone else's real wealth, the part interest being fixed in terms of money. As the value of money falls, the size of the part interest in real wealth diminishes.

Interest is a phenomenon that identifies money wealth, because money wealth connotes interest-bearing property. Interest is the periodic income, also fixed in terms of money, that is payable to the holders of money wealth. The right to receive this periodic income is what gives money wealth its value and distinguishes it from mere money, which has no value. Therefore interest too, along with money wealth, is at the core of the process of inflation.

Money Wealth

Interest is a hobgoblin that haunts all economics. Lord Keynes included it among the holy trinity in the title of his *General Theory of Employment, Interest, and Money*. Manipulation of interest rates downward was at the heart of his work. Low interest rates were the obsession of economists and central bankers alike, and high interest rates were a matter of terror. Interest is a simple article of commerce that has been subjected to attempted price control constantly and in every country. Interest is a simple and minor article of commerce that no one has been content to leave to the pricing of an open market. The reason is that Keynes and others tended to think of interest as a kind of economic universal, the very heartbeat of capitalism. The fact is that interest is not a universal nor even very important at all, scarcely more important than valueless money itself.

It is sometimes said that interest is the rental price of money. It is more frequently thought even than said. This is the root of the error. If interest were the price of money, according to the law of supply and demand interest rates must go down as the supply of money went up. The Keynesian objective of low interest rates could then be achieved by monetary inflation.

Interest is not the price of money, any more than a motorcycle is the price of the money which buys it. Money, having no value, has no price of its own, but money is the price of all other things of value. Interest, or more specifically the money contract which bears interest, is the subject matter of the purchase and sale involved in lending money, not the money itself. It is the interest that is being bought with the money and not the money being rented with the interest. A borrower does not rent money in the usual sense of keeping it and returning it later. He sells his own contract to pay interest now and principal later, and he quickly respends on something else the money he receives for selling his contract.

The point is not merely academic in the slightest. If interest were the price of money, interest would be as universal as money is and might have something like the importance that economics and finance attach to it. In reality, interest is merely the market price prevailing in but one of the markets of commerce, the market for debt, the market for bonds and credit and other interest contracts. It happens that this market was a rather large market in the United States, but nothing about capitalism requires it to be. A market for money contracts is no more vital or indispensable than a market for, say, frozen orange juice futures contracts. Moreover, the correct understanding of what governs interest rates becomes exactly inverted by thinking of interest as the price of money. Instead of going down as the supply of money goes up, interest rates likewise go up, and usually more than as much. Interest is governed not by the total quantity of all money in all markets, but by the relationship between supply and demand in the one small market for money contracts. Inflation causes an oversupply of eager borrowers and a disappearing demand from fearful lenders, so that the prices of money contracts fall and interest rates rise. If demand for interest contracts should totally disappear, as it should do in an inflation if lenders really knew what they were about, interest rates would be infinite at the same time that the total supply of money was also excessively abundant. Monetary inflation causes high interest rates, not low ones.

Still we found economic management striving artificially to lower the market price of interest rates, uttering the ultimate absurdity that the cure for high interest rates is more money. By 1969 and 1970, in spite (or rather because) of the monetary flooding of the previous decade, interest rates in the United States became the highest since the Civil War. Interest on long-term corporate bonds of the highest caliber approached 9 percent per year. This situation caused consternation among the devotees of low interest rates, and interest was temporarily reduced somewhat by a renewed outpouring of money on the part of the Federal Reserve. This temporary reduction held sway for about two years, after which interest rates ascended again to still higher peaks in 1973. Despite the first tiny steps in 1951 toward freeing money from interest rates, the Federal Reserve like any good banker still guided its money policy far too much by the state of the interest market. This made no more sense than staking the economic health of the entire nation on supporting the market prices of frozen orange juice futures. It is wondrous to dream what boons might be won if the government just once set free the market for interest contracts to do its own job, legitimate but modest, in exactly the same way as the market for frozen orange juice futures.

Paradoxically, the *real* interest rates of 1969 and 1970 and 1973 were far from being the highest in American history, but were among the lowest. Nominal interest is not the same as real interest. Nominal interest might have been 9 percent or more, but real interest was much lower. If the intrinsic value of the money contract was being taxed away by inflation at the rate of 6 percent per year—this was the effect of the steady money expansion at that time—the largest part of the 9 percent nominal interest payment represented not interest at all but a return of capital, a repayment of principal. Ordinary income taxes, moreover, were payable on the nominal interest rate of 9 percent; part of the return of capital was therefore being taxed as ordinary income. After taxes, in most cases, the rate of real interest was actually negative. Interest rates of 9 percent were high, but not nearly high enough. To achieve the same after-tax yield as a real interest rate of only 3 percent, if the income tax rate is 35 percent and the inflationary tax on capital is 6 percent, nominal interest rates would have to reach about 12 percent. But no holder of money wealth could seem to grasp this.

Negative real interest rates resulting from deliberate inflation are not accidental. Lord Keynes knew very well what he was about in his attack on the interest rate. He did not frankly acknowledge that his goal was to be gained by a secretive inflation tax, but he did frankly acknowledge that his goal was to reduce the prevailing rate of interest to zero or a negative quantity. His goal was the "euthanasia of the rentier," which is to say the extinction of the holder of money wealth. He described the assault by inflation on money wealth with approval as "a process of continuously disinheriting the holders of the last generation's fortunes." The strangest of all his predictions was that the rentier capitalist would wither away when his purpose had been served, very much as Karl Marx expected the state to wither away when socialist utopia had been attained. Keynes said:

> "I see, therefore, the rentier aspect of capitalism as a transitional phase which will disappear when it has done its work."

It did not happen in the way that Keynes expected, but it did happen. Interest rates did indeed become negative. The rentier was indeed giving away the use of his capital *gratis*. But the situation was unstable. It came about not because capital was so plentiful that there was no alternative for capitalists, as Keynes expected, but because the rentiers who tolerated these negative yields did not understand what was happening. When they did, it would happen no longer. Persons incautious enough to become holders of money wealth should beware that the announced intention of Keynesian economics was to effect their extinction.

Just as the vastness of money wealth is essential to the success of an inflationary tax, so too is the numb insentience of its holders. Lenders never seem to understand what is happening in an inflation, no matter how long it continues or how explosively it compounds itself. They increase their interest rates as a crude way of defending themselves, but they never increase their interest rates enough. The lender habitually seems to think that the loss of value of money wealth is about to end, although the government cannot permit it to end. Each fresh quantum leap to higher interest rates so dazzles the lender that he believes yields will never be so high again; in fact, in most cases they will not soon be so low again. In Germany, until the day the inflation finally ended lenders were continuously losing real value by lending, even at interest rates above 22 percent per day. So perversely does this work that the money wealth actually grows faster, the more vigorously the government mines it by inflation. It is like a breeder reactor in atomic energy which produces more fuel than it consumes. The more the government steals from lenders, the more enthusiastically they lend. The money wealth of the United States which stood at only about $1.8 trillion in 1962, when the inflation began, had increased to $3.2 trillion by 1971.

That holders of money wealth are the sheep to be shorn in an inflation is a natural consequence of Lord Keynes' rather hostile attitude toward rentiers. He thought of them as idle rich men and coupon-clippers, who were fundamentally less useful than active entrepreneurs or workers. Ironically, however, the rentiers are not the rich men, and it is not the rich who pay. The rich tend to be relatively bright men and therefore to be net debtors, not creditors, in an inflation. The dull-witted rentiers who stand still for the shearing are the more modest savers of lower income, even the workers themselves. Pension plans, savings deposits, and life insurance companies alone accounted for more than $700 billion of the net money wealth of the United States in 1971. These are what the less wealthy savers invest in, and those who do are the rentiers. The rentiers who pay for an inflation are not the high-income classes but the low. Karl Helfferich observed that the same was true of the German inflation. It is a strange perversion of Keynes and of standard liberalism to find that their assault falls on the small wealth of the smallest citizens, frequently for the direct benefit of the very rich rentiers such as stock speculators.

As money wealth expands and interest rates rise in an inflation, the very size of the money wealth and height of the interest rates compel the government to continue and accelerate the inflation. This principle is as important as the Law of the Exponential Inflation. Indeed, it is very largely the underpinning for that law. The working elements of a populace will only tolerate a certain maximum burden of real debt. Only so much of the fruits of their efforts will they allow to be drawn off and distributed to rentiers. Lord Keynes pointed this truth out with respect to government debt, but it is equally true of private debt. Inflation overexpands the aggregate load of debt to the point that it is simply out of all proportion to the real wealth of the nation. The debt structure then cannot be permitted to constitute real value, because that would result in diverting to the holders of money wealth more of the real product of the nation than its other citizens can bear. Therefore the real value of the money wealth must be either eroded by inflation or amputated by bankruptcies. Inflation is easier, but the more the money wealth is eroded by inflation the more it grows so that it must be eroded more rapidly. Similarly, as interest rates go higher in partial defense against inflation, the government is compelled to inflate by more than the interest rates have anticipated. No borrower in America could for long stand any substantial amount of debt paying interest at 9 percent in real value. Those interest rates must be cheated upon. Every day that passed while long-term debt at these levels became more prevalent guaranteed all the more unshakably that the government must rob the money wealth at rates of at least 4 or 5 percent, merely to hold the real burden of money debt to tolerable levels. Prosperity was no longer the objective, but only solvency. The government would have to inflate by just that much more to gain the old prosperity in addition to solvency. Because of these compulsions, inflation by the government is never a voluntary act once inflation has begun. The government is in every sense a prisoner of its past.

Keynes' concept of interest as an economic universal would have meant that an attack on the interest rate would be an attack on all of capital, but it is not so. Interest is the yield on money wealth, and money wealth is only one small

Money Wealth 183

part of the entire range of capital. Real capital consists of such assets as land, factories, other buildings, and equipment, and either direct ownership or common stock ownership of this capital is completely different from money wealth. Inflation touches none of this; the attack on the interest rate touches none of this. It is possible, of course, to define interest so broadly as to include the rates of return on all classes of capital, including these, but this is simply to define away the problem. The inflationary tax can only reach the value of money wealth and not other kinds of wealth. Interest rate manipulation can only reach the interest on money contracts and not the yields on other capital. This fact is manifested by the inflation's inversion of the traditional relationship between interest rates and the yields on common stock. Common stock traditionally yielded more than debt, because of stock's higher risk, but that was reversed in the inflation and the gap continuously widened. Debt obligations became the true risk investments. Stock yields hovered near 3 percent, the historic gilt-edge interest rate, while debt interest rates increased to the liberal levels formerly reserved for stock. Lord Keynes conceived of his assault on the interest rate as laying a burden on all of capital, for the benefit of consumption, which capital could not escape. In reality it laid a burden on only a part of capital which all of capital could easily escape. Keynes underestimated the hardihood of the resilient capitalist, who simply decamped from money wealth in favor of equity investment.

Money contracts bearing interest are so thoroughly nonessential that it is perfectly possible to conceive of a highly-organized, smoothly functioning capitalist economy having no fixed interest contracts at all. Fixed interest, like gold, is a barbarous relic of the nineteenth century, when prices were stable and money contracts had a constant real value. In the modern age, when prices are not stable and money contracts are subjected to an exorbitant inflationary tax on value, interest exists only until capitalists become discerning enough to abolish it. One alternative to fixed interest investment is equity investment. Another alternative would be constant-value lending. In a constant-value money contract, payments of both interest and principal would be multiplied by a constant-value factor based on some price index, so that each payment to the lender would have the same real value and not merely money value as was originally intended. Constant value is of course difficult to define precisely, but almost any index such as consumer prices or wholesale prices or even the price of wheat would serve better than money does. Constant value would restore to lending the relationship that it was always supposed to have, namely an obligation of a borrower to pay his lender a fixed amount of real value regardless of the good or bad fortunes of the borrower. Naturally a borrower could not incur constant value debt as freely as he incurred money debt. He could not afford under any circumstances to pay 9 percent interest at constant value. Even at 4 percent he could not incur constant value debt without considerably more due care than he employed in the inflation, but that was how debtors were always supposed to incur debt.

Constant-value loans or "indexed" loans were advocated as long ago as the late nineteenth century by the great economist Sir Alfred Marshall as an antidote to the damage caused by unstable prices. Constant-value factors were still surprisingly little used in the United States, considering its persistent inflationary history, although they were more widespread in other countries which had a fuller experience and more complete understanding of inflation. Since constant-value lending defends lenders, no borrower would offer it until lenders refused to lend on any other basis. In an advanced stage of inflation when lenders finally awoke, constant-value lending would become more nearly universal as it did in Germany.

If constant-value lending became general in the United States, its effects would be magical. All of the unjust and economically damaging redistributions of value between creditors and debtors which occur in either inflations or deflations would be eliminated. The catastrophic destruction of debtors in the Great Depression caused by rising real value of money wealth would have been entirely avoided. Likewise, inflation's tax through the falling real value of money wealth would be instantly ended. Nominal interest rates could be expected to fall, although real interest rates would rise. A 4 percent interest rate at constant value would obviously be a better deal for lenders than 9 percent fixed in money in the American inflation. As this new safety became apparent to prospective lenders, floods of money which had taken refuge in the most marginal of equities might return to their rightful place in legitimate lending. This would be the way to reduce interest rates, if the government's economic management really wished to reduce them.

A conventional fixed money loan represents a lender's gamble on not one but two risks, the borrower's solvency and the government's manipulation of the money unit. The first belongs, the second is an intruder. A constant-value loan eliminates the intruder, removes the risk of the money unit, and locks the lender's safes against the government's pilferage. The borrower's solvency might then be a more serious risk, but that is always a proper risk of lending. If money had a constant value as money is supposed to, money would be the simplest and most universal possible constant-value factor to use in money contracts. But if the government deliberately or incompetently destroys the constant value of money, private persons may substitute another at will and thereby abolish fixed money interest. In the United States of 1973, while the government assiduously inflated by 6.5 percent per year, it was incomprehensible that any lenders still entered into long-term money contracts without the protection of complete constant-value clauses, but do it they did.

The specter of constant-value lending may be as sinister as it is attractive. It shuts out the government's tax collector, but that is bad as well as good. As surely as constant-value lending erects a complete defense for the lenders, it puts a complete end to the effectiveness of the government's inflationary tax. The government's principal source of real revenue is then closed. All those billions upon billions of dollars of real value which the government was able to collect for prosperity are now gone. The money wealth which the government must erode in order to keep the nation afloat cannot be eroded. Interest rates which the government must defeat in order to buy prosperity cannot be defeated. Monetary inflation, the single and universal economic tool which worked for decades, can no longer work. The government must look for something else. It is true that the supply of money itself would still remain available for inflating even if all debt were constant-value, but as a source of real values through the inflation tax the money supply is puny. Far worse rates of inflation would then yield far more meager returns. The desertion by creditors of fixed lending in favor of constant-value lending is one of the infallible indicators that the collapsing stage of an inflation is beginning.

Keynesian economics stake everything on the interest rate as a capitalistic universal, but it is not. Interest not only is not universally important, but it is not really important at all. Fixed interest might well disappear altogether and still leave a capitalistic nation operating better than ever. The inflationary assault on money wealth succeeds quite nicely for a time, but only until money wealth finds that it can erect a convenient and complete defense by simply abolishing fixed interest. For the government to rest all economic health on a single massive tax like inflation, which is perfectly avoidable and depends on the continuing gullibility of the persons who select themselves to be taxed, is hazardous in the extreme.

28
The Economics of Disaster

The economics of inflationary disaster are a simple process which need not detain us long. The economics of disaster are as simple as the inflationary economics were complex. The government was the managing proprietor of the inflationary economics, but the economics of disaster are conducted by persons other than the government and are largely beyond the government's control. Inflationary economics required motive power supplied by the government, but the economics of disaster are self-propelled. It is the government that decides when and how fast the inflationary reservoirs shall be filled, but it is something else that decides when the dam shall burst.

The economics of disaster commence when the holders of money wealth revolt. It is as simple as that. The government has little or nothing to say or do about it. Its policies are scarcely worse or different than they have been all along. They may even be better, as they were in Germany in 1922.

Holders of money wealth express their revolt by the simple act of getting rid of their money and money wealth and declining to hold it in the future any longer than necessary to get rid of it. They do not fly flags or demonstrate in the streets to express their revolt; they simply get rid of their money. When a sufficient inflationary potential has been laid up by the government in all the available reservoirs, that is all that is necessary. If the simple desertion of the money becomes widespread or universal, the latent inflation surfaces in the form of disaster. The duller the holders of money wealth are, the longer the government can go on storing up inflation but, by the same token, the more cataclysmic must the eventual dam burst be. The Germans were among the dullest and most disciplined of all holders of money wealth, and this alone permitted the government to build up so huge a pool of unrealized inflation before the burst.

The desertion of the money holders has many of the aspects of a panic, like any desertion in the thick of a struggle. All may be orderly in one moment and in full flight in the next. As slow and imperceptible as the inflationary economics were, the economics of disaster are sudden and unexpected. A filling of reservoirs which may have taken years may be emptied in a day.

The reservoirs where the inflationary potential has been stored are those we have already described. Money velocity which has lagged behind its natural level throughout the incipient inflation may suddenly multiply itself many times over as holders dump their money. Prices of desirable things rise accordingly. Government debt which for long has immobilized some of the inflated money now is deserted by existing money and turns into money itself. Fractional-reserve banking turns the new money into multiples of additional money. Money which has been engaged in servicing the enormous money wealth now deserts the money wealth and seeks real assets instead. Even the money which has been occupied in markets for real investments such as industrial stocks may lose heart in the face of falling profits and hard times, and come forth in search of surer value. Even the money which has been occupied in buying and selling goods and services, many of them useless, deserts them in favor of essentials like food and land. In a collapsing inflation, people's powers of discrimination between real values and spurious values become suddenly acute, and the apparent supply of saleable real values falls. Foreign holders of the money take fright too, and their money elbows its way into the markets and reverses any balance of payments deficit. Finally, the government finds itself deprived of its inflationary tax while its regular taxes yield little, and it resorts to still more money inflation as a means of finance. In so doing, the pathetic government trails far in the dust of the fleeing citizenry.

Like any panic, the economics of disaster tend to overshoot the inflationary potential. If the government did nothing to add any more money to the flood, some but not all of the inflation resulting from the bursting of the dam would subside. Money velocity is a good example. We saw earlier that velocity can easily increase tenfold in a bad inflation, and if it does prices must also increase tenfold based on velocity alone. But velocity is transitory, and if the inflation stops, velocity will subside and prices must fall again by nine-tenths. The same is true of investment in real values like industrial stocks. If inflation stops and normality is recovered, money will return to sound investment and the prices of other kinds of values must decline accordingly. But the inflation based on the abandonment of the former money wealth and spurious values tends to be permanent, and this amount of inflation is more than enough to leave a tremendous destruction in its wake. Moreover, the government seldom stops inflating cleanly or soon. The bursting of the dam is not to be minimized.

There is no good way of estimating what point is the breaking point for the economics of disaster. There is also no use in planning for what to do in the event of disaster, since nothing much can be done about it. The United States even in 1973 was still far short of the revolt of its money holders, even after a decade of continuous theft from them. There was not the least sign of any dumping of dollar property by either citizens or foreigners. The unrealized depreciation of the dollar was probably no more than a fifth as great as that of the Reichsmark when the flight from the mark began. In the turmoil of the time, the Germans had much more psychological cause to take fright than Americans did in 1973. This book does not proclaim that the bursting of the dam was at hand. It does say that the reservoirs were already partly full and filling. Americans must learn to live with this fact like the people who live out their lives in a valley below a great dam, but when a freshening stream of inflation was found issuing from a crack in the dam it could not be treated like an innocent brooklet rising from a pure little spring in the hills.

The point to be taken to heart by any American government is that the degeneration of an inflation into a catastrophe is not the willful act of the government. A government does not remain safe from disaster simply by abstaining from extreme misdeed. No government collapses its currency because it wishes to or because it flagrantly does not care. When at last it sees the choice, it has no choice. People take over, and the government is relieved of its command. Neither is a government safe because the point of mutiny is still far off. When once a government embarks on the course of monetary inflation, it is forced ever forward by the iron Law of the Exponential Inflation. The government is trapped between, at its back, the money wealth and the necessity to mine from it at an increasing rate, and, before it, the necessity that the holders of money wealth voluntarily permit the mining. No matter how distant they may be, revolt of the creditors and inflationary collapse are ultimately certain unless at some timely moment the government and the people elect the supreme act of self-denial by stopping the inflation and swallowing the accumulated stores of hardship and injury. O how we earn an awful fate, when first we practice to inflate.

29
The Crux

Here we come to the crossing of the ways, or the crux of the matter as the Latin usage would have it, and it will pay us to pause and look at the road signs at this crossing of the ways before we leave it. Here the two divergent paths of thought in American economics converged. Here there was a confluence of dissimilar streams of thought that sprang from remote and uncongenial sources. Here the issue was joined, the battle lines were drawn, and to our surprise we find that the battle was a draw.

The travelers down one of the two paths—adherents of what is commonly thought of as the main force of Keynesian economics—declared that they can purchase prosperity with a policy of continuous government deficits and easy money, that if this caused a little inflation it was not possible to have sufficient prosperity without a little inflation. Experience in the United States proved them correct.

The travelers down the other path—monetarists who are loosely allied around the banner of Milton Friedman—declared that the policies of the first group amounted to nothing but monetary inflation, that their economic stimulation resulted from the government's tampering with money, that inflation also resulted from the government's tampering with money, and that if a little inflation was tolerated it must constantly increase to more and more inflation. Experience also proved them correct.

Both were correct. Neither was wrong. Each of the two kinds of economist held the truth of half a theory, and ne'er the twain had met as yet. In the existing economic organization of the United States, sufficient prosperity could not be obtained without monetary inflation, but to obtain sufficient prosperity continuously monetary inflation must compound itself exponentially to the point of ultimate collapse. Which way then to economic health? The answers that economics gave suggested that there was no way. They remind us of the Maine Yankee who, when asked directions to a nearby place in Maine, replied sadly, "You can't get there from here."

On its face, this is absurd. On their face, the answers of economics were absurd. You can get to anywhere from anywhere else, if you are willing to blaze your own routes. To say this is no mere uninformed bravado. In the nature of things, it is true. We need no evidence to prove it. In the nature of things, a nation which is as economically strong and as untroubled by real handicaps as the United States was must be, if not healthy, at least capable of being healthy. It could do better than economics had done so far.

But not by traveling the established roads. From this crossing, the road signs do us no good. One road leads only to accelerating inflation, and the other road leads only to worsening stagnation. The traveled ways do not go where we want to go. To get there, we have no choice but to take leave of the traveled ways and strike out across country. Bring your hiking boots.

30
Taxes

The idea of taxes is a strangely neglected idea. There is no lack of taxes in the modern world, to be sure, but the conception of what the taxes are doing economically is sorely neglected. Taxes are the great engine and the sole motive power of the government's economic management, but the government fails to understand its engine. If there was one single cause of the inflationary failure of economic management by the government, it was the failure of the management to understand taxes.

Inflation, we have seen, was the one kind of tax that enabled the government's economic management to succeed even temporarily. Mysterious and surreptitious as it is, inflation is still a tax. It works because it is a tax, and more especially because it is a certain kind of tax, a capital tax. It must follow that any other tax of equal amount and comparable incidence would work just as well. And if inflation, although it works, has other serious drawbacks, it follows too that the remedy for inflation's evils is to find other equivalent taxes that do not have such drawbacks. All government finance consists of branches of tax policy. Even monetary policy is a branch of tax policy. An inflationary policy represents a decision to include the inflation tax on capital in the tax structure. A deflationary monetary policy would represent the decision to include the deflation tax on debtors in the tax structure. Fiscal policy too, meaning deficit or surplus in the government's budget, is a part of the monetary branch of tax policy. Since it is not possible for the government to run either a deficit or a surplus in real terms, but only to secrete the monetary inflation or deflation tax in their guise, fiscal policy represents merely an indirect choice to include either the inflation tax or the deflation tax in the tax structure. A monetary and fiscal policy which was perfectly non-inflationary and non-deflationary would represent a decision not to use monetary manipulation as part of the tax structure at all, but to rely instead on overt rather than covert taxes to accomplish the purposes of economic management. The government has no power not to tax to the full extent of its expenditure, but only the power to select one kind of tax rather than another. The most complex questions of government economic management thus mostly boil down to matters of the design and selection of taxes.

In view of the vastness of all taxes, including inflation, in the economic system, the complete failure of the economic management and the economic profession to grasp the fundamental importance of tax design during the American inflation was astounding. Keynes' *General Theory*, their theoretical foundation, contained not a single word of discussion of tax structure, which is astonishing for a work that claimed to be a general theory of the economic problem. Sophisticated economics, searching about for the magic talisman to economic health, devoted itself to every other kind of gimmick such as low interest rates, cheap money, budget deficits, and investment incentives, but all of these amounted to no more than an uncomprehending use of the inflation tax. The cleverest use of true taxes that economics could devise was to raise taxes as a whole for a budget surplus, or more often to lower them as a whole for a budget deficit. Either way, this undifferentiated manipulation of taxes as a whole was the crudest imaginable sort of tax policy.

Taxes are not a monolithic mass. Taxes are of many kinds. There are income taxes, sales and excise taxes, property taxes, and inheritance taxes, and then there is the inflation tax. The variety of different kinds of possible taxes is virtually infinite. Everyone knows this, and there was even a certain amount of study by tax economists of the differences in incidence of different kinds of taxes, which means which kinds of people bear the burden of particular kinds of tax. But this study was rudimentary at best, and understanding of the different effects of different kinds of taxes, including the inflation tax, was inadequate.

Economic life runs in two parallel channels, and the important difference between taxes is their relative drain from these two parallel channels. The two channels may be called saving and consumption, or they may be called capital and labor for the classes of people who are most closely identified with saving and consumption, respectively. Most people's lives participate at least a little in both channels. Most people work and all people consume, and therefore they are a part of the labor and consumption channel. On the other hand, most people also save something and hold some sort of capital, even if only by participating in some employer's pension plan, and therefore they are also a part of the capital and saving channel. The opposition between the two channels is therefore not a class conflict of one group of people against a separate group of people, but a counterpoise of two separate streams in all people's lives.

The government's duty of economic management consists of nothing more nor less than regulating the relative flows in these two separate channels—saving or consumption, capital or labor—so that they are in balance, not necessarily equal but in balance. The proper object of this economic management is not to benefit disproportionately one group of people which they or someone else decide is disfavored, nor is it to deprive some other group which someone decides is too well favored. Since both channels are of equal merit and both contribute equally to economic well-being, the proper object of economic management is to balance their flows in such a way that both channels flow most copiously for the benefit of everyone.

The way economic management balances the flows in the two channels is to draw flow from one channel—taxation—and divert it to the other—expenditure. In an early stage of economic development, the necessity of sound economic management is to draw flow from the channel of labor and consumption and to divert it into saving and the formation of capital. In a mature stage of economic development such as the United States had gained at the time of its inflation, the necessity is exactly the opposite, namely to draw flow from oversaving and the abundant fruits of capital and pour it back into consumption.

The early stage of development is well illustrated by the industrial growth of the United States in the nineteenth and early twentieth centuries. At that time, as in any economically undeveloped nation, the total flow in both of the two channels combined was meager, because the aggregate product of the nation was low. There might have seemed to be great hardship involved in diverting a substantial part of that meager product away from consumption by the workers who produced it and channeling it into the formation of capital, which meant building factories and railroads and capital equipment for the capitalist barons who would own it. Yet that was what was required, and it made no difference whether capitalist barons or the government owned it, except that it would happen more quickly if capitalist barons had the lure of private ownership. Without that kind of injustice and hardship, no nation would ever develop. Without taking a painfully large part of a painfully small product away from consumption and investing it in capital, that small product could never be made larger. That was the requirement of economic management in the earlier days of the United States, and by the purest historical accident it was met perfectly by the *laissez faire* inaction of a government that was quite unaware of what it was doing. The super-full employment of that time, the low exploitation wages of the workers, the low consumption because of low wages, and the absence of taxes and other regulatory burdens to impede the burgeoning capital empires all contributed mightily and well to the explosive industrial growth of the United States. That growth could not have been achieved without any of those factors, and no similar growth will ever be achieved again, anywhere, without a similar balance of factors.

The mature stage of economic development which the United States later reached was exactly the opposite in almost every respect. The task of economic management was theoretically much easier, because the total flows in the two channels had become abundant, but paradoxically the government experienced much greater difficulty attempting to master this much easier task. In the mature stage, the capital installation is largely completed, total output is large, and workers are much less needed either for current output or for the formation of new capital. As Keynes correctly pointed out, there is a chronic tendency in an advanced economy to excessive saving and insufficient consuming. The larger total incomes are, the more inclined people are to save larger parts of those incomes, but the less need there is for the formation of still more capital that could absorb these large new savings. The Keynesian solution to this was to stimulate new investment artificially, but there is a clear practical limit to how much artificial new investment can be stimulated, and the problem soon outruns the solution. What is needed most is that the abundant production of the existing capital system be consumed, and that the people through labor *or otherwise* be able to obtain the means of consuming it. What is needed is that the flows in the two channels be balanced by constantly drawing some of the flow from oversaving and diverting it back into consumption. In the extreme case of maturity where all possible needs of all people were supplied by capital, no workers were needed, no further capital investment was possible, and all saving was excessive, the holders of capital would hold all the means of producing but the rest of the people would have no means of buying, and capitalists and other people alike would be destitute unless enough of the fruits of capital were diverted to consumption to allow people other than capitalists to buy the product of capital. It is not a matter of moral rectitude that capital should partly support consumption in this way, any more than it was morally right that exploited workers should support the formation of capital in an earlier century. It is not a matter of justice, but merely of necessity.

The government's duty of balancing the flows is performed in two basic steps. The first is to draw values from its citizens, and this step is *taxation*. The second step is to redistribute the same values to its citizens, and this step is *government expenditure*. The economic balancing aspect of this two-step operation lies in the relative *difference* between the groups of citizens from whom values are drawn and those to whom they are distributed. *Redistribution* of values among citizens is thus the essence of the government's economic management. Where the imperative of economic management is to draw from capital and distribute to consumption, the government's mandate is to tax more heavily those who save or hold capital and distribute more liberally to those who consume.

Of distribution through government expenditure, more will be said in a later chapter.

Taxation is the intake side of the two-step process. Tax design is much the more important and difficult of the two sides, the other being expenditure policy. In an ideal tax system, the government would have an array of different kinds of taxes, each bearing more heavily on one economic sector like capital or consumption than on the other. Sales taxes, for example, are a direct restraint of consumption. Property taxes, inheritance taxes, and corporate income taxes are taxes on capital. Income taxes are mixed taxes but weigh somewhat more heavily on consumption power than on capital. Judiciously using the complete array of these taxes, the government could raise the capital taxes relatively when saving was too high and consumption too low, and raise the sales and income taxes relatively when consumption was too high and the formation of capital too low. Broad enough taxes like these would act as sluice gates in the two conduits and, shrewdly enough used, would give positive regulation of the flows in all conceivable economic circumstances.

The need in various times might be for flexible taxes, but the need in the United States at the peak of its inflation was for capital taxes. Since the necessity in a mature economy was to draw continuously from capital and distribute continuously to consumption, taxes on capital must be heavier than on income or consumption, and over the course of time they probably must grow still more disproportionately heavy. In the past, the need for a large and heavy capital tax had been met successfully, but only by the government's reliance almost exclusively on the inflation tax. Money inflation operated on both the tax side and the distribution side, because much of the value levied by inflation moved directly from creditors, who saved and held capital, to debtors, who spent and consumed. The tens of billions of dollars of value each year which the government levied from capital and distributed to consumption by inflation represented the only source the government had found rich enough to do the job. Talk of stimulative deficits and low interest rates and investment incentives was nonsense. The policies underlying the talk did accomplish the purpose, but the way they accomplished it was by redistribution from capital to consumption through the inflation tax.

If monetary inflation worked because it was a simple tax on part of capital, but inflation was bad, then of course some other comparable tax on capital could work just as well and might not be so bad. Counting inflation, the United States already had all the heavy taxes on capital it needed. Something like a moderate net-worth tax on all of capital, which was unknown in the United States but effectively used in many European countries, could easily have substituted for the inflation component in the capital tax structure. More about particular taxes will be said in the next chapter. The point here is that if deliverance from inflation were ever to be achieved, new capital taxes of comparable magnitude must be instituted. It was not so important exactly what the capital taxes were as that they be large.

Taxes are never fun. No one would rather be taxed than not be taxed. The idea of capital taxes strikes fear and rage into the heart of capitalist America, although in fact capitalist America throve quite nicely under an existing load of capital taxes which were adequately heavy when the inflation tax was figured into account. Disproportionately heavy capital taxes are not anti-capitalist, but the reverse. Only by means of capital taxes can a capitalist economy be made to work at all in an advanced state of development. A well-balanced economic management is as much better for capitalists as it is for workers and consumers. If capitalists who increasingly monopolize productive power do not allow enough buying power to be diverted from themselves to their consumers, there will be no profits for capitalists either. The correct level of capital taxes is high and growing higher, but not confiscatory. The correct level of capital taxes is that which achieves the maximum flow in the channels of both capital and consumption. Higher capital taxes than that are bad, and everyone, capitalists and workers and consumers alike, will be worse off. Lower capital taxes than that are also bad, with the same result. Capital taxes of the proper high level are as beneficial to capitalists as to any other member of society.

High taxes on capital do not destroy capital, as is sometimes charged, nor do they inhibit the formation of new capital, either of which effects would be bad. When a man pays a property tax on his house (a capital tax), he does not saw off a piece of his house and give it to the tax collector, thereby destroying that much of his capital. Not at all. He takes some of his income from some other source, measured not by the income but by the value of the house, and pays that to the tax collector. The house is intact. All taxes, including capital taxes, are income taxes in the sense that the means of paying them must come from income. A capital tax is a tax paid out of income but measured by the voluntary exercise of the privilege of holding property. Until the tax becomes so high that the privilege is no longer attractive, capital taxes neither destroy capital nor dampen the formation and acquisition of new capital. The privilege of holding property is a deep and powerful motivating force. It is this unique privilege that caused capitalistic systems to succeed, and capitalistic systems can continue to reap ample harvests from this fertile source. People do not cease to own houses because the property taxes on them are high, nor to hold investments because they are taxed heavily. No one should fear to tax the privilege lest people might be driven to foresake it, and on the other hand if the privilege is not taxed it will wither.

If there is one precept which even the archest conservative must receive from Lord Keynes, it is that an economy as complex and interdependent and as completed as mature America must be managed by the government. *Laissez faire* in the strictest sense no longer would do. Conservatives who did not accept this would find they were conserving a desert. Not only must the economy be managed, which is a declaration tinged with desperation, but it can be managed, which is a declaration steeped in hope. Past failures by the kinds of economists who most strongly advocated government intervention were no evidence that management could not succeed. Government management could continuously redress chronic economic imbalances, like that between capital and consumption, to the end that the economy produce the most for everyone. Government management cannot create wealth, but it can set free the efforts of willing people to create wealth. In all of this, the first and strongest set of tools the government can have is a comprehending use of its taxes.

31
American Taxes

If tax structure is at the heart of the modern economic problem, the American tax structure in the inflation was from every relevant viewpoint a monstrosity. It was scarcely less absurd than the tax structure that forced Germany into the World War I inflation, lacking even so much as a single broad-based tax available to the central government rather than the component states. American taxes began with a 1913 framework that was poorly conceived at its building and was never fundamentally remodelled. They progressed through myriad clumsy modifications until the labyrinthine handiwork that remained resembled what the Capitol building might have looked like if the elected legislators had been allowed, in committee, to draw the plans and erect the stonework.

The principal absurdities of the American tax structure fell into two main categories. The first was a complete inability to mount capital taxes sufficiently broad and massive to relieve the need for inflation. The second was an extreme proclivity for needless complexities and artificial distinctions which stimulated the useless, hindered the useful, and bewildered everyone. Many of the principal absurdities had a foot in each category. The principal absurdities that bear mention were in the areas of net worth taxes, inheritance taxes, capital gains taxes, corporation taxes, and progressive income taxes.

Net worth taxes in the American tax structure were absurd by their absence. Comprehensive net worth taxes were unknown to the United States, although many of the Continental European nations including Germany, the Netherlands, Luxembourg, Switzerland, and all the Scandinavian countries had smoothly functioning net worth taxes as important parts of their tax structures. A net worth tax is the broadest and most direct imaginable tax on all of capital and only capital. If ever any tax promised to be broad enough and massive enough to take the place of the inflation tax on money wealth, it would be a net worth tax on all of wealth. A net worth tax sufficient to do the job in the American structure would not have to be a heavy tax. A tax in the range of 2 percent of value in normal times, perhaps less, and higher only in times of emergency such as wartimes, would be enough. A net yield of perhaps $30 billion of new revenue would be about right. This net worth tax on the value of capital, in addition to a regular income tax on the balance of income from capital, would be what imposed on capital a total tax burden heavier to the correct degree than on personal income. Even so, most kinds of capital would bear a lighter total tax burden than they did under the existing American hodgepodge of capital taxes including corporate taxes, double dividend taxes, and inflation taxes.

A net worth tax could incorporate into a uniform structure the welter of local real estate taxes that threatened to crush many localities of the United States. Real estate taxes were peculiar to the English-speaking countries. Those countries of Continental Europe that used the greatly superior net worth tax generally did not have appreciable real estate taxes in addition. In the United States, cities and suburbs especially groaned under real estate tax loads running often to 3 percent of market value per year or more, while it was estimated that the nationwide average of real estate taxes was only about 1.4 percent of value. Large amounts of property therefore were being inadequately taxed solely because of the localization of the taxes. It seems obvious that incorporating a uniform tax of no more than 2 percent on real estate into a net worth tax on all property could provide the same amount of revenue for all the same purposes without crushing anyone.

A net worth tax does present one technical problem in the accurate valuation of property. Sales taxes and income taxes do not have this problem, and the problem is not negligible. The problem is not insurmountable, however. Valuation is successfully accomplished every day in the administration of estate taxes, local real estate taxes, and the European taxes on net worth. The great advantages of the tax command that the problem simply be surmounted. The need for a comprehensive capital tax is so insistent that the goals of phasing out inflation and phasing back in prosperity may well not be attainable without general net worth taxes.

The inexplicable absence of significant *inheritance taxes* was another strange mystery of the American tax law. There were Federal estate and gift taxes and state inheritance taxes, of course, and the inheritors who bore them thought they were unconscionably heavy, but the fact was that they were ludicrously light. The annual Federal revenue from estate and gift taxes was only about $3.6 billion, which was less than the annual revenue from excise taxes on alcohol and scarcely more than one-tenth of one percent of the value of all private property in the United States. Estate tax rates were so low that an estate's value must be larger than $1.5 million ($35 *million* if there was a marital deduction for a surviving spouse) before it paid even as high a percentage of tax (34 percent) as a single man earning a mere $25,000 paid every year on his income.

The absence of adequate inheritance taxes was doubly strange because an unbroken line of distinguished authorities observed that an inheritance tax is among the wisest and justest of all taxes. Philosophers and economists like Adam Smith, John Stuart Mill, Bentham, Marshall, and Keynes, and statesmen and wealth holders as diverse as Jefferson, Lincoln, Theodore Roosevelt, Franklin Roosevelt, Hoover, and Carnegie expressed views similar to this of Hoover:

> "The estate tax, in moderation, is one of the most economically and socially desirable, or even necessary, of all taxes."

If ever there was a painless time for society to tax heavily the wealth a man has accumulated, it is when he has died and finished with it. The tax is a pure tax on capital which the nation needs badly. Apart from the revenue, society might, by diminishing the flow of wealth downward from creator to descendant, diminish also the drearily familiar American institution of the useless or underproductive rich heir. By the same means society might stop depriving itself, through the immobilizing effects of excessive inherited wealth, of the best efforts of those who genetically ought to be among its most capable potential contributors. These social reasons are among the reasons why the nation's greatest men, including rich men, unanimously endorsed inheritance taxes.

Despite the critical acclaim, inheritance taxes languished. A perceptive observer said,

> "Its inadequacies methodically increase from one act to another. An excessive exemption is combined with inadequate rates, and these are joined by significant loopholes."

This is perplexing because inheritance taxes do not face the rebellious resistance of millions of voters which almost any other sound tax does. Sage thinkers like Mill and Keynes pointed out that there was better reason for heavy taxes on inheritance than on high incomes, but American taxes turned this comparison upside down to tax incomes heavily and inheritances lightly. One can only surmise that the inherited rich had more time and money than the working rich to influence tax-making Congresses.

The remedy for inadequate inheritance taxes is to treat inheritances as income and tax them at the same rate as any other income. The economist Henry Simons endorsed this idea in a 1938 book, and before that the very first income tax act in 1898 had treated inheritances as income. To a recipient, inheritance is a simple addition to his means like any other income. If existing progressive rates of tax on income were too heavy as applied to inheritances, that was the fault of the progressive income tax and not the principle that inheritance is income.

Besides treating inheritance as income, revision of the inheritance taxes would have to eliminate major channels of avoidance such as the huge $60,000 exemption, to some extent the marital deduction, and the ability to skip whole generations of tax by the clever use of trusts. If the basic exemption were eliminated, millions of smaller estates would become taxed substantially where they were previously not taxed at all. This is proper. A small legacy from a small estate is just as much windfall income to its recipient as a huge legacy from a huge estate. The millions of smaller estates are where the bulk of the capital and the revenue are, not in the few large estates. The great weakness of inheritance taxation always was that it was enviously concerned too much with breaking down great fortunes and not enough with drawing adequate revenue fairly from the capital of everyone. If the income tax rate were a flat 35 percent and it applied to inheritances, inheritances might yield something like $35 billion per year to assist net worth taxes in replacing inflation. A 35 percent tax rate would still leave 65 percent of every estate to satisfy a decedent's wish to be generous to his heirs, and on the other hand would be heavy enough to break down a great fortune to a mere 27 percent of its original self within two generations after the death of its creator.

Massively increased inheritance taxes would have an

inevitable tendency to lower the market prices of property of all kinds. The taxes could not be paid out of current income, and portions of more estates would have to be sold to pay the taxes. Market supplies of property for sale would be increased, and prices would be lower as a result. This is at least as good as it is bad. Tax revenues based on value would be lower than otherwise, but that is not fatal. For every owner or seller that saw the value of his property decline, there would be a buyer who was enabled to buy it more cheaply than he formerly could. Even the seller or owner is not damaged because the earning power or other usefulness of the property is the same as ever, and he pays lower taxes on value. The effect of all these complex results is simply to lower the cost of property relative to personal income, and this is desirable. A mature society in which the stock of capital and other property is largely complete must find a way of constantly recycling this limited supply of capital away from existing holders at their deaths and into the hands of the society's new contributors. The opportunity to acquire property is the capitalist system's most attractive prize, and the system is only as vigorous as it is capable of redistributing its prizes continuously to its new live contributors rather than to the heirs of its old dead ones. Moderately high inheritance taxes, forcing liberal supplies of property constantly on the market at lowered prices, do this.

The *capital gains tax* at least was not an absentee, but was only half present in the American tax structure. Since 1921 there had been special favors in the tax law for capital gains, most recently a tax at just half the rate that applied to other income. No arbitrary distinction in the American tax law contributed more mischief to American life than the distinction between capital gain and ordinary income. Whole subchapters and hundreds of pages of the tax code were devoted to complex provisions whose sole reason for existing was the artificial favoring of capital gain over ordinary income. Every new tax act compounded these complexities further. The alluring tax advantages of capital gains sucked money into the most speculative and insubstantial kinds of investment, seeking capital gains in preference to old-fashioned income like dividends and interest. The capital gains tax was at the bottom of many an unhealthy American stock market boom. Lord Keynes advocated extra-heavy transfer taxes as a deterrent, certainly not extra-light taxes as an inducement, to the American love of speculation. If a capital gain is a real gain and not an inflationary paper profit, there is no possible justification for taxing it in any way except like all other income. If the progressive ordinary tax was too heavy for large one-time capital gains, that again was the fault of the progressive income tax and not of the principle that capital gain is income.

Capital gains taxes actually work in powerfully conflicting ways at different points in an inflation. In the early inflation boom like the 1960's, when huge capital gains were found under every stone and they were real gains because there was no price inflation, taxes at only half ordinary rates were far too low and were unjustifiable. But in a later inflation like the 1970's, when capital gains were still everywhere because of the price inflation but they were mostly paper gains and not real gains, taxes even at only half the ordinary rate were taxes on capital and not on gain and were far too high. The solution to this problem was not too difficult: the cost or "tax basis" of each investment might be adjusted by the factor of inflation since its purchase, and the balance of gain, being real gain, might then justly be taxed as ordinary income. In the circumstances of 1973, this might actually amount to a substantial reduction of taxes on capital gains, which is unfortunate but proper. A properly designed capital gains tax would never be a large revenue producer at any time except an early inflationary boom, because in real terms and conditions of stability there would be comparatively little capital gain in excess of capital losses. Other kinds of capital taxes must take up the slack.

Corporation taxes were another set of arbitrary distinctions in the American tax law. These distinctions were pure at heart, but their reason was weak. First, the income tax rate of corporations was higher than that of most individuals, although lower than that of some individuals. There was no good reason for any difference. Second, after a corporation's income was taxed once at the corporate rate, it was taxed again if it was paid out to stockholders as dividends. It was not taxed twice this way if it was paid out to a creditor as interest, nor was it taxed twice if the business organization was a partnership or something other than an ordinary corporation. A more irrational arrangement for taxes on business could scarcely be conceived.

These irrationalities were pure at heart because they did manage in a bungling sort of way to raise the taxes on capital to a passable level. Most capital was still held in corporations, and the largest of them still did pay dividends. The higher corporate taxes and the double taxes on dividends therefore did raise the overall tax burden on capital in comparison with the tax burden on personal income and consumption. In so doing, they created more hundreds of pages of tax code complexities founded solely on the artificial differences between corporations and other taxpayers or between dividends and other income. What is worse, these differences let far too much capital (paying no dividends or earning no income) go scot free of its share of taxes, and they created too strong an inducement to corporations to accumulate income when the most economically efficient use might be to distribute the income to stockholders as dividends and let them re-employ it elsewhere.

Correct reform of corporate taxes would make the income tax rate applicable to corporations the same as applicable to all other taxpayers, and furthermore would tax dividends only once, in the hands of either the corporation or stockholder but not both. Like a rationalized capital gains tax, this would amount to a tax reduction, but the improvement in rationality and efficient economic functioning would easily be worth the loss of a few billion dollars of revenue. Other capital taxes could make up the difference.

The shining jewel among the crowning absurdities of the American tax law must be, by acclamation, the *progressive income tax*. Even the name "progressive" is a bit of public relations propaganda, because it sounds like something forward-looking and therefore good when it really is no more than an attempted banditry of the rich few by the less rich many. A "progressive" income tax merely means a tax whose rate is not uniform at all levels of individuals' income. The American tax began at zero tax on the lowest incomes and rose to 70 percent of the highest incomes.

No feature of American tax was more questionable and less questioned than the progressive income tax. Its cardinal failing was that it did not work. There were so many loopholes that the rich simply did not pay the highest progressive tax rates. The progressive tax produced very little revenue above what a uniform moderate rate would do. The progressive tax did spawn hundreds more pages of complexities of the tax code, either creating loopholes or trying to close them. It did give useless employment to thousands of tax lawyers and accountants, waste millions of hours of the best citizens' best efforts seeking to avoid the tax, and artificially distort the use of resources by diverting them into less productive but less heavily taxed channels. The progressive tax did weaken the morale of citizens and strike most heavily at the moderate incomes of the middle citizens who contributed most to society but had least access to the means of tax avoidance. The effects of the progressive income tax as compared with a uniform rate of tax were all bad. One of the oldest judgments of the progressive tax, made in 1845, still held good:

"The moment you abandon . . . the cardinal principle of exacting from all individuals the same proportion of their income and their property, you are at sea without a rudder or compass, and there is no amount of injustice or folly you may not commit."

In the face of all the valid criticism, no reasoned defense of the progressive income tax exists. No need for a reasoned defense is ever recognized. The tax just *feels* right. As indefensible propositions go, the progressive income tax is a durable one.

The progressive income tax is an economists' and politicians' tax. People who know better, like lawyers and administrators and taxpayers themselves, know it for a fraud. Economists, however, are prone to think more grandly about what they call "equity" in taxation, and to them it seems eminently more equitable that lower incomes should be taxed less than proportionately to higher incomes. To them the progressive income tax is an article of faith, and it is faith and not reason that perpetuates it. Equity is among the slipperiest of all philosophic conceptions. No competent ethical philosopher would dream of offering equity as a tape measure for economic calculations, but economists had no such compunctions. In practicing equity rather than economics, economists appeared to be practicing philosophy without a license, and practicing it rather poorly. If free markets are working correctly, and if income from inherited wealth is separately dealt with by sufficiently heavy inheritance taxes, the size of an individual's income is exactly proportional to his contribution to the rest of society, and it is difficult to see why a larger contributor is proportionately less deserving at the hands of society than a smaller one.

As for politicians, the beguiling appeal of the progressive tax is easy to explain. The progressive tax was a feature of the first income tax law of 1913, and it was then an outgrowth of the softheaded Populist quackery of the late lamented nineteenth century. None of the other mad follies of Populism survived into practice, but this one did. The rich should be soaked, it was thought, and the way to do that was by the progressive income tax. Fortunately the soaked proved to be more nimble and fleet than the soakers. In final analysis, the progressive income tax existed only as a political sop thrown to the hoodwinked masses.

The obvious solution to the irrationality of the progressive income tax was simply to abolish it. The Federal income tax should be a flat percentage of every dollar of every taxpayer's income of every kind. The amount of the tax would depend on the varying need for revenue and on the varying balance between capital taxes and income taxes, but the most desirable range would probably be in the vicinity of 35 percent. Taxes on higher incomes would be reduced to this rate, and the rate is low enough so that inheritances and capital gains could be taxed as income.

If the income tax were to be truly a single-rate tax, taxes on lower incomes would also be raised to this rate, and other concessions like personal exemptions and some personal deductions would be eliminated. These changes would amount to a tremendous tax increase of the order of a hundred billion dollars a year, and the increase would fall on the vast numbers of lower incomes which benefit from the most numerous votes and the most legislative solicitude. This tax increase would therefore be totally impossible unless something else were done to compensate the smaller taxpayer for the tax increase. That something else is the national dividend which is to be proposed in the next chapter as a substitute for all government subsidy systems including subnormal tax rates and large tax exemptions. The hundred billion dollar tax increase represented by a uniform income tax contributes about half the cost of the national dividend. Every lower-income taxpayer who works would have more cash in hand, after the higher taxes on his income but supplemented by the national dividend, than without either. So long as this is true, no one need be shy of proposing the massive tax increase of a single-rate tax. The uniform tax and the national dividend are pieces of a matched set. This shop does not sell them separately.

Tax structure is the key to the enforced retirement of the inflation tax, and the renovations that were necessary to the American tax structure were deep and wide. They were deeper and wider than had been made to the American tax structure in the previous sixty years of its life. A political realist might gasp at the assignment of doing all at a stroke what could not be done in sixty years of patching and fixing. But it had to be done. There was plainly and simply no other way to disestablish inflation from the tax structure. Inflation would gladly persist and wait until the plight became so intolerable that that kind of fundamental rebuilding was politically possible.

32
Government Expenditure: the National Dividend

The other side of the government's economic management from taxes is expenditure. What taxes draw in, and often more, expenditure must pay out. The government never fails in this duty. The task is easier than drawing in taxes. The government finds myriad ways for getting rid of the surplus profits of national effort to someone, somehow. The question of this chapter is whether these ways are the best ways.

Government expenditure is often falsely maligned, especially by conservatives. Government expenditure is no more innately evil or good than expenditure by any other quarter of society. It is true, as conservatives say, that government expenditure tends to be somewhat more wastefully spent than expenditure by private persons; but it is also true, as liberals say, that expenditure on services that only governments can provide tends to be excessively niggardly in comparison with the overall affluence of the American society. Most emphatically of all, government expenditure is not inflationary of itself. The government could spend the entire gross national product without inflation, if it contrived to tax away that entire product from its producers. Doing that would be bad for other reasons, but not for reasons of inflation. Conversely, reducing the level of government expenditure does no good whatever in abating an inflation. Doing that merely cuts the supports from under a large number of Americans and leaves them in want, while the inflation goes on.

A stunning truth, seldom seen in clear view, is this: in the United States by the time of the inflation, the primary economic role of the government had become *to support the people* by its expenditure. No longer could the government confine itself to providing the services that a government normally must perform, such as paying its soldiers and buying them equipment, paying its judges and legislators and building them buildings, building highways and parks and providing schools and mails and railroads and airports if no one else would. All these things the government must still do, but where once these were its whole job, now they were the lesser part of its job. The main objective of the government's expenditure was not to buy anything or build anything, but simply to give away purchasing power to help support consumption by the people.

No one should lament the passing of the day when there was plenty to do for everyone who was willing, so that the government could justly leave everyone to fend for himself. It may well have been a better day, but that kind of attitude to it is ordinary nostalgia and is not constructive. The passing of that day is not a socialist plot, and the trend toward the government's supporting the people with its expenditures is a correct response to a plain necessity. The less urgently workers are needed to operate the system, while their need to consume is as great as ever, the more the government must draw taxes from capital and distribute freely to the people for consumption. The truly conservative view would not be to deny or deplore the necessity, both of which are futile, but to take care to see that the method of redistribution is well designed to increase and not diminish the efficient operation of the system.

The American government had a patchwork of ways to give away purchasing power to support the people, most of them masquerading as something else. They were similar to its patchwork of taxes. First there were the frankly gratuitous distributions which economists call "transfer payments," such as welfare payments, unemployment compensation, and Social Security. Next there were huge subsidy programs like farm price supports and shipping subsidies. Next there was the vast amount of government employment, and private employment supported by government spending, which pretended to obtain a useful product or service but really was for the support of the persons employed. Another form of distribution to support the people was the government's inflationary redistribution from creditors to debtors. Still another was the income tax concessions that the government gave to lower-income individuals through large exemptions and deductions and low rates. Finally there were the artificial legal devices to prop up the prevailing wages in private employment, such as minimum wage laws, government-spending wage laws, and governmental support for the wage-raising powers of unions. All of these were ways of channeling purchasing power to the people.

This collection of distribution schemes did the necessary job after a fashion, but as a distributive system it was uneven, unjust, ugly, wasteful, ineffective, and actively destructive of American well-being. It was obviously uneven, because highly-paid administrators, capitalists, and workers in government-supported channels were handsomely kept, while multitudes of other citizens received next to nothing. It was palpably ineffective, because poverty still existed. It was wasteful because programs were so outlandishly complex that most of their expenditures were dissipated in administration. It was unjust and ugly because it was selective; the basic idea that some distributee must be allowed to spend some of the values that taxpayers have produced is less repugnant than the idea that some government functionary should select the distributee. Worst of all, the system was actively destructive of the potential richness of American life because it purposefully prevented people from doing useful work that they would be glad to do. It is shocking to observe that payments under every one of the principal social programs—welfare, unemployment, and Social Security—were made on the one condition that the recipient refrain from working. Spurious employment in government industry also precluded workers' doing some other useful work, and artificially high wage costs also directly prevented people from working. The existing distribution system did its best to make everyone idle as the intentional price of receiving its dole, and this was incredibly evil. It is incomprehensible how any nation could expect to grow and thrive by using all the surplus fruits of its efforts to induce people not to create any more.

Suppose now, just suppose, that all of the government's existing distribution systems were swept away at a stroke and replaced by a single distribution system, masquerading as nothing but a distribution system, and benefiting every resident American citizen equally whether rich, poor, old, young, able, unable, working or idle. The surplus prosperity of the nation which was drawn in by the government through its appropriate taxes would be in effect apportioned among all the citizens, equal shareholders in the commonwealth, as a national dividend. At the price levels of 1972, this national dividend might as a starter amount to a stipend of $1,200 per year to each adult and $600 to each child under 20. Later, as the system began to work and to generate more surplus while dispensing with other government expenditure, the dividend might well rise considerably higher, but it must always remain modest in comparison with the income people earn by actively contributing to the society. This rationalization of all the government's irrational distribution schemes into a single comprehensive distribution program, coupled with adequate capital taxes in place of inflation, would constitute the most

Government Expenditure

momentous breakthrough the United States could make into the sunlight of the modern age.

The theory of the national dividend is that the nation has surplus prosperity enough to take care of the most basic requirements of each of its citizens, such as food, clothing, housing, and medical care, with no further strings attached. Attaching strings accomplishes nothing but to create evils. So the government simply pays for these things. Beyond those most basic requirements which he has received free, every man is on his own and every man is treated exactly equally. He earns as much or as little more as he cares to work for, he is paid no more or less than the fair value of what he contributes, and he pays the same percentage of tax on whatever additional he earns as everyone else. It is a two-tier system, admittedly the purest socialism to the extent of minimum requirements, but also the purest individual enterprise for the much larger remainder of all activity. In comparison with the patchwork that preceded it, this system is even, just, and no longer ugly because all citizens share equally; it is no longer wasteful because its simplicity makes the cost of administration virtually negligible; it is effective because involuntary poverty should end; and it ceases to destroy the potential richness of American life because it no longer restrains anyone from working who cares to.

A national dividend as a general distribution system, coupled with an array of taxes including capital taxes, provides the government with a complete set of valves to balance the flows between saving and consumption. If consumption is too high and saving too low, both the national dividend and capital taxes may be reduced. If saving is too high and consumption too low, as they were in the Depression, both capital taxes and the national dividend may be increased. If the people choose to work hard, the flows may increase; if they shirk, the flows must diminish. It is up to the people. The people control the total flows; the government just balances them. Even if capital grows so dominant as to eliminate all need for employment, the government can valve off from the fruits of capital, and distribute by the national dividend, enough consumption power to keep the system working smoothly. No other arrangement can do that.

The cost of a national dividend would be apparently very high. By simple arithmetic, $1,200 per adult and $600 per child would appear to cost the staggering sum of $212 billion, which was about 18 percent of the gross national product in 1972. But the cost is only apparent. The national dividend actually costs nothing, because it constitutes no more than a restructuring of an existing patchwork of distributions that already cost just as much. Let us emphasize the *quid pro quo* of the national dividend: no more welfare, unemployment compensation, Social Security, farm subsidies, shipping subsidies, other subsidies, income tax personal exemptions and deductions, low tax rates in lower income brackets, superfluous government employment and government-supported industry, and legal props under the wage cost of private labor. Unless all these prices were paid, the national dividend would be unworkable. If all were paid, there would be no new cost. Social Security, unemployment compensation, and welfare were already costing $78 billion per year; subsidy programs were costing $25 billion; leveling the income tax at, say, 35 percent without exemptions or deductions would yield perhaps $100 billion more per year; and the balance of the national dividend can easily be made up from increased capital taxes and reduced government expenditure in other sectors.

The ways in which the national dividend could strike off the shackles from the American system are virtually limitless. People would be set free to do useful work again without forfeiting some government giveaway by doing so. Employment could once again be allowed to enjoy the fertility of a free market. Wages paid for work done could be allowed to find the natural value of the work, rather than some inflated level, without depriving any worker of his full share of the prosperity for which the national dividend would be partly

Government Expenditure

responsible. Valuable kinds of work that could not be economically done in the United States might be done again. Workers might come to look on great new strides in automation as a boon to their total prosperity rather than a threat to their livelihoods. The national dividend as a general subsidy to every kind of employment and activity would harness the nation's wealth to make it the strongest competitor in the world rather than one of the weaker. For the poor, a fund of buying power would be provided from which to finance housing, clothing, medical care, education, televisions, or whatever else they may desire most. The people themselves might decide what is of value, rather than the government deciding for them. Criminal convicts could help pay for their own incarceration. Small farmers might be enabled to stay on their marginal farms against the tide of factory farming. Workers who had had to gravitate to the grim cities for work or welfare might take their national dividends and disperse back to less lucrative but more satisfying surroundings. The magnet of urban welfare would be demagnetized. Materialism itself and the sovereignty of the dollar might be moderated. The citizen might choose to take some of the surplus prosperity in leisure rather than more work. The visions are infinite.

The idea of the national dividend is not althogether unknown. Lady Grace Rhys-Williams in England advanced the proposition of a universal "social dividend" with many sound arguments in her book, *Something to Look Forward To*, in 1943. Milton Friedman's 1962 book, *Capitalism and Freedom*, offered the proposal of a negative income tax as a replacement for the welfare mess. Like any good enlightened conservative, Professor Friedman was an advocate of simple, direct, and efficient remedies for obvious problems. To the question of what should be done to help the poor, he would answer, "Give them money." The negative income tax and the national dividend are remedies of a similar character, but the more limited negative income tax seems too timid for the size of the problem.

The national dividend does present a few serious problems of potential abuse. One is the population problem. An unlimited national dividend would be an obvious inducement to breeding parents of a certain sort to turn out babies as a sort of cash crop. A national dividend which operated as a baby bounty would be worse than no national dividend at all. This problem is likely enough and serious enough that a workable national dividend would have to forestall it by paying no additional stipend for any future child which was, say, the third or later child of either of its parents, but instead carving out that child's rightful payment from his parents' existing shares.

A second problem is that of incentives. It is the question of how people as a whole would respond to a national dividend. If they were paid enough for a decent minimum living without working, would they work? Even without a national dividend, dropping out of the system was moderately widespread. Under a national dividend, it could not be less widespread. The forces of necessity exact at least a little work from persons who are only marginally interested in working, and who might well lose that little interest if necessity were removed. The principle of the unconditional national dividend is that it is every man's own business if he chooses to drop out, and that it is both meddlesome and not worth the effort of the government or anyone else to try to motivate him in some other direction, by withholding his share of the prosperity or otherwise. On the other hand, if everyone dropped out to retire on the national dividend, the surplus prosperity of the nation would quickly evaporate and so too would the national dividend. There is still too much work to be done, day in and day out. The day when no work is required is still far off. So the question still is, if there were a national dividend, would most people still work about as hard as ever in an effort to improve upon the minimums provided by the national dividend? What little evidence there is suggests that they would. Most people, including most of those the nation needs most,

Government Expenditure

seem to work because it is their nature and not just because they are driven by need.

I do not underestimate this problem of the national dividend. It is the crucial problem. If a national dividend would wither the will to work, then a national dividend would not succeed. But if that is true, it is also true that there is no other way for people to acclimate themselves to an overabundance of prosperity. If it is true, people cannot cope with success. The people will be as great and grow as rich as they care to, no more and no less. If the response to full prosperity is to cease trying and want no more, the people will decline. Granting the people a national dividend might let them grow when denying it will no longer make them grow. In the end, the people should be allowed to decide.

33
Employment

Of all the sacred cows of modern economics—among them interest, money, employment, investment, and growth—employment must be deemed by all odds the reigning bull. All good economic performance is measured first by the fullness of its employment, and all bad performance by its rate of unemployment. All other economic consequences including inflation are subordinated to employment. We are constantly being instructed about the "trade-off" that is supposed to be necessary between inflation and unemployment, so that neither can supposedly be reduced without an increase of the other. As a consequence, we have both more inflation and more unemployment than ever before.

Just as interest and money were found not to matter earlier, employment will be found not to matter now. (Investment and growth will have their turn later.) This is not to deny that employment may be something that everyone may need, but rather to say that employment could take care of itself quite nicely if it were simply allowed to take care of itself.

Employment

Employment is not by any reasonable reckoning the ultimate end of human existence. Employment has two distinct aspects, the work done and the wages earned. The economic system wants the work done, and the worker wants the wages. Economics' obsession with full employment on behalf of the workers acts as if the main object of employment, even to workers, was the work. It is not; it is the wages. To a worker, the main object of employment is to gain access to the means of consumption, which is wages. Work as having something to do may have a value of its own separate from the wages, but to a worker that is secondary and he can quite ably fill that need for himself.

In the simpler days of old, work and wages were inseparably bound up together. Work was the only known way of obtaining the means of consumption, and on the other hand the economic system needed all the work it could get from its citizens in return for giving them the means of consumption. In the more modern day, employment and consumption are no longer completely inseparable. The economic system has productive power which increasingly exceeds the need for work. The system does not need and perhaps cannot even use all of the work its citizens can supply. The system therefore can and perhaps even must make some of the means of consumption available otherwise than in exchange for work done, which means otherwise than through wages.

The national dividend, as a substitute for full employment policy, does this. It divorces the divorcible. It separates to some extent the distribution of the means of consumption from the wages for work done. It frees employment to perform no more than its natural function of getting done the work that must be done at a natural wage price, while letting people look elsewhere to the national dividend for a part of their total shares of prosperity. Work is rightly the servant of men, and a national dividend allows work to stay in that place; the enthronement of full employment as the sole source of all bounty, on the other hand, makes men the servants of their work. When economic managers harness the people to artificial employment as the price of their purchasing power, they resemble kindly masters of pet dogs who relieve their pets of the desperate necessity to hunt and kill for their livelihoods but then will not give them their dog biscuits until the dogs have gone through some cute tricks that the masters like to see.

Full employment policy, as the sole method of distributing adequate prosperity among the people, has a number of side effects, all of them bad. For one, it directly causes inflation. For a second, it directly causes unemployment. And for a third, it directly causes stagnation. In order to distribute an abundant prosperity among the people, full employment policy must seek not only adequate employment *but also adequate wages.* Adequate wages in an abundant prosperity means unnaturally high wages, wages that are higher than the fair market value of the work done. Inflation, unemployment, and stagnation are all caused by excessively high wages. It is paradoxical but true that the more effort there is to stimulate employment artificially, the less real employment there is. Nothing could increase available employment more vigorously than to allow its wage cost to decline to a free market level.

Inflation results from high wages in full employment because money inflation, itself the cause of price inflation, is the only known stimulant strong enough to create work when excessively high wages do not permit a free market for work to exist. The trade-off which is alleged to be necessary between inflation and unemployment (the so-called "Phillips curve") is completely uninevitable. There is no necessary connection whatever. If there were a completely free market for labor, there could well be no involuntary unemployment whatever even while there was also no inflation.

Unemployment too is caused by nothing but unnaturally high wage levels. If a prospective worker will accept a wage which is no higher than the fair value of the work he can do, he will be employed. The normal market response of a seller who cannot find a buyer, including a worker who cannot find

Employment

an employer, is to lower his price until he does find a buyer. If a worker will not make this response in selling his work, he is *voluntarily* unemployed at most. Lord Keynes, be it remembered, defined full employment as the point where workers do not offer any more of their labor at the prevailing market price, not necessarily the point where all prospective workers are working. Actual unemployment there might still be at this point of full employment, because to a prospective worker the prevailing wage offered to him was too low to be worth foregoing his leisure, but if so the unemployment would be voluntary and not the proper concern of full employment policy.

Stagnation accompanies unemployment and inflation among the consequences of unnaturally high wages. The higher wages rise in order to provide workers their fair share of prosperity, the more useful work prices itself out of existence. The workers suffer from lack of the work and wages, and that is unemployment. The system also suffers from lack of their productive effort, and that is stagnation. As the nation grows richer, one by one the most useful and worthwhile—but not lucrative—activities can no longer be carried on in the nation. The nation cannot let its wages fall, lest many of its people not share in the richness. But it cannot get work done, because the wages are too high. A paralysis of affluence sets in. The nation finds itself so rich that it cannot allow itself to work. The nation reposes on its collective posterior in order to keep its affluence up. It is preposterous. And it is all because the wages of work are relied on exclusively to distribute the surplus prosperity as well as to pay for the work.

A nation in this predicament is living on its capital in the truest sense, because it is the capital investment accumulated over past centuries, which could never be accumulated again, that makes all this possible. It is grotesque that there should be any unemployment, any stagnation, or any spurious employment, all cultivated by full employment policy, when the needs for useful work confronting the nation are still enormous. There was no shortage of work to be done in the United States. The supply of workers exceeded the need only in relation to the useful work that the nation *was doing*. In relation to what the nation *could be doing*, there was plenty of useful work for everyone for decades to come. Whole cities of slums waited to be pulled down and replaced with decent housing. Decrepit transportation systems ached to be restored. The building of complete pollution systems for every city, town, mill, and factory could engage every available worker. In fifty years, perhaps, the work might run short, but not sooner. If there were a free market in labor, all these things could be done. Only by shaking off an indolence enforced on the nation by the inflated wages of full employment policy could the work be allowed to begin and employment to become truly full.

A free market in labor means simply that the wage cost of labor is set purely by supply and demand for workers, without artificial influences like wage laws, unions' manipulation, or restraints on the supply of workers. If the supply of workers is large and the demand for them is moderate, wages must be moderate and a competition among workers may develop. A free market in labor, something that had not been seen in the United States for at least forty years, would be the complete remedy for all problems of unemployment and stagnation. Not for inflation—capital taxes take the place of that—and not for adequate prosperity—the national dividend must help with that—but for all the remaining problems of work for the workers and productivity for the nation. A free market in labor might well lower the average market price for labor, but the combination of lower free market wages and the supplementary national dividend would improve the total lot of every worker of the nation over his lot with unnaturally high wages alone. The national dividend would maintain fully his share of the prosperity, while he in common with all other citizens would participate in the renewed richness of the system which free market wages and employment made possible.

Employment

What would happen, if there were both a national dividend and a free market in labor, would seem to be this: Wages might be lower, but total prosperity of everyone would be higher. The lot of workers could easily be so much improved that they might voluntarily choose to work shorter weeks with more leisure rather than earn more. Automation could be welcomed for its further improvements in the national dividend, rather than feared for its losses of employment. If there were no more money inflation, wages must remain not only lower but constant. No law or government authority would decree that they remain constant, but both prices and wages simply could not be raised in the market if there were no more money. The biennial strike for higher wages would be futile, and it might as well not occur. Because of increased competition among the less skilled kinds of workers, it would be wages for unskilled work that would be lower, but wages for the scarcer skilled kinds of workers probably would not be any lower. The incentive to workers to improve their skills so as to get better jobs would increase, and the chronic shortages of skilled workers might abate. Even in unskilled work, wages could not fall far; employers setting wages would be competing against a somewhat reduced need of workers to work, because of the national dividend, and that is a more humane competition than against the brute force of unions but equally effective to keep wages up to presentable levels.

In a free labor market there would be no involuntary unemployment—none. Some workers might unemploy themselves because they did not like the wages or the work, but that would not be unemployment. No man is involuntarily unemployed while any job is open, anywhere, at any wage, that he could perform or learn to perform. The purpose of a labor market is to adapt the available workers to the available work by inducing the unemployed to move, to take the available wage, or to retrain themselves, and the motive force causing the market to function is that the worker's only alternative be voluntary unemployment. So long as the voluntarily unemployed are not impoverished, because of the national dividend, the market can be allowed to operate on its own.

Although there would be no involuntary unemployment, there might well be considerable *dissatisfied* employment, which means workers who did not unemploy themselves but still were not satisfied with the wages or the work. This too makes a labor market function, because it impels the dissatisfied to improve themselves as workers for the better jobs, and it impels the workers already in the better jobs to improve themselves too in defense against the dissatisfied candidates outside. This kind of competition is not altogether enjoyable, but it makes the system go and over the centuries it proved to be endurable.

The free market in labor finds blocking its way, like the glowering ranks of the Philistines, the whole institution of labor unions. Unions are the principal reason why free markets in labor do not already exist. Unions are dedicated to no one principle so much as the extinction of free markets in labor. Competition among workers is the cardinal anathema to the unions' theology. Unions routinely engage in anticompetitive practices which, anywhere else but in labor relations, would win them long prison terms under antitrust laws. Unions' commission is, after all, to raise wages higher than their market value, and like any good market-rigger they do that by eliminating competition from the market in any way they can.

The ways that unions use are familiar. Union contracts suppress competition between one worker and another by equalizing wages and by exalting seniority over all other qualifications. They inhibit better workers from working better than other workers. They restrain the amount of work done and increase the number of workers required, which is known as featherbedding. Unions often regiment entire industries so as to eliminate competition between the workers of one employer within that industry and those of another. Employers in the industry often happily participate in this process so as to help eliminate at least that aspect of competition among themselves. Unions restrict, often by simple fear, the entry of hungrier new workers into an industry which is on strike or which they monopolize, as in construction or longshoring. Unions resist the introduction of more efficient uses of labor or the movement of industry to more economical labor areas. All of these things suppress free markets in labor. They restrain competition, increase cost, and make industry less efficient. They cause unemployment and stagnation. They make the total pie divisible among all the people smaller than it otherwise could be. The theory of these methods, if there is any theory, must be that they gain workers larger slices of the smaller pie, and supposedly that is better for them than merely fair shares of a larger pie. That theory is disputable.

Of course the continuing crusade to eradicate free markets in labor is never wholly won, or even predominantly won. The surviving vitality of American industry attests to that. The native industriousness of workers themselves springs up persistently despite all efforts to keep it down, and some unions too are less union-like than others. But the fact remains that the least healthy industries are those in which unions have most nearly succeeded in extinguishing free markets in labor.

Unions' efforts to extinguish free markets have the direct aid and comfort of the Federal government, without which they could not prosper. Far from seeking to foster competition as it does in industry, the government silently supports and assists the unions' efforts to suppress it. Most of these forms of assistance are traceable to unfortunate meaures adopted by President Franklin Roosevelt's administration to try to cure the Depression. They were generally ineffectual for that purpose but left the nation's economic system loaded with labor shackles for the ages to come. One form of assistance is the various minimum wage laws, such as the Fair Labor Standards Act, the Davis-Bacon Act, and the Walsh-Healey Act, which, like every effort to dictate prices to a market, succeed only in drying up demand for labor and creating unemployment. Another form of government assistance is the millions of jobs of spurious employment engendered by the government's spending, which produce nothing but reduce the supply of labor and inflate its cost. The most important form of assistance is the government's commissioning the unions themselves as a kind of fourth arm of the government, through mainstay laws like the National Labor Relations Act and the Norris-LaGuardia Act, to act as the government's own regulatory agency imposing discipline and fair labor conditions on industry.

This is ingenious. The government's laws are hands-off laws, meaning that they do not so much abet the unions' regulation as forbid governments, courts, and employers from interfering with it. With the help of this kind of law, unions can regulate very effectively. Unions are possibly the most efficient of all government regulatory agencies. They regulate not by the tedious government methods of hearings and regulations and injunctions, but by the more instant and muscular methods of strikes and boycotts. With these tools, any government agency could probably regulate efficiently too.

These laws are not bad laws in principle. The government should indeed keep hands off labor disputes between an employer and its own employees. Employers should indeed be prevented from interfering with their own employees' organizing into unions if they wish. But that is as far as it rightfully goes. There should be no way for unions to bring the weight of the labor side of a whole industry to bear on one employer or on all the employers in that industry. There should be no way for striking employees of one employer to call in the coercive support of anyone else. There should be no way for unions to monopolize employment in any industry. Expert hired representatives, unions may properly be; brokers of hired power, they should not.

Labor unions are a complex and mixed subject. The institution of unions is not all good and certainly not all bad. Unions contributed mightily to the strengthening and perpetuation of American industry by equalizing the two equal partners, capital and labor. They still contribute a legitimate service as a kind of professional adviser to workers. Unions have earned an honest place for themselves, but they have not proved themselves any more fit to act as a fourth arm of the government than industrialists are. Unions are not the same thing as their members. Workers working are among the most deserving of all citizens, but unions militating on their behalf are not necessarily so. One thing that labor unions are not is farsighted. They do not grasp sophisticated notions of the well being of workers, such as the idea that other things might be indirectly better for workers than artificially high wages. Unions do not represent the interests of workers first and unions second if they are different, as they would be if the wages for work were to lose part of their function of distributing prosperity. Unions still adhere to simple-minded philosophies like the famous "More!" of Samuel Gompers and the view of workers in society as an eternal war between Us and Them. Both kinds of view are anachronisms. Unions have too fond a taste for anachronism.

Employment is not really a difficult technical problem. A free market in labor would solve it, and a free market would spring back into existence if the government merely released its restraints. Given a free market, full employment is as easy to provide as the useful work that needs doing is abundant. A free market in labor would go far to restore the American nation to its former strength, health, and ability to grow. Coupled with a national dividend, it would generate a greater prosperity shared fairly among everyone. Conversely, the kind of labor mentality that regards a free market with the ultimate loathing is the blank wall that bars the way.

A free market in labor, once gone, does not come back easily. No one knows whether people ever would permit it to come back once labor unions and labor mentality had driven it away. In this section of the book, we are indulging the luxury of ignoring practical possibilities. There is nothing that says a free market in labor must come back. The nation can do without it; not well, but it can do. It is not a matter of life and death, but only of more prosperity or less, more employment or less. Intransigent labor can continue to demand an ever-larger share of an ever-smaller pie, until in the end it owns the entire share of an empty plate. That is exactly what it will do if it decides that even that is better than the terrors of a free market.

34
Investment and Growth

If employment is the sacred bull, investment and growth are the sacred calves of modern economics. If employment is what economists try to achieve, investment and growth are how they try to achieve it.

Investment is undeniably the cornerstone of all economic development. Investment is what built the industrial system, and investment is what made the system as fruitful as it is for the people who inherited it. Investment in this sense means the formation of capital, and that in turn means using some of the product of men's labor to build physical productive assets instead of consuming the output as it is produced. A primitive farmer, for example, who spent some of his scarce productive time building a water wheel to grind his corn more efficiently, or building a plow to plant it more efficiently, or building a fence to protect his corn from animals, was *investing*. He was forming *capital*. His allotting some of his total time to investment instead of just to producing corn was economic *saving*. Investment was the opposite of *consumption*, which was what he did with the corn he grew. The more efficiently his capital helped him grow corn, the more corn he could grow, and that was *growth*. And the more his production was increased by investment, the more production capacity he had in excess of the requirements of subsistence so that he could grow still further. Or, on the other hand, the more capital investment he had made the less he would have to work to produce an adequate total output.

Investment is unquestionably a good thing if it is good investment, and growth is unquestionably a good thing if it is good growth. In the old days, when each primitive farmer was allotting his own productive time between output for consumption and output for investment, the sacrifice of time to investment tended to be rather shrewdly chosen. As a result, the investment was mostly good and the growth was mostly good.

In the latter day, investment and growth are elected not by either producers or consumers, but by governments and economists. Modern economics turned the whole chain of goals upside down. It made the object of the whole economic game not sufficient production, but sufficient employment. It said that no longer does man work in order to produce, but man produces in order to work. It said that man must make capital investment not so that he can work less, but so that he can work more. Only a professor could persuade himself of the truth of such sophistry.

The pivotal tenet of the modern economics is that investment of any kind, good or bad, produces more employment (the "multiplier") than is spent on the capital investment itself. The more investment of any kind there is, the more employment there will be. This makes of investment no longer a means to a desirable end, but an end in itself. That is *investmentism*. This transforms growth also from a desirable objective to a necessity. That is *growthism*. In pursuit of these goals, modern economics is willing to resort to all manner of distortive devices to encourage indiscriminate investment. The

Investment and Growth

principal one is artificially low interest rates, which do encourage investment because larger numbers of investment opportunities will have profit margins higher than the interest rate and therefore attractive for borrowing and investment. Since artificially low interest rates can only be obtained by money inflation, investmentism translates itself into inflationism. What little thought economics gives to the design of taxes concentrates itself, not as it should on the balance between capital and consumption, but on what tax devices will artificially stimulate investment and therefore employment. The misbegotten tax investment credits of the inflation era were an example.

The result of the economists' obsessions for investment and growth was not outright failure, strictly speaking. There was investment and there was growth. The percentage gains in the gross national product did continue to flow in as numbers on paper. But a kind of Gresham's law operated—bad investment drives out good—so that what investment there was was not merely indiscriminate but mostly bad. Bad investment means the building of superfluous factories, office buildings, office equipment, airliners, and highways, even while urgent needs for other good investments like houses, pollution facilities, and transportation systems go unsatisfied. Bad growth means constantly increasing production merely for the sake of production and not for the sake of satisfying the wants of people. No one person's opinion of what investment and growth are good or bad is valid. The people and the entrepreneurs would decide that, voting with their purchasing power. Good investment and growth are definable as whatever investment and growth would remain if all artificial stimulants by the government and economists were removed.

Even if investment and growth were all good, their fatal flaw is that they cannot continue to infinity. Investment and growth are inseparably accompanied by a growing permanent destruction of irreplaceable resources, by a growing permanent creation of indestructible wastes, and by a growing permanent propagation of insatiable populations. In the far distance, the point waits where no more investment or growth can be tolerated. If an economic system supports itself by relying exclusively on artificial investmentism and artificial growthism, it is sure of eventually reaching the point where it cannot support itself at all. Investmentism and growthism clearly have a limited life, and the economic system that ties itself to them will have a limited life too.

A slavish commitment to investmentism and growthism is a belief that an economic system cannot live without growing. That is as plainly false as to say that a man cannot live without being young. Investmentism and growthism are a refusal to let maturity arrive. They are a quest for eternal youth, and they are as neurotic and futile as such quests always have been. Economic youth, like any other kind of youth, may have been an exciting time of building and looking ahead, but maturity is said to have its rewards too. None of this is to say that the economic youth of the United States was necessarily over and past, but rather to suggest stripping away all the artificial youth to see what real youth there might still be, or what real maturity might quite pleasantly take its place.

An extra word or two about population growth is in order. The disastrous future consequences of unrestrained population growth were at last being noticed in the United States. Restraint of population growth was being urged even at the same time that economic growth was being stimulated, often by the same people. The two goals are irreconcilable. Economic growth is heavily dependent on population growth. If population growth actually slowed down, growthism would be more difficult to pursue and full employment impossible to achieve. An expanding population growth produces more consumption, which the system needs, than workers, which it does not need. Hordes of babies and children consume loyally but they do not work. The reverse would be true if population growth slackened. All those hordes of former babies and children would then need work, but for scarcity of new babies and children consumption would fail to increase. The problems of insufficient prosperity of the past were as nothing to what would come if population growth did indeed abate. Employment, investment, and growth not only are not friendly to stabilization of population but probably could not either endure or survive it. One side in this conflict must yield.

Fortunately, the same device that sets employment free also sets investment and growth free. The problem never was employment, but an adequate distribution of purchasing power. If employment was not the problem, then artificial investment and growth were not needed to provide employment. If adequate distribution of purchasing power were provided by a combination of capital taxes and a national dividend, in addition to wages for work, then employment, investment, and growth could all be set free to go their own way. And a better way it would be. As was true of employment, the less effort there were to stimulate investment and growth artificially, the more good investment and real growth there might be. If there is purchasing power in hand, people will buy what they want, grow as they wish, and invest as they need to. Purchasing power begets its own employment, investment, and growth. What it begets is good by definition, because it is what the people elect, having at their disposal the means to choose. Risk takers can best decide what risks to take, investors what investments to make, people whether to grow, and workers whether to be employed. No wealth and no prosperity was ever manufactured in the office of an economist or a bureaucrat. They spring only from the efforts of the people. Economists and governments can best confine themselves to providing the people the freedom to choose, and, having done that, they will have done well.

35
Dogma

Dogma is the mummified form of theory. Dogma consists of tenets of mind that have ceased to grow and adapt. Dogma is living belief become petrified, working theory become embalmed in stone.

America was shut into its inflation by formidable walls of dogma on every side, as high and blank as a sierra. One wall was conservative dogma. Another wall was liberal dogma. Still another wall, the most formidable of all, was economic dogma, which was the mummified theory of the very profession which was trusted to know the way out. Among them, these dogmas effectively closed off every avenue of escape from the American inflation.

For probably as long as men have consorted with other men, they have divided themselves naturally into two irreconcilable camps corresponding to what we nowadays call liberals and conservatives. The liberals at Athens, for example, were those who favored conciliation with Persia or Sparta, and at Rome they favored uplifting the poor from their pov-

Dogma

erty with bread and circuses. Conservatives thought all that futile. Never in history have liberals and conservatives compromised their differences appreciably, and they probably never will.

The problems of the inflation stood as close as it was possible to stand to the center of the conflict between the warring camps. The questions of who shall be taxed, who shall benefit from the government's largesse, who shall work, and who shall benefit from work were their main line of battle. It is not difficult to predict which of the ideas this book advances would be embraced by liberals and which by conservatives. Liberals would adore, and conservatives abhor, the massive new capital taxes, inheritance taxes, net worth taxes, and capital gains taxes, and the massive new distribution system through a national dividend. Conservatives on the other hand would celebrate, and liberals denigrate, the abolition of upper income tax rates, lower income tax rates, income tax exemptions, double corporate taxes, welfare, unemployment compensation, Social Security, government subsidies, artificial employment, and legal supports for unions' restraints of trade. Virtually every member of both camps would embrace about half these measures. Hardly anyone would embrace them all, though the fact is that none should be adopted unless all were. In the eternal stalemate between the two camps, it is better that nothing be done than that either camp prevail.

The conventional liberals and conventional conservatives who inhabit both camps are essentially impostors. They are not true to either liberalism or conservatism. They are usurpers of their own names. The words themselves, "liberal" and "conservative," are both good old words, they are both names of commendation, and they entail no necessary conflict with one another. "Liberal" connotes liberty, liberality, abundance, and progress, and who could condemn any of those? "Conservative" connotes conservation, frugality, and mindfulness of the future as well as the present, and those traits too are laudable. Both conceptions in their true form could easily coalesce upon policies of *maximum present munificence consistent with permanent continuation of that munificence into the future.* Half of that idea is foreign to conventional liberals and the other half to conventional conservatives.

Individual men who stood tallest in history often could not be readily classified as either liberal or conservative. They were both liberal and conservative in the true sense, but neither liberal nor conservative in the conventional sense. They seldom had many close followers. They were dwellers in the no-man's-land between the two camps. No liberal is a true liberal who is not obliged to admit also being conservative, and conversely, and the conventional members of both camps were of a purer and therefore falser strain.

The conventional conservative gives his camp a reputation for not only conservation but parsimony. He conserves for the sake of conserving, and he resists change for the sake of sterile stability. He acts according to a belief that whatever is, is right. He speaks usually in defense of some kind of vested interest, such as existing wealth or entrenched power, and he opposes any kind of progress that would be hurtful to those vested interests. He tends to show a lack of humanity toward less able and less fortunate people. He insists on natural selection by individual accomplishment in its uttermost rigor, especially for other people. He is too fond of laws to repress the natural forces that actuate other people which he considers ignoble.

By the time of the American inflation, the conventional conservative had become an endangered species. His numbers were reduced and his strength had waned. This decimation of the conservatives was itself a danger, because, like the pest that keeps other pests under control, the militant conservatives had long kept the militant liberals trimmed in numbers and cowed in audacity. If one kind dies off, the other will multiply, and multiply was what the camp of the liberals had done.

What passes for a liberal in modern times is a complex fellow. He clothes himself in the raiment of generosity and

Dogma

love. His motives are of the purest and his goals of the loftiest. He seeks to benefit his fellow men. He concerns himself, for the most part sincerely, with the weaker and less successful of society's members. No one but the harshest misanthrope could really quarrel with a liberal's objectives. But beyond the purity of his motives and the altitude of his goals, the conventional liberal flounders. If softness of heart is his virtue, softness of head is his flaw. He can be counted upon to follow all the worst-conceived, least efficient, most costly, and most wasteful routes toward his goals, generating malignant side effects, breaking down the fruitfulness of the system, doing great harm to the objects of his own benevolence, and finally failing to reach the goal itself. A liberal's benign goals, if they are achievable at all, are invariably achieved most efficiently by hardheaded conservatives.

A conventional liberal is congenitally unable to count the cost, feeling perhaps that it would seem mean of spirit to look at anything so crass as the price tag when a humane goal is in view. He labors under a quixotic belief in the perfectibility of life, scorning mere improvability. He is an activist, but his headlong activism is akin to the fibrillation of a diseased heart, while it is the slow and plodding beat of a healthy heart that moves the good fresh blood. He too trusts naively in the magical efficacy of mere laws to generate and guide natural forces, resembling nothing so much as King Canute decreeing that the tides of the sea be still and sending his royal bureaucrats to flog the waves when they fail to obey.

With his exclusive concern for all those who finish out of the running in the footrace of society, the common liberal is in constant peril of making a cult of inferiority and a stigma of excellence. Any society which exalts inferior over superior, cultivates its most barren fields ahead of its most fertile, and reserves its best prizes for anyone but its best contributors is in deep trouble as a going society.

With his effort to elevate altruism as a ruling principle beyond the requirements of humane charity, the common liberal introduces a disorganizing force into the operation of society. The society which is most liberal for everyone is that society in which every member is induced to contribute the most he is able in exchange for the maximum possible gain or income to himself. The liberal's altruism deprives society of the efforts of both himself and his distributees.

The conventional liberal loves too well to meddle in the lives of others. He is allergic to individual liberty. The last thing he wants is to set up his fellow men on their feet and let them find their own way. He wants to hold their reins, like an overprotective parent. And like such a parent, he usually harms more than helps his dependents.

The ordinary liberal is usually several steps removed from real life. That is how he can be so foolish. He is almost always either wealthy, or academic, or artistic, or political, or in some other way has escaped from the need to do productive work for a living. Workers are often allied with liberals for their own gain, but they are seldom liberals themselves. As more and more of a society's members become removed by affluence from direct exposure to the sweaty production of wealth, the society's most urgent task is to preserve an instinctive memory of what the sources of that wealth were. Liberals fail to remember.

Most troublesome of all, the conventional liberal suffers from great difficulty learning. His beliefs are impregnable. He is impervious to evidence that his best-loved schemes mostly cost too much, backfire, and fail. His defense is simple and complete. He denies the evidence. That is the way of dogma.

John Maynard Keynes once wrote a plaintive article entitled, "Am I A Liberal?" In it he looked about him in England and found no party fit to join. The Tories were diehards. Labour were a party of class aggression. The old Liberals were moribund. Dogma was on all sides, and reason nowhere. It is the same with Republicans and Democrats, or indeed with all parties of every land in every age. Keynes' conception of an individual capitalism continuously working itself lean was congenial to hardly anyone. Keynes expressed it this way:

Dogma

"The Conservative Party ought to be concerning itself with evolving a version of Individualistic Capitalism adapted to the progressive change of circumstances. The difficulty is that the Capitalist leaders in the City and in Parliament are incapable of distinguishing novel measures for safeguarding Capitalism from what they call Bolshevism. If old-fashioned Capitalism were intellectually capable of defending itself, it would not be dislodged for many generations."

Some years later, in 1939, he said this:

"I am ever more convinced that there was deep wisdom in those seventeenth and eighteenth century thinkers who discovered and preached a profound connection between personal and political liberty and the rights of private property and private enterprise. The fact that the lawyers of the eighteenth century perniciously twisted this into the sanctity of vested interests and large fortunes should not blind us to the truth that lies behind. As Count Kalergi has recently reminded us, 'in all ages private property has been an essential element in liberalism, a bulwark of personality against the omnipotence of the State, and a stimulus to seek comfort and culture,' and it was recognized in the French Revolution by the seventeenth paragraph of the Declaration of the Rights of Man as an 'inviolable and sacred right.' "

Keynes was a dweller in the no-man's-land between the liberal and conservative camps, a highly unpopulated place. To be on the right track, one must dwell there too. One must learn to like the solitude. Being alone is perhaps no assurance of being right, but having plenty of company is a fairly strong suggestion of being wrong. America's challenge in the inflation was to take the scarce best from the dogma of each camp, leaving the copious dross behind, and then to blast a breach through the walls of dogma to open a way beyond them.

Economic dogma was an even more formidable barrier in the American inflation than the dogma of conservatives and liberals. After Keynes, dominant economic theory had taken an increasingly mummified form. The American inflation was an economists' inflation, just as the German inflation had been.

Learned economists were given their head as they had seldom been given before, and the direct result of what they learnedly directed was disaster. The direct result of what they deliberately chose to do was the inflation and nothing but the inflation. No command post in the whole directorate of American life was more vital than the economic command, and none was more poorly served. If economists had performed half as creditably as the industry and labor against whom they loved to pontificate, America would have been blessed indeed.

In the face of its own failure, economic dogma remained serenely unchanged. Dogma is like that. At the crest of their own inflation, the economic priesthood were still nodding and polling themselves and fingering their talismans and murmuring their incantations of employment, investment, and growth. Their assignment was still what it always was, or should have been: let everyone work who wishes, let everyone have a fair share of the prosperity, cheat no one, and *let there be no inflation*. The priesthood and their dogma were still failing in that as completely as ever. They showed no awareness of what had happened and no idea of what to do next. As experts, they appeared not to know what they were doing. Strangest of all, their sorely tribulated flock still listened to them as respectfully as ever.

Prevailing American economics had degenerated since Keynes from a live and developing science to a kind of witch-doctor sect. It was like medicine of the day when George Washington's physicians had all but bled him to death before he finally asked to be allowed to die unassisted. It was like geography of the day of Columbus, when the idea that the earth was flat was the dazzling New Geographics and the much older orthodoxy of the round earth was virtually discredited. It was like physics in the days of the quest for perpetual motion, but alas, the conservation of energy still held economics in bondage too.

The aberration of the New Economics in America bore perhaps the strongest resemblance to the Lysenko aberration in the agriculture of the Soviet Union. Trofim Lysenko was the official genius of plant genetics in the governments of Josef Stalin and Nikita Khrushchev. He nailed official Soviet agriculture to a set of his own revolutionary theories that promised miraculous and effortless gains in crop yields, just like the gains in economic abundance promised by the New Economics. Unfortunately for Russia, Lysenko was a mountebank, an honest one perhaps but still a mountebank. His theories failed and so did the Russian crops. Only after the mighty effort of expunging the Lysenko aberration completely could Soviet agriculture return to the sweaty and unmagical work of hewing out real gains. So too with the New Economics.

Milton Friedman was fond of quoting an aphorism attributed to Poincaré, the French president, that war is too important to be left to generals. Professor Friedman adapted it to say that monetary policy is too important to be left to central bankers. It is equally true that economics is too important to be left to economists. Even generals can bungle their commands without consequences as dire as if economists do, and few generals ever bungled as purely as economists did in the American inflation. What is true of generals, central bankers, and economists is perhaps true of every other species of experts as well: government is not safely left to politicians, law to lawyers, education to educators, or information to journalists. An expert has devoted himself so exclusively to probing all the thickets in his own forest that he understands less well than an intelligent outsider where his forest fits into the landscape. He is no blinder than anyone else, he just looks that way. A rare man can overcome this handicap, but only a rare man. An expert may not necessarily be unfit to preside over his own domain, it is just more difficult for him. A rare general is fit to assume the ultimate responsibility for war, too. The rare economist who can assume it for economics can do so not because of his expertise but in spite of it.

Economists are only men, after all. They are good men

and true, one and all, and each one undoubtedly desired the good health of their patient, the American nation, fully as ardently as George Washington's physicians desired his. Economists are all intelligent men too, better able than average citizens to apply difficult and sophisticated conceptions which they receive from elsewhere. But when something goes awry with the received conceptions, the average intelligent economist is not enough to set them straight. The mind capable of original creation is as rare as it ever was. All the doctoral degrees in Academe do not necessarily add up to a single such mind.

Economists seem susceptible to catching various occupational contagions which impair the effectiveness that they as individuals otherwise would have. Being academic, they suffer from the same insularity from the rigors of real life that liberals do. Economists often sound as if they thought employment and unemployment were something that comes in bottles, like tincture of iodine, to be mixed up in a laboratory beaker and applied as needed. Plying a shovel out in the economic ditches with the rest of us might be good for that ailment. Economists are in the constant scholar's danger of over-refining their material to a pile of fine dust, learning more and more about less and less until they know everything about nothing. They develop a liking for paradox and a love for making problems look more difficult than they really are, the better to justify their experthood. Economics is swept by a constant epidemic of mathematics, substituting equations for ideas and computers for brains, as if mathematics lent scientific legitimacy to the black art. Many an economist, deprived of his mathematical language, is speechless. Struck on the head by Newton's apple, he would probably consult his computer to discover that apples will almost invariably fall outward into space, except on very rare occasions, predictable by enormously complex computer calculations, when they will fall downward instead on unguarded heads. Playing with their computers, economists too often develop a disturbing taste for playing with the levers that operate the lives of other people. Their charming name of "model," a computer term, aptly describes their conception of the rest of us, like a transcontinental toy train set complete with cute little figures that move about at the press of a button just like real people.

Economists are not all of one mind, let it be said. Economists disagree among themselves as sharply as most men. Many a good economist knew better than economics as a whole did in the American inflation. But dissent was too scattered and too polite. Denunciation is a mode of expression that is not often used within the cloister, but nothing less than denunciation of the old dogma could make it known outside the cloister that a priestly doubt existed. Laymen cannot cogently denounce experts, and if experts will not, error will persist. If experts shall lose their expertise, wherewith shall they be expertised?

The fact that only the rare economists can be entrusted with economics is not reason to discard economics, but to go and find the rare men. Milton Friedman regularly advocated a government of rules instead of men in economics, as a solution to the deficiencies of men. But rules are not superior to men; they are no better than the men who make and observe them. The remedy for a defective government of men is not more rules but better men. The death in 1928 of Benjamin Strong, the dominant central banker of the United States, dissolved the shrewdest economic government of men (with Norman of Great Britain and Schacht of Germany) that existed in the twentieth century, and perhaps caused the Depression and later war. The remedy for the death of a man like Strong was to go and find another.

American economics in the ordeal of the inflation left much to be desired, but for the same reason left much room for improvement. The tremendous forward strides which were already past in sciences like medicine and physics were still ahead in economics. The assignment was still the same, no one had changed the specifications: let the people prosper, find a stable cruising speed, cheat no one, and permit no inflation.

In a nation still as strong and as rich as the United States, the assignment simply could not have been as impossibly difficult as economists made it look. The problem was not the impossibility of the task, but the incapacity of the men who had thus far tried it. All that economists needed was someone to show them how.

Lord Keynes once said,

"If economists could manage to get themselves thought of as humble, competent people, on a level with dentists, that would be splendid!"

And if economists as dentists could manage to stop agonizing over the metaphysics of toothache and just learn to *drill* the blooming thing, that would be splendid indeed!

THE LAST ACTS

The American Prognosis

36
Act Two, Scene One: President Nixon Begins

I can remember, as a student, being taught the structure of a well-wrought traditional stage drama as an inverted V form. After a prologue or some other prefatory material, the flow of the drama was supposed to turn upward and rise steadily to a turning point, which occurred almost unnoticed somewhere in the second act. After that, the action was to turn downward and proceed equally steadily to a final dénouement which was to occur near the close of the third act. In this design, a good inflation is something like a good play.

The administration of President Richard Nixon, beginning in 1969, clearly embraced the second act of the great American inflation which had been initiated years earlier under President Kennedy. It might well encompass the third act as well, but the second act clearly.

Richard Nixon was predictably a different sort of president from his two predecessors who had presided over the earlier formative stages of the inflation. He was a Republican as they had been Democrats. He had been vice-president as part of the Eisenhower administration, which itself had constituted the last years of stability before the renewed inflation began. And Mr. Nixon had failed by only the narrowest of margins to win the presidency from Mr. Kennedy in 1960. It was foreseeable that the attitude of Mr. Nixon's administration toward the inflationary mess would be altogether different from that of the Kennedy-Johnson regime. By both temperament and philosophy, President Nixon and the Republicans were well suited to try to rectify the terrible inflationary damage, some of which the Democrats had already done and the rest of which they left waiting to happen.

In this effort, however, the Nixon administration failed. It proved to lack the wit to know what needed to be done, the will to do it if it had had the wit, and the power to do it if it had had the will. After years of the mightiest efforts the presidency could bring to bear, the nation had nothing but a recession and some hard times to show for its pains and had gradually grown weaker and more vulnerable than President Johnson had left it. Both the current rate of price inflation and, what is more important, the Index of Latent Inflation were higher by 1973 than they had been in 1969. All of this meant that the sternest measures of this sternest of presidents had achieved no forward progress at all against the inflation, but at best had only held the line and succeeded in losing ground more slowly.

To say that President Nixon failed is no great criticism of Mr. Nixon himself or his administration, for the task that confronted them in 1969 was one that demanded economic skill bordering on genius. Genius merely failed to appear. It was a far more difficult task than would have confronted Mr. Nixon in 1961 if he had won election to the presidency then. The United States in 1961 had no serious economic problems and a base of firm stability. By comparison, the challenge of 1969 was the severest economic challenge faced by any president since President Roosevelt tried, with equally scanty results, to meet the challenge of 1933. Mr. Nixon's failure was a failure to subdue a monster that others had bred and raised to full maturity. Measures like those of Mr. Nixon would have been quite sufficient in 1961 to forestall the birth of monsters.

The situation that President Nixon inherited on his inauguration day in 1969 was truly frightening. Any person who fully grasped the depth of the problems that existed must have marveled at the intrepidity or the foolhardiness of any man who wished to assume the presidency at all under such circumstances. The Viet Nam war was then at its worst, with the rates of dollar cost, of American casualties, and of civil protest at home against the war all at their peaks. The rate of the Federal budget deficit was at a peacetime record which was then considered to be incredibly out of control. The rate of price inflation was the highest since 1951 and rising. Money inflation had risen to a rate of almost 8 percent per year, which was far faster than the fastest rate that had previously been seen since 1946. The American social fabric was in an appalling state of strife, disunity, and ferment. For the more fearful among those who could see the gravity of the situation, it was possible to foresee that some sort of collapse must surely come within Mr. Nixon's first term, no matter what he might do. This collapse, of course, did not come within that time span, although it did approach ever nearer.

President Nixon's years divide into two distinct periods at approximately the middle of 1970. The first of these, lasting for about eighteen months, was the first scene of Mr. Nixon's second act, and the difference between the two scenes was so extreme that the dividing line between them may well turn out to have been that momentous turning point of the entire inflationary drama.

During the first scene, the government strove mightily to throw a harness on the dragon of inflation by imposing various economic restraints of a rather stringent sort. After a few months of office for taking bearings, the campaign went forward vigorously. It proceeded on two fronts, both quite conventional for such campaigns. The Federal Treasury reduced its expenditures and strove for a balanced budget, which it did approximately achieve for the fiscal year from July 1969 through June 1970. At the same time, the Federal Reserve System tightened money. From having been clipping along at about 8 percent per year, the rate of money inflation began to drop sharply in May of 1969, and by the following year it had amounted to only about 3.8 percent. In essence, the campaign was as simple as that.

The sequelae of this government strategy were perfectly predictable, and they occurred in a perfectly predictable sequence and time scale. The almost instantaneous first result, as always, was that the stock market fell. Within two months after May 1969, average stock prices had fallen by 14 percent, and within another year they were down by 31 percent. At the same time, interest rates instantly began a steady rise to the unprecedented heights of the spring 1970 credit crunch. These were the first results. Much more slowly, in fact not reaching the worst until late 1970 after the strategy had already been abandoned, business began to turn sour, profits began to plummet, workers were laid off and unemployment rose, and recession came.

The one result that did not follow was an end to the price inflation. Prices were still climbing about as fast at the end of this scene as at the beginning. This circumstance led the government to believe that the strategy was failing and that the old rules did not work any longer. This inference was totally wrong. There was nothing intrinsically wrong with the government's "game plan," as it liked to call it. But the government expected far too much of this strategy, right though it was, and expected the desired results far too quickly. The government's only mistake was to underestimate how deeply entrenched was its enemy. It had taken three full years of far tighter money to reach price equilibrium in 1948, and there was no reason to expect success sooner in 1970.

The money expansion rate of 3.8 percent per year during the tight money was only half of what had preceded it, but

Act Two, Scene One

it was certainly not non-inflationary. It was nothing like the zero money growth of 1948, or 1957, or 1966. It was about as high as the inflation rate which had started it all in the first four years of the inflation under Presidents Kennedy and Johnson; it was as high as that which produced the boom and inflation of 1956; and it was almost as high even as the deplored inflation of the Korean War. It was no lower than the current rate of price inflation, which meant that it was merely keeping pace and making no inroads at all on the Index of Latent Inflation. This rate of money expansion would have been good for a perpetual inflation of at least 3 percent per year, accompanied perpetually by the recession which was impending. That at least would have been better than a perpetual inflation of 6 or 7 percent, accompanied eventually by the same sort of recession, such as would have followed if the tight money had not been imposed.

Though President Nixon's timid tight money was at least on the right track, the government's extreme budget cutting of 1969 was a mistake. The fiscal solution of the balanced budget was greatly overplayed. When so much of the nation depends on government spending for its livelihood, budget-cutting merely cuts the props from under these people and leaves them unemployed, doing nothing to help inflation. Avoiding that budget shock wave might have ameliorated the resulting recession and permitted the government's healthful tight money to continue for a longer time, possibly even for a long enough time. But it was not to be.

By the summer of 1970, the government had reached its Rubicon. The next presidential election was then little more than two years away, and Mr. Nixon knew well from his 1960 experience that economic restraint must not be allowed to persist any closer to an election than that. In the event, the abandonment of economic restraint turned out to be almost perfectly timed to allow recovery just before the election. In addition to politics, there was the problem of solvency. The Penn Central Railroad had just collapsed, Lockheed Aircraft was on the brink of bankruptcy, and money was so tight and interest rates so high that a national wave of financial collapses seemed to be in the making along with the worsening unemployment and contracting business.

So the government laid down its arms, burned its forts, deserted its positions, and fled. What this meant simply was that the government turned on the money inflation and government deficit spending again full blast, as full as ever. Commencing approximately with August 1970, the government's budget deficit dived to new peacetime depths, and a remarkably steady new money inflation rate of around 6.5 percent began and continued throughout the next years. Those three percentage points of increased inflation, a mere six billion dollars of new money a year, made all the difference in the world. Interest rates plunged, the stock market soared, and the nation was back on inflation's high road to prosperity.

The government's brief defense along the line where it had dug in at the beginning of the Nixon administration was forgotten, and no further effort was made to dig in along any line. To say that the government thus failed in its assignment, which is true enough, is not necessarily to say that this line of defense could have been held. Without other fundamental economic reorganizations, none of which was even being considered, tight money and depression very possibly could not have been tolerated long enough to have any effect on inflation. In other words, the government's defense lines very possibly were going to be overrun anyway. Be that as it may, the government's relieved abandonment of the defense in the summer of 1970 is what marks the end of Act Two, Scene One, and perhaps that elusive turning point of the entire drama. For it was not at all certain that any further effort to stanch the inflation by correct methods, even as resolute as this irresolute one, would ever be made in the future. There was no longer any practical possibility that inflation at least as bad as then existed would ever be arrested, short of some kind of traumatic dénouement.

37
Act Two, Scene Two: Price Controls and Other Follies

Scene Two of President Nixon's administration was the silly season of the inflation. Everything was the opposite of what it appeared to be. The nation appeared to be in better health economically, but it was worse. The government appeared to be trying to hold the line against inflation, but it was actually fostering the inflation at a prodigious rate. And the strangest and silliest of all the delusions that dominated the consciousness of that day was that ultimate folly of inflation fighting, price controls. This chapter is basically about price controls, because price controls were all that the government had left after it abandoned all its real defenses.

The factual course of the period was simple. After the government turned on its deficits again, it kept them on. After it turned its money pumps back up to that 6.5 percent annual rate, it kept them there. The government persuaded itself that that rate of money expansion was about right for "noninflationary growth." Never mind that that was well above the rate of the worst inflation after World War II and before 1967.

That was a nice moderate rate of inflation and the government would keep to it, which it did. The government's conduct was steady and it was unremitting, that much must be said for it. It did not vacillate any more. It followed a good straight course, and it moved along as constantly as it could. It was much like Napoleon's retreat from Moscow.

The natural effects of this new combination of policies were as predictable as those of the old game plan had been. The stock market rose and interest rates fell. Later, after the usual long wait, business and employment turned up again, the recession went away, and prosperity appeared to return. By the end of 1972, when the presidential election came to pass and Mr. Nixon was re-elected, the nation was in a boom. A year later, however, this time without any reduction in the rate of money inflation, the stock market had fallen again, interest rates had risen again to surpass even their previous peaks of 1970, price inflation was worse than ever, and recession seemed to be impending again.

Strangely enough, the rate of price inflation, which had not improved during the stringency of 1969 and 1970, also did not improve when it was ended. The government should not have expected the price inflation to do anything but become worse once the government renewed its money inflation, but it did seem to expect otherwise. The government professed great perplexity that the price inflation was still cruising along at somewhere above 4 percent, gathering its breath for a new upsurge with the boom to come, in August of 1971 after a year of renewed money growth. So the government roused itself to the most dramatic kind of grandstand play that it could envision, and that was President Nixon's famous announcement of Phase I of price controls on August 15, 1971.

Another international money crisis was then in progress. The constant outflow of cheap dollars from the United States had inundated the Europeans again, and since May they had more or less discontinued supporting the old exchange rates but were resisting an upward revaluation of their currencies

Act Two, Scene Two

against the dollar. Most of the aspects of Mr. Nixon's August plan were directed to the international money situation. Among other things, he announced immediate detachment of the dollar's value from gold, a sort of floating of the dollar; he announced an import surcharge of 10 percent to force other nations to raise the exchange value of their currencies; to enliven the sluggish domestic economy, he announced removal of excise taxes on automobiles, as if the proliferation of automobile economics was not already overblown enough; and above all he announced a ninety-day freeze of wages and prices as Phase I of his new commitment to wage and price controls.

The commitment to price controls is important. Nothing much else about the August edicts was important. The continuing international money crisis was temporarily resolved later that year by the international agreement known as the "Smithsonian agreement," which re-established fixed exchange rates for the time being and generally devalued the dollar. The other effects of the August edicts were largely miscellaneous. The commitment to price controls, however, was commitment to a new first line of defense against inflation that was totally incapable of doing any good and quite capable of doing active harm.

Price controls were the darling of liberals of every kind, and especially the liberal wing of economists who were the same wing that had created the inflation in the first place. If ever there was an apt example of King Canute commanding the tides to be still, and mobilizing his minions to flog the waves when they would not, it is price controls. Price controls appeal wonderfully to the King Canute complex among liberals. For years, and more particularly since the despised President Nixon had come to power, they had been preaching for price controls to hold down the natural forces that they themselves had insisted be unleashed. In the end, President Nixon, who was not a man to go down fighting in an outnumbered cause merely because he was right, switched to the enemy camp and thereby got command of it. It was very clever. Leonidas the Spartan should have mastered that maneuver. When the people screamed for controls, President Nixon gave them controls. When they screamed against the resulting shortages, President Nixon removed controls. It was a Greek farce. And since nothing else was being done, the farce must continue.

Price controls have as long and honored a history as inflation. In four thousand years of inflation, price controls have a perfect record of four thousand years of total failure to control inflation. Two of the best examples were World War II in the United States and the German inflation during and after World War I, when price controls were termed by Lord Keynes "not the least part of the evils." Always and everywhere, price controls have failed to escape any part of an inflation in the long run and have usually helped considerably to make inflation worse. It is not possible to mount a really catastrophic inflation without the able assistance of a first-class set of price controls, as the United States of 1946 and Germany of 1922 well learned.

It would be idle to assert that price controls do not control prices. Obviously they do. Controlled prices are lower than they would be without controls. Many critics who are philosophically opposed to price controls do their own cause a disservice by claiming that controls are ineffective on prices, as they did during the relatively successful Phase II of President Nixon's program. If that were true, price controls would be doing no harm either. Price controls do hold prices down. Their effectiveness in World War II America or in inflationary Germany cannot be disputed. But controlling a price below its natural level or its natural rate of increase does not destroy one single percentage point of inflation. Like matter, inflation is indestructible. Price controls merely postpone inflation, cover it up, hide it away, and store it. Price controls merely transfer the inflationary potential manufactured by the government to the reservoir of latent inflation instead of being realized on a

Act Two, Scene Two

pay-as-we-go basis. That is all that price controls can ever do. If this were the worst that price controls did, they would do no active harm. If the government's policies were no worse under price controls than they would be without price controls, postponed inflation would be no worse in total than immediate inflation. In real life, this seldom happens. Inflation deferred is inflation forgot, and not merely forgot but joyfully ignored. The only inflation a government can understand is inflation it can see, and if it can see none because of price controls it feels free to act as if there were none. This is why a first-class set of effective price controls is indispensable to a first-class inflationary collapse. Without the self-deception of price controls, the government is forced by the rising prices to find some less facile way of financing than unlimited money inflation.

The interesting example of the Korean War price controls bears mention. This episode was sometimes offered as a case of successful price control without retribution, and contrasted with the case of World War II price controls. After the removal of World War II controls, latent inflation exploded, but after the removal of Korean War controls, nothing happened. This shows merely that the Korean War controls were unnecessary and were accomplishing nothing, although they also were doing no harm but to waste the time of everyone. There was no latent inflation at the time of the Korean War. The government over-reacted with its controls to an inflation that was not there. That episode should have offered no comfort to the United States of 1973, however, because the situation then was increasingly like World War II and not like the Korean War.

The full flavor of the foolishness that prevailed in the United States after the commitment to price controls in 1971 is difficult to convey. This was what made Scene Two in Mr. Nixon's act the silly season of the inflation. Having abandoned the last serious efforts at defense, the nation gave itself up to sound and fury signifying nothing. In place of policy, there was only obscuration. The government laid down smokescreens to conceal the absence of any defensive forces. Day in and day out, newspapers were filled with column upon column and page upon page of doings and dissertations of the Price Commission, the Wage Board, the Cost of Living Council, the president, the unions, most of the bureaucrats, all of the politicians, and every conceivable kind of self-appointed expert on what the price controls were doing, what they were going to do, what they should do, whether they were succeeding or failing, and so forth. Phase followed phase of price controls. At every turn the inflation was worse. Now there were consumer boycotts and protests, followed by counter-protests and boycotts by producers, and the government chiming in like King Canute with price freezes and defrostings and new kinds of controls. It was all of no consequence whatever.

Inability to see beneath superficialities is the stamp of every severe inflation, and never was this more conspicuous than by 1973. If there was a sudden flareup of rising prices like meat and food, the nation could become alarmed and incensed and demand legislation about it. If there was a temporary abatement of rising prices, as during the controls of 1972, the nation could believe that there was nothing wrong any longer. If the inflation was superficially less bad and the prosperity superficially better in 1972 than previously, the nation was able to feel that its economic health was improved when actually it was worse than ever. The hopefulness of the nation, its government, and its people, peeping around each new corner in hope of finding the inflation gone away and health restored, was both touching and pathetic. Neither of those boons was ever going to be found on the path it was then taking.

The incredible Watergate affair afflicted the nation almost more than anything else in its travail. Watergate was an absurd little political gaffe committed by some of the more foolish of Mr. Nixon's political troops in the re-election campaign. The forces of the liberal opposition, who had been

Act Two, Scene Two

soundly thrashed in the election, immediately set about to undo both the election and the president with the Watergate incident. Only in America could political trials have the President of the nation as the quarry, and all the mechanisms of law in the nation be bent on the lynching of their own leader. The most important segments of the nation's press, which had uniformly indoctrinated the public with misinformation and misjudgment of the inflation, now diverted all useful attention away from it to the Watergate affair. All the nation attended the circus while Rome burned down at home. The Watergate hounds baying after the president bore a similarity to the downfall of Matthias Erzberger in his 1920 libel trial with Karl Helfferich, and the economic consequences might be just as grave.

The simple fact was that the nation by the beginning of 1973 had still paid hardly more than half the cost, in price inflation, of the fun and games it had been buying for itself over the ten years since 1962. Such prosperity as the nation still enjoyed was still false and still totally dependent on the continuing and accelerating inflation. The price inflation since 1969 when Mr. Nixon entered, bad as it was, only about equaled the money inflation in the same time. The price of the six years under Presidents Kennedy and Johnson that preceded Mr. Nixon was still due and payable, and the implacable creditor of inflation was pressing. The failure to rein in the money inflation in 1964 and especially 1965 was far more important to the inflation that was raging in 1973 than anything that was being done in 1973. It is possible that the die for all the remainder of the inflation had been unalterably cast by the close of 1965.

The dangerous part of any inflation is the part that cannot yet be seen. The inflation that can be seen is past doing any more harm. In 1973, as at any other point in the American inflation, there was no power under the sun that could excuse the nation from seeing its prices continue rising ultimately to the equilibrium that past money inflation had already fixed.

If the Index of Latent Inflation had been correctly estimated, that would mean in 1973 that prices must rise by the additional 22 percent of that index even if the money inflation should stop the next day. Moreover, the money inflation was not about to stop the next day. The money inflation was still rollicking along at the same old steady 6.5 percent a year, which, according to all the evidence of the preceding twenty-five years, meant that the price inflation too must rollick along at a minimum rate of at least 6 percent per year forever, on top of the 22 percent one-time head of pressure that had already been built up. The nation could not bear to let the money inflation diminish. As Karl Helfferich used to say in Germany, that "would have brought about a collapse of wages and prices, probably accompanied by crises and catastrophes," but no one seemed to notice that the nation must face up to those very crises and catastrophes *someday*. On top of everything else, the nation even at 6.5 percent per year inflation had the look of entering into the kind of recession and inadequate prosperity that in the old days were only found in the company of zero inflation. That might mean the government would have to turn up the money pumps another notch.

The situation in 1973 was not good. It had seldom been worse. Confidence was unfounded. Complacency was ill-informed. Hope was misplaced. If the prospect that confronted President Nixon at his inauguration in 1969 was frightening, that which confronted him in 1973 was fundamentally more so. Any man who grounded his course of conduct on a belief that stability and health were not far away simply did not understand.

38
The Way Out

One of the few philanthropisms of inflation is this: technically, it is a matter of the sheerest child's play to stop an inflation, *any* inflation. At least that is true if the underlying economic system is in passably good working order, as those of both Germany and the United States were. Inflation can be brought to a halt at any stage, early or late, before collapse or after collapse. It is even possible to halt an inflation overnight, as was done in the German inflation. In some ways it is easier to do after a collapse, when all the wreckage has been obliterated, and in other ways it is easier before a collapse, when the system is still working well. But it is easy at either time, and the steps necessary are essentially the same at either time. All that is demanded is that the nation finally pay up the perfectly payable price of its past greed. No voluntary cooperation by the people is necessary, the government can accomplish it without anyone's help. A nation succumbing to inflation is like a man drowning within arm's reach of a shore he does not see.

Make no mistake about this further fact: it is not a matter of child's play, in fact it is not possible, to stop an inflation at any time without paying the price. The price of past misdeeds is always there, is finite in amount, is usually greater than is thought, invariably rises still higher the more it is evaded, is ineradicable, will not go away, and in the end *will be paid.*

There are only three basic requirements for bringing any inflation to a halt. They are, first, that prices must rise; second, that money must stop rising; and third, that the money wealth must be devalued to tolerable levels. No more is required, but no less will do either.

The first of these requirements is that prices must rise. The final end of an inflation is of course that prices stop rising, but that can only happen after they have risen enough. The essence of an inflationary situation is that equilibrium prices are higher than current prices are. When prices are allowed or encouraged to rise to their equilibrium, and not before, they will stop rising of their own accord. If the Index of Latent Inflation accurately estimates the distance from current prices to equilibrium prices, then inflation will end when prices rise further by the amount of the index. In the United States at the beginning of 1973, that estimated amount was about 22 percent. Efforts to hold prices below their equilibrium by price controls and the like, which are common to all inflations, are futile. The only way to purge an inflation is not to control it but exactly the opposite, to *get it over with.*

Purging an inflation by letting prices rise is of course very painful. As the pains grow more acute, there is a natural doubt that the rising prices will ever stop, as expressed by President Truman's desperate special message to Congress in 1947. The answer is to keep calm, salve the pain, be confident, and wait. Inflation will stop when it is ready to stop.

Purging the inflation may proceed either quickly or slowly, depending on how much latent inflation there is and how rapidly the prices rise. If the government really wished to use its price control powers effectively to bring inflation to an end,

The Way Out

it would use them not to hold prices down but to force them up. For example, if the United States used its price controls to compel every seller to raise his prices overnight to the estimated equilibrium level, which by the end of 1973 would probably be about 168 percent of 1962 prices (a rise of 30 percent for the full year 1973), and at the same time to raise the wages he paid by the same amount as his prices, the latent inflation would be quickly eliminated. Prices and wages could then be released from controls to act according to market forces, and they would rise no more if the latent inflation had been accurately estimated. That is the overnight ending of an inflation. It is like fighting forest fires with backfires. The ground we burn intentionally is going to be burned over anyway, and if we burn it ourselves we can prevent the fire from going beyond it.

The second requirement of stopping an inflation is that the quantity of money stop rising. Raising prices to eliminate inflationary potential works only as permanently as no more inflationary potential is added by money growth. This means that the increasing quantity of money must stop completely. Zero money growth is requisite. Every central bank knows how to stop the growth of money if it wishes, and if it does the inflation too will stop as soon as latent inflation has eliminated itself through rising prices. The reduction of money growth to zero may be as abrupt or as gradual as one likes. As long as the rate of money expansion is constantly lower than the rate of price inflation by at least some amount, the inflationary potential is eliminating itself and the inflation will someday stop. The more gradually it happens, the longer it will take, and the pain will be less acute but more prolonged.

The third requirement of stopping an inflation is a more subtle one. Prices must rise enough to devalue the nation's money wealth to a level of real burden that its debtors can bear. Remember that the money wealth was the mother lode of the inflation. Inflation's principal function was to mine this lode, using the proceeds to buy prosperity and at the same time lightening the load on debtors. Debtors can only tolerate so much debt if it is real value, and inflation has the paradoxical tendency to cause debt to grow far out of proportion to real wealth. If inflation is to be finally abandoned, it must remove one last, huge chunk from the value of the money debt before departing. This means, in its simplest signification, that the assured further price increases represented by the latent inflation (to a level of 168 percent of 1962 prices at the close of 1973, according to the estimated Index of Latent Inflation) might very well not be enough price increases to lighten the debt load sufficiently. A further large infusion of money inflation might be necessary before bringing inflation to a stop. The nice question is how much is enough. The government at the end of 1973 might, for example, have put out in a single day perhaps 100 billion new dollars before proceeding to extinguish the inflation by raising prices. That would have raised the money supply by about 37 percent, the equilibrium price level to 230 percent of 1962 instead of 168 percent, and the necessary total price increase for the year 1973 to 77 percent instead of only 30 percent. That would certainly devalue the debt enough. Somewhere between that and the actual latent inflation that was probably the right amount of price rise to devalue the debt. Balancing the survival of debtors against the injustice to creditors was a matter of delicate judgment.

The part played by this one last burst of inflation is vital. Germany was an example. The astute German managers of the Rentenmark plan shut off the further growth of money only after "an immense access of inflation," far larger than anything that had gone before. The Germans had to leap ahead of the astronomically rising price inflation with a still more astronomical amount of money inflation, and then instantly turn about and face down the prices and say "Halt!" It required great prowess, and they made it work. No one should underestimate the necessity of this feat. The fantastic amount of paper wealth accumulating right up to the last day of an inflation could not be allowed to exist as real value in the new stability without ruining the debtors. The reasonable expectations of the creditors that their credits would be good had to be disappointed, and the unreasonable expectations of the debtors that their debts would be written off had to be realized. It was not just, it was just necessary.

The reduction of debt to a tolerable level will take care of itself in one way or another, if not by a final burst of inflation then by wholesale bankruptcies. Bankruptcies are wasteful and inefficient and do not really help the creditors, when compared with the ease and efficiency of writing down the entire debt structure by a single stroke of the government on a single day. If anyone should protest the injustice to creditors of this stroke, he may be answered first that it is necessary, second that the government had been doing the same for decades, third that it is in the creditors' interest too that the nation regain health, fourth that the loss is smaller than the possibly complete loss creditors may expect if the inflation proceeds, and finally that the devalued wealth was probably not well earned real wealth anyway but only easy wealth owed mainly to the inflationary boom.

These three steps are all of the technical prerequisites for ending an inflation. Ending the inflation in the United States presented a fourth major problem, however, and that was the problem of providing sufficient prosperity for the people after the inflationary drugs were removed. Strictly speaking, providing for prosperity was not a true prerequisite to ending the inflation. Any moderately competent American economist knew how to stop the inflation by stopping the money, if that was all that was asked. The nation would soon be economically prostrate if no more than that was done, but, strictly speaking, that would not alter the fact that the inflation was over. Even Karl Helfferich knew all this. It was those "crises and catastrophes" that would ensue that led him like everyone else to believe that inflation was less bad than the alternative. The same prosperity that lured the nation into inflation in the first place also deterred it from leaving. Providing for prosperity must therefore be taken as a fourth necessity for leaving inflation for all practical purposes, forgetting about strictly speaking.

Notice that the problem of prosperity was peculiar to the American inflation and not characteristic of all inflations. It was what made the American inflation more difficult and more dangerous than any previous inflation of history. In Germany of 1924, by contrast, there was no enduring problem of prosperity after the inflation had ended. There was an adjustment in the form of depression and unemployment for less than a year, and after that employment and prosperity became quite satisfactory through the normal forces of economics and without help from the government. The United States in 1973 was different. Americans had been accustoming themselves to the unreal degree of inflated prosperity not for a year or two as the Germans did, but for literally a generation. Millions of Americans had never known any kind of prosperity but unreal prosperity. Readjusting themselves to real life was not going to be as easy for them as it had been for Germans. Although the American inflation was less severe than the German, its much longer duration made its psychological scars likely to be even worse. Still more importantly, the United States was much more mature economically than it or any other nation had ever been. It could not possibly employ all its available citizens and supply them with adequate earning power without either using progressively worse inflation or drastically reorganizing its economic structure. In short, the United States was so rich that it could not be sufficiently prosperous in its existing organization without inflation. No other nation, inflationary or not, had ever faced this problem.

Technically, this new problem of prosperity was no more difficult of solution than the old problem of inflation itself. Practically, it was far more difficult. Eliminating inflation could be done by the government with no cooperation from

The Way Out

the people, but regaining prosperity could not. Prosperity required a far more extensive program of radical surgery on the economy. It required intelligent legislation, where merely halting inflation required no legislation. It also required legislative treading on some part of the jealously guarded preserves of practically every important private interest group in the nation, and that is seldom successfully done by democratic legislation.

The technical program for severing prosperity from inflation, allowing the inflation alone to die, has been outlined earlier in this book. At the barest minimum, there must be massive new capital taxes to take the place of the inflation tax, and there must be some effective method of distributing the proceeds of the capital taxes to the people for consumption. The abundance of the new prosperity would, I think, be in the direct proportion that the nation adopted the whole program and not merely the minimum program, the whole program being the adoption of net worth, inheritance, and capital gains taxes; adoption of uniform income taxes and elimination of low rates and exemptions; elimination of double corporate taxes; establishment of a universal national dividend and abolition of all other distribution systems; removal of all government legal props under artifically high wage rates; and introduction of a free market in labor. The minimum program would produce a less abundant prosperity, but even the minimum program would at least allow the nation to navigate safely past the rocks of depression.

The kind of prosperity that could still exist if inflation were renounced might well be a different kind of prosperity. Many people might not like it so well. It would be above all a real-life kind of prosperity, and that might well be humdrum in comparison with the unreal prosperity of the inflation, like a return to sobriety after a trip out on hallucinatory drugs. Every dollar would be hard earned and therefore carefully spent. There might be less luxury. The stock market would be becalmed. Wage increases would be difficult or impossible to get, and wages themselves might be unspectacular. Employment would be useful and therefore humbler, less glamorous, and perhaps less fun. The prosperity might not seem like the promised land. It might be a bit boring. On the other hand, every man could have a job. Purchasing power would be good, not lavish perhaps but still good. The most useful citizens would be the best rewarded. Poverty should decline. Real well-being should begin to rise again. Leisure might increase. *And there would be no inflation.* America could find a stable and mature cruising speed. It might not be too bad either.

The problem of prosperity was independent of inflation in more ways than one. Merely continuing the inflation was no assurance of continuing the prosperity. Insufficient prosperity was going to emerge in the United States again whether it renounced inflation or not. That was because of the Law of the Exponential Inflation, which made it necessary to compound the inflation continuously in order to keep the prosperous effects, but compounding to infinity was not possible. The choice between inflation or a renunciation of inflation was not a choice between an easy and familiar route to prosperity or a more difficult route to prosperity. Not at all. Without radical transformation, the nation would soon have both inflation *and* depression. It was a choice between prosperity or no prosperity, between living poorly or living well, and between living in a declining state or in an improving state.

Notwithstanding all that, in 1973 the choice between inflation and a renunciation of inflation appeared to be a choice between easy times immediately or hard times immediately. Inflation was still potent enough to postpone the hard times a while longer into the future. It was actually a matter of hard times immediately or harder times later, but that was not fully apparent, and in any case hard times while they stay in the future are not very painful. For that reason, virtually no one in the United States really wanted to end the inflation. Despite all the verbal indignation that was heaped on inflation in all its stages by the people, their leaders, their spokesmen, and their press, it was all purely verbal indignation. Almost literally no one really wanted to end the inflation with all that that would entail. It would repay anyone handsomely to note that well.

39
The Way Ahead

The way that actually lay ahead of the United States in 1973 seemed not very likely to be similar to the way out of the inflation. This chapter takes a look at all the preliminary drafts by the master playwright for the third act of the American inflation. As with any good drama crafted with validity and truth, there were only a few basic variations which would not exceed the bounds of reality. Each variation flowed with inevitability from the conduct of the players in the drama.

Since this chapter looks to what was the future in 1973, the reader should be charitable toward whatever errors of foresight may appear. From the first day after these words were written, the reader possesses better information about the unfolding inflation than the author had. These words might even be read at a time when the final conclusion of the American inflation is known, and in that case the reader's privilege of comparing the prognosis with the autopsy is an enviable one.

The Way Ahead

Which course the third act of the American inflation might take was a purely political question and not an economic one. There were no economic problems in the American inflation, only political problems. If the government did A, then X would follow economically, and if the government did B, then Y would follow economically; but the choice between doing A and doing B was a political question.

There were really only three possible basic drafts for the third act of the inflation. The first of these was one called "Tight Money." This was the one in which the play would end with the band of hardy strugglers finding their way safely out of the deep and perilous forest, much battered and wounded but safe at last. This was the draft ending which was elaborated at length in the preceding chapter, entitled "The Way Out," and it was the one course of action which could hope to reduce or eliminate the American inflation without deepening harm. In the absence of this course of action, the American inflation would most certainly never be reduced or eliminated without first writing off the dollar and the dollar wealth.

Tight money had been tried by the government intermittently over the course of the inflation, abortively in every case since 1962, and it was possible that it might be tried one or more times, probably abortively, again. If the major structural changes which were described in the preceding chapter were not made, however, and it seemed exceedingly unlikely that they would be made for the reasons given there, then the economic depression and unemployment which would follow from tight money made it practically certain that the tight money would never be tight enough or persist long enough to reduce the inflation significantly. In theory, even in the aggravated circumstances of 1973, a naked policy of tight money alone with no great structural changes could still do the job, ending the inflation and leaving the economic system alive and breathing, but just barely. The accompanying depression would certainly be deeper than any that had occurred since World War II, and it was not a strong possibility that any political government would allow itself, or be allowed, to let that happen.

The second basic scenario for the last act of the inflation was one called "Stabilized Inflation." According to this draft, the drama would have no clear-cut ending in the classic sense. It was the not-with-a-bang-but-a-whimper ending. This complex of conditions would come to pass if the government despaired of ever making any significant reduction of the inflation and simply surrendered to it. It would adhere to a constant and moderate rate of money inflation such as the 6.5 percent per year which was prevailing in 1973. By so doing, the government would accept the prevailing inflation *de facto* and simply resolve not to cause it to become any worse, and forever after the inflation would simply go on at the same steady rate. The curtain would fall whenever everyone was willing to give up on victory and persuade himself that the defeat was really a tolerably honorable draw.

Stabilized inflation has some good points in the real world. Its principal good point is that it is achievable in the real world. The body in motion is allowed to stay in motion, at the same speed and in the same direction. The dismaying consequences of trying to escape from an inflation need never be faced. A truly stabilized inflation, in which prices are truly free to rise at their own speed, is fully as stable as a condition of steady prices, and there is no necessary tendency to degenerate into a worse inflation.

On the other hand, a truly stabilized inflation in the United States would not be by any means the long-sought condition of prosperity. If prices were genuinely free to rise at their own speed, and they adjusted themselves to a steady 6.5 percent money inflation by rising steadily at perhaps 6 percent per year themselves, the economic condition of the nation would still be a condition of insufficient prosperity. It would resemble in all respects the condition traditionally known as Tight Money. A steady 6.5 percent money inflation, in the

The Way Ahead

presence of a steady 6 percent price inflation, would be exactly as tight a money policy as zero money growth in the presence of stable prices. Prevailing interest rates would have to be of the order of 10 percent to 15 percent per year. The money inflation, having no marginal speed advantage over price inflation, would yield no beneficial stimulation, and the state of unemployment and insufficient prosperity would therefore be exactly as bad as before the inflation ever started.

If prices were *not* permitted to rise freely at their own speed, then the inflation would not be a stabilized inflation. If only the money inflation proceeded at that steady but moderate pace, and prices were artificially restrained to a slower pace, the danger represented by the large latent inflation would increase. Since the marginal speed advantage of the money inflation over the price inflation was being maintained, this course of action might temporarily continue to have some beneficial effects. Prosperity might be a little better, interest rates a little less high, and unemployment not so bad as in a truly stabilized inflation. But the relative safety of the stabilized inflation would be sacrificed, and unlike the stabilized inflation there would still be every danger that the situation might degenerate into a worse inflation.

By 1973, the stabilized inflation was about as conservative a course as the most conservative political government could be expected to follow for any extended period of time in the United States. Undertaking the terrifying journey out of the inflation seemed out of the question. The spirit of the times was not to seek difficult victories, but to settle for moderate defeats. A stabilized rate of money inflation was the course that President Nixon's government seemed to be following throughout the three years from 1970 through 1973 with a remarkably constant money growth of about 6.5 percent per year. There was frequent talk, alternately, of tight money conditions and easy money conditions being maintained by the Federal Reserve System, but in fact there were neither. There were unusually steady money conditions. Arthur Burns, chairman of the Federal Reserve Board, was an adherent of the Friedmanite school of thought that any kind of monetary trend, tight or easy, if it was a steady trend, was better than the constant alternation of tight and easy money that had bedeviled the nation for decades. The Federal Reserve seemed to be testing this thesis, and it was a most interesting experiment.

Though the prerequisite of steady money growth was being satisfied, however, the relative safety of a truly stabilized inflation was still far from secured, mainly because prices were not yet being allowed to rise at their own speed. As a result, interest rates were not nearly high enough and insufficient prosperity was not nearly bad enough for a stabilized inflation. As 1973 wore on, however, interest rates were rising past their old peaks to new historic highs, prices were being forced free to rise by shortages and market distortions, the stock market was deflated, and signs of approaching recession were appearing. All this came to pass without the least reduction of money expansion such as had always been the cause of these symptoms in the past. Stabilized inflation had not arrived, but it was coming. The acid test of the conservative government's mettle would come when the full rigors of the stabilized inflation began to be felt, with faltering business, worsening unemployment, insufficient prosperity, unheard-of interest rates, and cantering price inflation, all with the same old steady money inflation of 6.5 percent a year. The epic question then would be whether the government could still stick with its steady rate of money growth or must instead take the next quantum leap upward to money inflation of perhaps 10 percent a year or more in order to abate the depression. That latter course would be the way to the third and last of the draft scenarios for inflation's final act.

This last draft of the finale can be called the Geometric Inflation. It is another name for the big bang, or German, ending. It has a distinct flavor of the *Götterdämmerung* about it, and one must infer a certain Wagnerian influence on our

The Way Ahead

master playwright if he should elect this ending for the drama. Each new step in a geometric inflation would occur when the government, dissatisfied with the stagnation that accompanies stabilized inflation, lifted the rate of money inflation by a fresh quantum leap. The faster rate of money growth might temporarily restore the desired conditions of low interest rates, full employment, vigorous growth, and prosperity, but only until the price inflation was again restabilized at the new higher rate, accompanied again by all the old symptoms of unemployment and insufficient prosperity. The government can go through this as many times as the people will tolerate, but at every new level the choice is the same: either an entrenched and permanent inflation, with recurrent insufficient prosperity but without increasing danger, or a newly increased money inflation with temporarily improved prosperity, increased danger, and a guaranteed increase in price inflation in the future. This is the practical working of the Law of the Exponential Inflation. It is not a true economic law because the government always has the theoretical ability to draw a line and say, "No farther!" But the practical compulsions upon the government to take each new step of the geometric inflation are very great. And the only possible ending of the geometric inflation, if it is repeated again and again until it will not work any longer, is the German ending.

These three—Tight Money, Stabilized Inflation, and Geometric Inflation—were the only permissible drafts for the last act of inflation that did not violate reality. Of course, it was possible to conjure up other fanciful endings. It was possible to dream of a Saint George riding out of the mists with his magic sword to slay the dragon and leave everyone to live happily and prosperously ever after. This was just the sort of ending that people in the grip of an inflation do customarily trust in. It was just the ending which most Americans, people and government alike, were in fact trusting in. But it was totally fanciful. It belonged to the world of fairy tales and not of real life. Only certain kinds of endings for the American inflation were admissible in the real world, and the Saint George ending was not among them.

One other kind of dénouement for the American inflation is worth mentioning, not because it was likely to happen but because it was not. This was the Great Depression of 1929–1933, replayed. This was deflation. In this draft, the government would tighten money so hard that business and the securities markets would collapse, unemployment would soar, people would turn inward, prices would fall, and the value of money wealth would actually increase. Not long before precisely this sequence was set in train by the Federal Reserve in 1928, John Maynard Keynes himself was foreseeing the probability of *inflation* for the United States. Humility must rule before so distinguished a misjudgment, but still deflation was not practically possible in 1973. Inflation and deflation had been equally available to the government in 1928, and it was pure gamble for Lord Keynes to predict one rather than the other. They were not equally available in 1973. The burden of the total debt would have become doubly intolerable if the value of money had not merely stopped falling but actually risen, as in a deflation, and the government knew very well how to prevent that by inflating the money. The government's own enormous debt, a factor which significantly was not present in 1928, would force the government to issue money simply to service the debt. The deflationary ending was as fanciful as the Saint George ending, possibly more so. It is said that generals are forever preparing themselves to fight the last previous war, and the same was true of Americans in 1973 who were still arming themselves to fight the last previous depression.

As between the two most probable courses ahead for the United States in 1973, the stabilized inflation and the geometric inflation, which was more probable remained exceedingly unclear. Three more years of President Nixon's administration remained, and his previous administration had resisted worsening the inflation with reasonable firmness al-

The Way Ahead

though it had also done nothing whatever to improve it. On the other hand, his administration had also been willing to turn inflation on again forcefully in 1970 in the face of unpleasant economic conditions. In the likely event that similar conditions returned again with the inflation undiminished, his administration might be willing to turn the inflation on still harder by taking the next leap upward in the geometric inflation. It was uncertain. If the third act of the inflation had not been played out before the elections of 1976, which were to be the celebrated bicentennial of the republic, the choice of the person who would become president then might very well be decisive of the republic's fate.

The specter that waits in the wings of any inflation, including the American, is the general exodus of the people from the currency when they lose faith in it at last. When this specter steps in from the wings, the government's games are over and the final curtain is not far away. There had been no sign of this specter in the American inflation at any time through 1973. The stolid willingness of Americans to absorb inflated dollar wealth had been and continued to be enormous. The level of understanding of the inflation was of course very low at all times, and this had its good side in keeping the specter away. In 1973, Americans were actually deepening their commitment to money wealth by a tendency to invest more heavily in bonds and debt obligations as a result of the severe stock market losses of recent years. Americans had been standing docilely still for the fleecing for years, and there was no telling how long they would stand for being skinned as well before they would bolt.

The American position in 1973 was moderately grave. The Index of Latent Inflation at the beginning of the year was over 22 percent and could not fail to become worse unless the current rate of price inflation was consistently worse than the money inflation. This was smaller than the latent inflations in the United States at the close of World War II, or in Germany near the close of its boom in 1921, but still grievous in view of the nation's inability to cope with it. As Shakespeare's dying Mercutio said of his own mortal sword wound,

". . . 'tis not so deep as a well nor so wide as a church door, but 'tis enough, 'twill serve . . ."

Near the end of 1973, yet another economic crisis menaced the grossly overextended nation. As a result of another brief war between Israel and its Arab neighbors, Arab oil producers began to shut off the supply of oil to Western nations, especially the United States. Almost instantly, American industrial activity across its whole range began to contract. Crises like this one often passed over as quickly as they came, and moreover the crisis was technically no more insuperable than the inflation itself; but if the crisis did not pass, and if the government surmounted it no better than it did the inflation, the crisis could easily supply the final spark to the explosion of the inflation. Having stretched the dollar to its ultimate limit just to stay afloat in the best of times, the government had absolutely nothing in reserve for even slightly less good times. Any serious economic reverse such as a crop failure would operate in the same way. As shortages spread, the supply of values decreased, businesses closed, workers were laid off, and tax revenues fell, the government would be forced to inflate more than ever before in order to finance itself and answer the universal cries for help. Much the same role was played to the German inflation by the French invasion of the Ruhr in January 1923, followed by German passive resistance that shut down much of the German industrial machine.

Every inflation, from the first day that its proprietor government begins it, contains the seeds of the German ending. Each inflation also contains inbred compulsions upon the government to continue nursing these seeds to full growth. It is a commonplace of history that the nation which cannot learn from the past condemns itself to repeat it. To act in the confident belief that there was no valid comparison between the awesome German inflation and the still moderate Amer-

The Way Ahead

ican inflation was to flout that commonplace. If the United States could learn quickly from the German example, it could escape its own inflation and leave the two in final retrospect quite dissimilar. If it could not learn the lessons in time, the deeper similarities between the two inflations were bound to emerge more clearly as time passed. President Nixon, a conservative and businesslike president, might find himself playing the American role of the conservative and businesslike German Chancellor Wilhelm Cuno, who for the worst part of the German agony totally failed to arrest an inflation he never made.

40
Democratics

"Democratics" is a name that might be applied to the functioning of politics in a democratic system. The United States in its great inflation was still one of the most highly democratic systems the world had ever seen. If political problems and not economic problems were the root of the American inflation, and if the American system failed to solve those problems, then the democratics of the American system would be the cause of the failure.

Democracy's historical record of performance in inflations was never good. Numerous were the democracies which could not arrest inflations without undergoing either collapse of the currency or political convulsion or both. Few were the democracies which did not fail in this way once big inflations were established. Inflation is the plague of weak governments, and democratic government is in essence weak government. The American democracy had become fully as weak as the supremely democratic Weimar republic that failed in the German inflation.

Democracy's weakness is inability to act. No one, not the most ardent democrat, would maintain that ability to act is one of democracy's strong points. That is the very antithesis of democracy. Given the action to be taken, it is the autocracy which can take the action quickly, efficiently, and forcefully, and the democracy which cannot. This is not to advocate autocracy, which has many well-known failings of its own. It is merely to say that democracy is not in one of its fields of strength, but of weakness, when it needs to take immediate, drastic, intelligent, and singleminded action in a matter as perplexing, as fraught with factional conflict, and as vexed with difference of opinion as inflation. Rising against military attack comes easily to democracy; rising against inflation does not.

Democracy's very inability to act is one of its sturdiest virtues in other circumstances. The true genius of democracy is its ability to smother with inaction the wild notions and mad causes that send bodies of its citizens tilting in all directions in every era, and to smother them in so impersonal a way that the smothered citizen cannot identify anyone who has frustrated him except "the system." When inaction is the best action, as it is most of the time, democracy performs well. Impotence before a crisis like inflation is the price democracy pays.

Nothing inherent in the nature of democracy compels it to be impotent before a need for action. If all the citizen-members of a democracy were endowed with self-reliance, intelligence, and a measure of self-denial sufficient to reach agreement on the sacrifices affecting them all which were necessary to liquidate an inflation, their democracy could take the necessary action quite as readily as any autocracy. This ideal democracy of sturdy yeomen is as unknown to history as the ideal autocracy of the philosopher-king, but there are degrees of impotence and degrees of sturdy yeomanry. Some democracies would do better than others, and the American democracy itself would have done better in other times than in 1973. The American democracy had never in its history seemed more barren of statesmanlike impulse, more wholly dedicated to narrow self-interest, and therefore weaker, than it had become by 1973.

Two tendencies, both conspicuous in the American situation, are potentially fatal maladies to a democracy. Both of them are paradoxical, inasmuch as both are hyper-developments of two of the noblest privileges of democracy. One is equality, and the other is individual rights. Democracy is supposed to promote equality among men, and it does, but extreme egalitarianism is perversely the destroyer of democracy. Democracy is also supposed to promote the individual rights of citizens, and it does, but militancy in the prosecution of individual rights is the mortal enemy of the existence of rights. Between them, these two tendencies account for the extreme weakness of the most extreme democracies.

The problem of egalitarianism is easily stated. A democracy can hope to function best when the members of its government are more capable men than the average of its citizens. The people are the parents of their government, and not the other way round. Like parents occasionally begetting children more gifted than the parents, a democratic citizenry can sometimes elect rulers who are better men than the citizens. In a democracy, it must happen. It happens when voters have a deferential willingness to elect men they instinctively sense to be wiser than they, and then to leave the government to them. Even the miserable Weimar republic had many superior individual men among its Reichstag members. The United States itself had many superior individual men among its past Congresses, and they tended to have influence disproportionately greater than their numbers. No more.

The spirit of the time in 1973 was extremely egalitarian. Deference to elected government had been disappearing since the end of the Eisenhower years. The idea of deferentially voting for a better man than the voter was an idea whose time had gone. Every voter had become as good as any other

Democratics

man, and the elected candidate must be as much as possible a mirror image of the voter. In return for his election and his paycheck, he must accept the imposition of the voters' judgment and do the voters' bidding in all things. This trend in the American democracy gave the voter a heady and generally accurate sense that the government was his own, but it also debased the capability of the government. Under these circumstances, the government could stand no taller than the average of its citizens, which was far less tall than the American government had historically stood. The government was reduced to a constant pandering to base motives of greedy citizens, a constant pursuit of faddist causes trumped up by noisy cliques, and a constant bartering of self-interest among strong private factions to the exclusion of the broader interests of the nation. It was democratic without doubt. It was more democratic than governments ordinarily were. It was also potentially fatal. It was an exact replica of the Weimar republic. Heedless egalitarianism destroyed the Weimar republic as surely as it destroyed the First Republic of France, or the Fourth. A little less democracy is a stronger democracy. A little more democracy may mean no more democracy.

Militancy in the enforcement of individual rights is similar. In fact, this kind of militancy is the more general phenomenon of which egalitarianism is only a part. Militancy was the spirit of the age in America, and militancy as much as anything accounted for the spreading impotence of American democratics. Militancy is no more than the vigorous assertion by individuals of rights guaranteed to them as individuals by the democratic system. If the existence of individual rights is the most sublime privilege of democracy, and it is, then they should be all the more sublime the more militantly they are pressed. But it is not so. Individual rights can exist only so long as they lie mostly unused. If all individual rights are to be asserted by everyone to their ultimate extreme, there can be no rights. Militancy in the enforcement of rights is the exterminator of those rights.

Individual rights are a prickly thing, like a bag of burrs.

Without exception, the exercise of one man's rights is bound to be an infringement of the next man's rights. A blatant freedom of one man's speech infringes on the next man's freedom from undue disturbance. A criminal's right to be free from unjust procedure infringes the rights of other citizens to be free from crime. Individual rights of one man can be allowed to exist only in balance with the inevitably conflicting individual rights of other men, and balance can exist only if no one man insists on forcing his own rights as far as they can be forced. This is why rights are healthiest, strongest, and safest when they lie idle. From that principle flowed the ancient presumption that the man who most vocally demanded his rights probably least deserved to receive them. Immanuel Kant formulated the test for permissible social conduct by an individual as that which all, and not merely a few, citizens could engage in without harm to the functioning of society. Militancy of rights fails that test. A small minority of citizens militantly demanding their rights can be endured, but if all citizens did so the rights must be abolished. Forbearance alone allows democracy to flow and rights to exist. Militancy destroys them both.

An individual right so basic as not even to require stating in bills of rights is the right to pursue private self-interest. A man may seek his own interest, without required concern for any other man's interest, to the absolutely ultimate extreme that does not violate a law. That is a broad freedom. A man may strike, he may agitate and protest his living and working conditions and the goods that he buys, he may combine with other citizens in lawful coercion of third citizens, he may sue anyone he chooses with or without cause, above all he may petition and lobby his government for special advantage to himself that other citizens do not have. Other individual rights a man may exercise only occasionally in a lifetime, but self-interest is what he pursues every day and most of the hours of his life. This pursuit of self-interest is not in the least a vice, but truly the engine that moves the system efficiently forward.

Democratics

Harnessing self-interest is the heart of the political problem in an economic crisis like inflation. The self-interest of each group must balance with that of all others and not militate against them. But the government cannot harness self-interest; only the people can. The government can propose and enlighten, but the people must accept. In an economic difficulty like inflation, the problem of adjusting self-interests is the problem of persuading each segment of the people that action which appears to be opposite to their short-term best interest actually serves their longer-term best interest. It is the problem of persuading workers that conditions which prevent wages from rising are better, even for workers, than skyrocketing wages. It is the problem of persuading capitalists that better distribution of purchasing power from capital to other citizens is better, even for capitalists, than letting them hoard it. It happens that the longer-term best interest of every group is harmonious with that of every other group, and there is no conflict, but that is hard to see. It is not a matter of altruism but of more sophisticated self-interest. It is not a matter of being more humanely considerate of the other fellow, but of being more shrewdly considerate of oneself. But all that is hard to see.

Militancy in the pursuit of no right is more mortally damaging to free democracy than in the pursuit of self-interest. Self-interest in a democratic and libertied system like the United States resembles a sort of radial tug-of-war, each citizen holding a single rope that is anchored to all others at the center of force, and each citizen at liberty to pull on his own rope as strongly as he wishes in order to draw the center of force of the entire system toward himself. The right to pull is an attractive right, but only so long as no one exercises it. If more than a few citizens pull, all others must pull also to protect themselves from having the center of force pulled away from them. And if all citizens at last are forced to take up their ropes and pull with might and main in self defense, the system is immobilized. Each citizen then is exhausting himself to accomplish nothing more than if all the ropes had been left slack, but only to avoid being beggared by his fellow citizens. The ability to pursue self-interest has been effectively destroyed. Militancy destroyed it.

Governments are nominally in charge of what their nations do, and inflation in particular is caused by governments and preventible by governments, but the ultimate responsibility for what governments do lies with their people. It is too comforting to blame "the government" or "the politicians." Every nation gets precisely the quality of government it deserves. Every government, even dictatorship more than is generally supposed, is the creature of its people and not the reverse. Candidates for government do no more than offer a product for the people to buy. Anything that the people would buy, some candidate will be found to offer. Good government reflects credit on either the sagacity or the sound instinct or at least the deference of the people. Bad government likewise reflects more discredit on the electorate than on the elected representatives, just as the existence of pornography reflects more unfavorably on the audience than on the purveyors.

Contrary to the view that the United States itself tended to take, democracy is not a form of government for all peoples. The instinctive understanding that rights can be honored only in moderation is what marks a people capable of democracy. Such peoples are rare. The United States had been such a people for two centuries, but it remained to be seen whether it continued to be so. In the toils of the great American inflation, the democratics of the system were not working well. Excessively egalitarian, riven by militancy, paralyzed by self-interest, blithering of individual rights, and therefore weak—in this state of readiness the American democracy confronted the supreme challenge of inflation. It was an exact likeness of the state of readiness in which that other most democratic of democracies, the Weimar republic, faced the same test, and it might all too possibly forebode a similar failure.

41
Political Reorganization

The end of the road for a government that fails to control its economic problem is political reorganization. There is no other alternative. If governments do not find a way to liquidate inflations, inflations have a way of liquidating governments. A business corporation that fails to control its economic problem can become bankrupt and go out of business, but a nation cannot go out of business. It is obligated to exist. It must either succeed or reorganize. Political reorganizations may take any form from armed revolution to orderly constitutional remodelling, but their one common requirement is that they produce a different kind of government that is strong enough to control the economic problem.

The terminal inflationary conditions that compel a political reorganization to take place are familiar. No mere short temper on the part of the people brings on the upheaval. Quite the opposite. People show a long-suffering reluctance to resort to political reorganization against incompetent government. When the majority of people finally resonate to Hitler's judgment of the existing democratic government as "parliamentary bedbugs," or to Charles de Gaulle's contempt for "parliamentary *immobilisme*," and not before, will the existing government be dismissed. What drives people to this is nothing less than a breakdown of the economic system for providing the necessaries of life. In an inflation, this happens when a helpless government, trying to flee from hard times and at the same time to overtake price inflation, takes each new step of the geometric money inflation so often that it finally stumbles into the German ending. The people become convinced that the inflation will never cease to worsen, and they then spend their money so fast that the inflation redoubles again and again. Money wealth is quickly erased, but still the inflation is unsatisfied. Controls are imposed on everything, but that merely dries up the supplies of everything. Normal business breaks down, and people lose jobs at an accelerating pace. Money, in spite of its surfeit, is scarce, scarce, scarce. Every kind of spending that can be eliminated, is eliminated. The most dispensable activities, like culture, charity, comforts, and education, go first. Useful but temporarily dispensable values like housing and clothing go next. Last to go, naturally enough, is food. Barter can take the place of a destroyed money system to some extent, but in a highly developed and specialized system too many of the people are too far removed from the sources of subsistence to enable barter to keep them going. When the food goes, and usually not before that, does reorganization come.

Great inflations are traditional causes of political upheavals. History is strewn with the carcasses of governments that failed to control inflations. This is how Lenin's famous judgment, that the best way to destroy the capitalist system is to debauch the currency, comes to fruition. Irving Fisher quoted a French aphorism, "After the printing press, the guillotine," which of course alluded to the bloody terror that followed the assignat inflation of the French Revolution. As Napoleon ultimately followed the assignats, so Mao Tse-tung followed the Chinese yuan inflation, the dictatorship of Stresemann and later Hitler followed the Reichsmark, and Charles de Gaulle followed another inflation of the French franc. Political reorganizations are of course not all bloody. The classic case that was not bloody was the temporary dictatorship of Chancellor Stresemann in Germany that ended the inflation. Charles de Gaulle's constitutional remodelling was another. Germany's voluntary submission to the fatherly authority of Konrad Adenauer for many years after World War II was another. Even the shift of power to President Roosevelt in the American Depression was a subtle kind of political reorganization, responding not to an inflation but to an entirely comparable economic emergency.

Besides ranging from bloody to bloodless, political reorganizations may be of any political persuasion, leftist like Mao or Lenin, rightist like Napoleon or Hitler, or centrist like Stresemann or de Gaulle. Very often each political wing will be in the running when reorganization impends, as for example when both the leftist Communists and rightist Nazis were in the streets in force at the very moment in 1923 when the centrist Chancellor Stresemann snatched the dictatorship from them both.

Political reorganizations thus are different, but the more they are different the more they are the same. In every case, the shift must be from weaker to stronger government, from more democratic to less democratic process, and from more diffused to more personalized power. Inability to act was what caused the failure, and inability to act is what must be corrected. In the final throes it is technically no more difficult to overcome the inflation than it ever was, but that fact alone does not overcome the inflation any more than it ever did. Desperation was needed to reconcile the nation to harsh medicine, and in the final throes desperation is in good supply, but unfortunately even desperation alone does not overcome the inflation. The political reorganization that does it must be radical. It may be bloodless and it may be centrist, but it cannot cling to the old middle of the road without drastic change. Centrist does not mean that. To be centrist is merely to forsake the illusory idea that one class of citizens can prosper for long while other classes do not. Drastic change is essential, and that is radical. The programs of Stresemann, de Gaulle, or Roosevelt were all more or less centrist, but they were also as radical as any Communist or Nazi revolution, and the political reorganization that successfully brought the American inflation to a conclusion would have to be no less radical than any of them.

Political reorganizations often represent opportunities for the future as well as failures of the past. A new and better building can be built on the ruins of a disaster site more easily than the old building could have been renovated. It is a harsh fact that collapse may be necessary to permit progress to occur. Desperation does not automatically increase the ability to move forward, but it does tend to decrease the will to resist. Making the most of the opportunity offered by a political reorganization depends on the historical accident of what man happens to be standing in the way of the reorganization and inherits its leadership. It is largely a matter of luck. Germany enjoyed a spectacular improvement in fortunes when the dictatorship that ended the inflation in 1923 fell to Gustav Stresemann. Germany was less lucky with the political reorganization of Adolf Hitler. Charles de Gaulle was clearly a stroke of improved fortunes for France. The United States had poorer luck with Franklin Roosevelt. As political reorganizations go, there are good ones and bad ones. The rightist and leftist ones are nearly always bad, and the centrist ones can go either way.

The political reorganization that might lie at the far end of the American inflation was still a completely blank slate in 1973. There would be no dearth of leftist forces waiting to take charge. There never is. Like insects, leftists are always about. Virtually all radical currents of thought in America were dominated by generally socialist and Marxist ideas. The accession of these forces to power might be more like the bungling Salvador Allende of Chile than the ruthless Lenin of Russia, but in either case the termination of the traditional liberty and prosperity of America would be equally certain. At the other pole, rightist forces in the United States were hardly more than vestigial. The United States had no tradition of military coups and seemed unlikely to develop the taste. The United States enjoyed a long history of being politically phlegmatic. Americans were not a people to take to the barricades. In 1973, Americans were not exactly the same kind of people they had traditionally been, but their political inertia might still steer them between left and right to some kind of political reorganization of the radical center.

Looking into the mists of the future from 1973, one could see nothing clearly of the dénouement of the American inflation. It was difficult to believe that anything so drastic as political reorganization must eventually become necessary, but it was equally difficult to believe that it could be avoided. It was difficult to believe that any government, knowing what it was doing, could be so foolish as to take the next step upward in the geometric inflation, but it was equally difficult to believe that any government could resist the tremendous political pressures to take just that step in flight from hard times and pursuit of prosperity. If collapse and reorganization required that the government continuously fail to take effective countermeasures, the government could be fully trusted to fail to take them. If collapse and reorganization required that the government from time to time increase the inflationary impetus, the government seemed ready to supply it. If ignorance was indispensable to an inflationary collapse, ignorance of the requisite kind seemed to be one of the nation's most abundant remaining resources. Political reorganization in the eventual future was altogether more probable than it should have been.

42
Self Defense

An individual caught in an inflationary vortex has one primary concern, and that is what he can do to defend himself. As an individual he has no power, there is nothing he alone can do about the democratics of the situation, and the reasons why the situation has developed are of only faint interest to him. Finding shelter is his need. When the state loses its ability to defend all its citizens impartially, defense becomes a matter of every man for himself.

Self-defense in an inflation is essentially the defense of property. An individual's person is not in danger, except perhaps for the violence that sometimes accompanies political reorganization. An individual will be the same person after an inflation as before, except perhaps for the anguish which may scar him permanently. It is his property that is the prey. If he does not have property in the sense of stocks or savings, he usually does have a calling in which he may have invested much of his life for training and experience. That is property of an intangible sort and an investment of the most important

Self Defense

kind. Inflation stalks his property with the sole object of devouring its value. Self-defense consists of emerging from the inflation holding intact some part of the property value that he had formerly thought he had.

Successful self-defense in almost any inflation is not an impossibility. It is not easy but not impossible. There are, however, one or two rather gloomy aspects of the search for self-defense. One is that there is no sure safety anywhere. There is no safe refuge where one can hide for the duration. The defense is, as they used to say in war, fluid, and it must change from day to day. The second gloomy aspect of self-defense is that loss will predominate over gain. Almost all kinds of investment property are inflated in price in an inflation and must therefore suffer some erosion of real value before the inflation is over. The object of self-defense is to minimize the erosion. It is true that for every loser there is a gainer in inflation, but it is the holders of property who are the losers and others, such as debtors and spenders, who are the gainers. Making any real profits in a dying inflation is practically out of the question. With clairvoyance or hindsight it could be done, and there were probably a few Germans who did do it, but anyone who dares try to play a decaying inflation for anything but defense against loss is playing a perilously greedy game.

The very idea of self-defense of property in an inflation necessarily assumes that an operating economic system, preserving rights of private ownership of property, will survive the inflation. That assumption is by no means assuredly right. The German system did survive the chaos of 1923, but the Russian system did not survive the chaos of 1917, and whether the American system would survive the chaos of the American inflation was not known. If it would not, self-defense of property would have been in vain, but there was nothing much that could be done about it, and so one might as well prepare a self-defense on the assumption that the system would survive.

The universe of investment property has many classes, all differing from one another in their vulnerability to inflation. They include at least the following: bonds, bank deposits, and other paper wealth denominated in money; common stocks and other ownership interests in industry or property; land and other real estate; goods and other tangible personal property; and foreign money or gold.

Money wealth was by far the largest part of investment property in the United States. Total debt exceeded $3.2 trillion and was growing rapidly. Money wealth had traditionally been the safe haven in economically parlous times like the Great Depression, and that was why owners of property were to be found preparing their self-defense against the last previous depression. In the inflation, however, money wealth had become not the safest but the riskiest, most speculative, and probably worst possible form of investment. It represented the most assuredly guaranteed loss. Money wealth was the mine that inflation stole from. If the inflation went on, money wealth was what the inflation would destroy. Shorter-term money wealth was less terribly vulnerable than longer-term— money due in thirty days cannot lose as much value in that time as money due in thirty years—but all money wealth was nakedly exposed to the assault. It was immaterial how solvent the debtor might be; though it be General Motors or the Federal government, the debt was unsafe. No person in his right mind would have been found investing in fixed money wealth at the paltry prevailing interest rates of less than 10 percent in 1973 if he could have known *with certainty* that money wealth was bound to lose its value by at least the 22 percent of the Index of Latent Inflation, *plus* the 6.5 percent per year inflation that the government was forced to sustain continuously *plus* whatever increased inflation the government might have to try in order to stave off recession. Certainty is of course an elusive thing. Probabilities are what people must be content with, and those were the probabilities. In view of those probabilities, the tranquility with which

Self Defense

hundreds of billions of dollars continued to flow into straight dollar debt without the least form of protective escalator against inflation was truly astounding. Any general exodus from this straight dollar debt, on the other hand, would of course signal the beginning of a breakdown of the inflation structure.

All of this would be quite different if money wealth were "indexed" against inflation. If General Motors or the Federal government, for example, offered a mere 4 percent bond, with each payment of interest or principal to be multiplied by the factor of increase in the wholesale price index since the bond was issued, that bond would be reasonably secure against inflation. It would be as close to a safe haven from inflation as could be devised. It would clearly be preferable to a 10 percent or even 15 percent non-indexed obligation of any debtor. Such bonds were widespread in the late German inflation and were in fact remarkably solid in value. At the time of the American inflation, they were also widely used elsewhere in the world but unknown in the United States. If any general flight from ordinary dollar debt developed, so that straight dollar bonds could not be marketed, the run could easily be stanched by offering indexed debt in its place. If indexed debt did become prevalent, the government's ability to finance prosperity with inflation would be at an end, but that was the government's worry. Until indexed debt did become prevalent, money wealth was no place to attempt self-defense in the inflation. Money wealth was ground zero on inflation's target range.

Foreign money, especially the American dollar as irony would have it, had been the safest refuge a German could seek in 1921 and 1922. In 1973, there was some appearance that foreign money like German marks or Swiss francs might be a safe refuge for an American to seek, especially in view of the successive devaluations of the dollar that had steadily increased the value of foreign currencies in recent years. Possibly this appearance was accurate, but probably it was not. Foreign money is a safe refuge from inflation only if the foreign money's government will defend its value from inflation more successfully than one's own government. In 1922 the American government did, but there is never any very firm assurance that any government will. The American dollar in 1922 was as solid as Gibraltar, and the economic troubles of Germany and other countries were but ripples lapping at its base. In 1973, no currency was like that any longer. The lingering strength and stability of the German mark were largely residual from the remarkable management of the Christian Democratic party, under men like Konrad Adenauer and Ludwig Erhard, that ended in 1966. After that Germany began inflating as merrily as anyone. By 1973, hardly any nation on the face of the globe was doing an even minimally competent job of maintaining the value of its money. The earthworks had all been swept away, and all were floating along on the flood together. One or more foreign moneys might conceivably do a little better than dollars, or they might all do worse. It was anybody's gamble.

Gold, the international money, was a special case. Throughout the eons of the world, gold had been the classic refuge of owners of property trying to defend it from economic slings and arrows. But, like everything else in an inflation, gold was overvalued. It was overvalued even before the inflation began. Gold yields no income and costs money to store and handle. It is not very useful. If the American Federal Reserve System should no longer accept gold as international money and people in general should turn against gold for that purpose, its intrinsic value for industrial and commercial purposes could not have been more than a small fraction of its prevailing price. Most of the value of gold lay in that people expected it to have value, and that value could last only as long as the expectation. That expectation had endured over thousands of years, and it might endure forever. Or it might not. It was anybody's gamble.

Real estate is a classic hedge against inflation. The name

Self Defense

is apt. Real estate is a real value. The intrinsic value of real estate is indestructible, except by depreciation or physical damage. If a man owns a piece of land to live on, it is equally good for living on before, during, or after an inflation. Its intrinsic value for living on is not affected by prices, even land prices. As an investment, however, the value of real estate is not so invulnerable. The value of real estate for investment depends on its market price and not merely on its continued usability for a particular purpose. In an inflation, prices of real estate are as inflated as any other prices, some kinds of real estate more than others. Real estate as an investment is by no means neglected in an inflation, and its quality as a real asset is by no means unnoticed. There are usually no price controls on real estate, and there are no natural restraints like foreign competition to hold down real estate prices. Real estate prices therefore inflate more rapidly in an inflation than do other prices. From those inflated levels, real estate can easily fail to hold its relative market value as other prices rise. Particular kinds of real estate which may have been especially favored by the inflationary prosperity, such as luxury dwellings and overblown commercial developments, conceivably might be even more prone to lose real value in the breakdown of an inflation. Real estate thus has no broad immunity from all loss of value, even though real estate is more real and less capable of loss than, say, money wealth. A some is still a home no matter what, but beyond that real estate is right out in the battlefield along with all other forms of investment, fighting to defend itself.

Farmland is a special category of real estate. There is more farmland than any other kind of valuable real estate, and farmland is possibly the most bedrock of all real values because it produces what people must have, inflation or no, in order to live. Farmers thrive and the value of farmland excels in the dying throes of every inflation, and the great American inflation would probably be no exception. But even farmland as an investment has its own special difficulties. Although farmers and farmland do strikingly well in late inflations, they tend to be somewhat less prosperous than the rest of the nation in early inflations or in normal times. No parcel of farmland is like any other, but each suffers the individual perils of geographical place, including floods, storms, and the other vagaries of weather. And farmland ownership in the United States was not organized to receive large amounts of outside investment. Most farmland was either owned by or leased to a farmer—that was why American agriculture was so phenomenally efficient—and there was no ready way to buy a share of a farm or a farmland fund, as there was of a steel company or a mutual fund. Farmland was vast and its value would endure, but it was, as they say, spoken for.

Useful goods are one last kind of property that will ordinarily keep its value through an inflation although it is not generally thought of as a form of investment. If all other kinds of investment will have difficulty holding their value in inflation, it must be because the prices of goods will rise faster than the prices of investments. It follows that goods would be a better investment than investments are. Theoretically, this is true. Any German could have made himself quite rich by acquiring a large store of underpriced food or other goods in 1920 and then trading this store later in the inflation for houses, stock of solid industries, or whatever other real assets he might fancy at ridiculously low relative prices. The possibility of investing in tangible goods is, however, more theoretical than real. A nation produces only enough of these goods for current consumption. Using them for investment is hoarding, and if any significant part of the current output were hoarded for investment the ensuing price inflation would quickly remove the advantage. In addition, as with gold, there is a cost involved because goods produce no income, incur storage and carrying charges, and require a distribution system to be resold. Goods can serve as a profitable investment only in the one specialized eventuality of a catastrophic inflation coming within a very short time, and that eventuality is never assured enough to be relied upon.

Self Defense

These possible foxholes of defense against inflation, ranging from prohibitively bad ones to plain bad ones, mediocre ones, and theoretical ones, leave only one large remaining battleground on which to take a stand. This battleground is the stock market, and it requires a chapter of its own, which follows.

43
Self Defense Continued: The Stock Market

The stock market in the United States is a vast place. It consists of billions upon billions of pieces of paper ownership of the industrial might of America, passing from hand to hand in a few strange ballroom-like markets around the country. The pieces are paper, but the stocks are real assets unlike money wealth, as real as any land, as real as a part interest in a drop forge or an electric steel furnace. And, apart from money wealth, the stock market is the only receptacle huge enough to accommodate all the wealth of the nation that might be seeking investment.

The stock market not only is vast but is well patronized in an inflation. The stock market is the original home of inflationary madness in the early phases of any inflation. Later the stock market may fall into disrepute, but that is as misplaced as the original madness. Besides earning easy riches for everyone in early booms, common stock always enjoyed a traditional reputation as a secure hedge against inflation. By 1973, however, disillusion with common stock had set in in the United

States. As other prices went up, stock prices went down. That was a strange way for a hedge against inflation to act. Common stock's traditional reputation as a hedge was widely discredited, and a general aversion to common stock investment took its place. It was all very perverse, but it was all very familiar. It was not at all inconsistent with the reality of common stock as a repository of value.

The strange behavior of stock markets is not nearly as inexplicable as it is often thought to be. Stocks in a market are merely one of the kinds of values that can be bought for money, and the prices of stocks are no different from the prices of any other articles of commerce. Like all prices, stock prices are not sacred cows that rise and subside at their own whim and without answering to any law. The stock market dances to an inaudible tune that is played for it by the government's money inflation or deflation, just as all the members of society dance to the same tune every moment of their everyday lives without being able to identify the source. A man who fully understood what inflation was doing at all times would seldom be surprised by the stock market. Armed with that understanding and little else, he could participate profitably in every stock market rise, step aside safely from every stock market fall, and shepherd his property with reasonable security through the bombardment of inflation or deflation.

The stock market without inflation would be a sleepy place. Without inflation, prices in a stock market would be steady, like other prices, and moreover they would be steadily low by standards of the American inflation. There would be little reason to trade in stocks, because tomorrow's price would be much like today's. Without inflation, there could be no general capital gains. All of this was proved in those few brief periods in America, like 1948 and 1954, when there was a real absence of money inflation. It must come as a blow to those who invest their lives or tie their fortunes to the hope of rising prices of investments, and the blow to them is regrettable, but a booming stock market is no necessary part of an economically healthy nation. Capital gains are no part of real prosperity. More nearly the opposite is true: A rising stock market is a danger signal of the first order, and a falling stock market is a sign of returning reality. A low and stable stock market may not be good for speculators, but it is good for the owners and accumulators of new wealth seeking to buy liberal real values at reasonable prices.

The stock market as a whole rises because there is money inflation and for no other reason, and the stock market declines because there is a weakening of the money inflation. Business prosperity and price inflation also respond in the same way to the same impulses, but at much longer time intervals, and that is why the stock market frequently goes the opposite way from them. When the government first turns on money inflation in times of slack business, the money has no work to do yet and nowhere to go but into investment markets. So the markets rise, even though business is still bad. Later on, as business begins to hum and prices to rise, some of the inflated money must be sucked back out of the investment markets to service the business prosperity. So the markets fall. As other prices go up, stock prices go down. When business is worst, stock prices rise most; and when business is best, stock prices decline. A rising stock market signals nothing but freshening money inflation. It is the earliest and most sensitive indicator of the inflationary train of events to come. Conversely, a declining stock market is nothing but a returning of stock prices from inflated heights to their base of real value.

The stock market is at its base of real value only at the fully deflated market bottoms which occur after a reasonably prolonged absence of money inflation, in company with rather depressed business. Whenever stock prices have risen above these bottoms, they are inflated. If stocks are bought at those prices, losses can be confidently expected whenever prices fall back again to real value in the future. Stocks bought at any point above their real-value bottoms are not a hedge against

The Stock Market

loss, but a guarantee of loss. On the other hand, stocks bought *at* real-value bottoms have good prospects of holding their value in all events including inflation. The levels of stock market bottoms bear a strong proportion to the prevailing levels of money inflation. For example, the American stock market's deflated bottom in 1970 was precisely the same percentage higher than its deflated bottom in 1962, 43 percent, as the money supply in 1970 was larger than in 1962. So long as this relationship holds, the prices of stocks bought at the bottoms can be trusted to rise and thus keep their value at least as fast as the money supply and therefore the equilibrium prices of other things.

This ability of common stocks to float upward with equilibrium prices is what distinguishes common stock from money wealth, making common stock potentially a hedge against inflation while money wealth is inflation's chief prey. An example may help explain this difference. Suppose ABC Corporation, which manufactures something useful, has sales of $100, costs of $90, profits of $10, and pays out $5 in dividends to its stockholders. Its stock might perhaps sell for $100 in the stock market. If there is an inflation, and all prices including those of ABC double, all other conditions being the same, ABC will now have sales of $200, costs of $180, profits of $20, and will be in a position to pay out dividends of $10 to stockholders. The $10 dividend will buy the stockholder just as much in food or clothing or rent as the old $5 did. The price of the stock in the market may also have increased to $200, and the stockholder has suffered nothing from the twofold inflation. If he had bought a 5 percent bond of ABC Corporation for his original $100, ABC would still owe him only $100 and $5 a year in interest income, both of which would be worth just half as much in food or clothing or rent as before the twofold inflation. A common stock can float upward on an inflationary tide like a boat, while a debt investment, fixed in place, sinks deeper under water as the tide rolls in.

A degenerating inflation may distort things wildly for a time. The stock market may come to seem a very lonely place, and the faith of a believer in common stocks may be very sorely tested. Germany was an example of this. When inflation began to run away, the prices of stocks not only collapsed back to real value from their inflated peaks, but for a long time they did not rise again even while the prices of other things were soaring. This meant that the real value of stocks in terms of other goods was constantly decreasing, even though their money prices were not. The reason for this was fear. Confidence disappeared, and no one could feel sure enough that any business would survive to want to buy its stock. In the end, faith was rewarded. Stocks did recover and emerged from the inflation being worth about as many pecks of potatoes as they had been worth after the first crash.

The stock market can go the other way in a degenerating inflation as well. Germany showed that too. When a law was passed forbidding Germans to invest in foreign money like American dollars, there was no place for money to go but the stock market, and the stock market had its most astronomical rise ever even while business was in its worst state of collapse. Something similar might happen in the American inflation if trust in the money wealth should break down and there was nowhere else for the purchasing power to go but the stock market. At these times, the stock market is overpriced again and is sure to relinquish some of its paper gains, but if there is nothing more valuable to buy stocks remain the best thing to hold.

What is true of the stock market as a whole in an inflation is not true of every stock in it. The stock market represents real value, but not every stock does. Far from it. The American stock market in the inflation dressed up many of its emptiest bottles of air as the most glamorous bulwarks of investment value. This is not unique, but characteristic. The German stock market in the boom of 1920 and 1921 was even slightly crazier, but only slightly. The cult of the capital gain in both

The Stock Market

markets exalted rising prices over old-fashioned values such as earning power or dividend yields. Rising prices begot further rising prices. Individual stocks that became the darlings of capital gain cultists rose to prices much higher than the market, and much higher than their real value in conditions of stability could justify. They could not help but lose value back to that level. Many other kinds of businesses and the prices of their stocks had been disproportionately favored by the unnatural prosperity and the unnatural activities of the inflation, and they too could not help but lose real value if the inflation broke down. On the other hand, many of the most useful and basic kinds of business had been relatively disfavored by the inflation, their stocks had suffered accordingly, and in the purging of the inflation both their business and their stocks' values could be expected to improve at least as much as the prices of goods. Successful self-defense in the stock market was a matter of projecting oneself mentally into the post-inflationary world for a look around, seeing which businesses would thrive as well as ever and which would not, and then returning to inflation's midst to buy the stocks of companies which would be thriving later and were doing at least passably well even then. As different as the post-inflationary prosperity would be from the inflationary kind, just that different would the thriving businesses of that time be from those of the inflationary era. As had been true in Germany, there was a strong suspicion that many of the last might become first, the humble exalted and the exalted cast down, but beyond that suspicion any man's guess was as good as the next man's.

Much the same kind of reasoning applied to that most important investment most men ever make, the investment of their lives in the training and experience necessary to their life's pursuit of some trade or profession or other line of business. Inflation misleads men as cruelly in that investment as it does in the stock market, and the harm it does by that deception is some of the saddest harm of all.

The American stock market was a vast place, vast enough to take in all the refugees that might seek it. There was safety there too, somewhere, if it could but be found. Safety would not be easy to find, and some loss must be expected, but survival was possible. The tides of inflation were what governed everything, and if a man could understand them and be prepared to move his place of defense from day to day, he could probably weather the storms. Attempting to make profits from the stock market, or even to make sense of it, without completely understanding the universal determinant of inflation was like being at sea among uncharted rocks and shoals without so much as a tide table. Reasonable men might differ as to what it was that controlled their destiny, but if they placed their trust in some other force they had better be right.

44
A World of Nations

The United States did not struggle in a vacuum with its economic problem. There was another whole world of nations beyond its shores, and many of those other nations were keenly interested spectators and also unhappy participants in the struggle. More than any other nation, it is true, the United States and its economic problem were virtually self-contained, and this made the American problem simpler and purer than it would have been elsewhere. It did not alter the fact that the American inflation assumed for itself a worldwide consequence.

Internationally, the American inflation was the transmitter and the rest of the world the receiver. The United States was the actor, and the rest of the world the audience. Other nations were forced to participate only because the action spilled out of the stage and into the orchestra. The United States was the author and the cast, and it held the power of control of the worldwide problem for better or worse.

Inflation's courier to the rest of the world from the

United States was money. Just as inflation is a disease of money, the bearer of contagion outward from its source is an outflow of money. The constant outflow of dollars from the United States implicated the rest of the world in the American inflation, as an outflow of Reichsmarks had implicated the rest of the world in the German inflation. One striking implication, identical to that of the German inflation, was to leave foreigners holding a staggering portion of the dollar money wealth which was waiting to suffer future losses in the inflation. Virtually the entire growth of the Federal debt of the United States after 1967, or $55 billion worth, was involuntarily financed and acquired by foreigners. By 1973, foreigners' holdings of liquid dollar debt from all American sources had risen to more than $90 billion from only about $31 billion in 1966.

More unwelcome by far than the tainted dollar debt was the export of inflation. America's export was the rest of the world's import, and it was shipped by means of the same outflow of dollars that carried the tainted debt abroad. Europeans had complained for years that the inflation they suffered at home arose by import of the American problem, and in that they were entirely correct. Inflation had become the United States' principal, and by far its most profitable, export.

Another name for the outflow of money that carries an exported inflation from its sources, like the United States, to its victims, like the rest of the world, is a balance of payments deficit. A balance of payments outflow is a perfectly normal and logical effect of an inflation in one country. If there is more money around in the first country than is needed to service all its normal purchases and sales, some of the surplus money must naturally go abroad looking for the good things that can be bought cheaply there. There is a strong tendency for money to flow from a country of surplus money, or inflation, to other countries of no surplus money, or non-inflation. The correct cure for a balance of payments deficit is as simple as the cause: stop the inflation at its source. This, however, is not desirable to the source country because of all the good things that inflation does for it, including easy and pleasant buying at foreigners' expense. The balance of payments deficit is entirely beneficial to the deficit country. Contrary to popular protestations of dismay, it has no ill effects whatever. The money that has departed the country reduces, dollar for dollar, the pressure toward price inflation at home, while the export of the inflated money brings in real values from abroad fully as efficiently as the export of any real goods would do. That was why the exported inflation soon became the United States' most profitable export.

Central bankers had an ingenious system for recycling payments deficits so that they could go on generating inflation almost infinitely throughout the world on the basis of the recycled dollars. Every surplus dollar that moved abroad generated an inflated number of Deutschemarks or Swiss francs from the German or Swiss central bank in payment for the dollar, but then the central bank took its newly-acquired dollar and lent it back into the United States so that the surplus of dollars there was as large as ever. The same dollar could flow out and generate money inflation in the rest of the world as often and as rapidly as the central bankers could recycle it back to the United States.

Here enters the matter of foreign exchange rates. Foreign exchange rates are the relative values between one currency, such as the dollar, and another currency, such as all the others. They have a considerable part to play in this. Recurring exchange rate crises, with their attendant speculative flows of money from one currency to another, were the most visible manifestation of the problem in the advancing years of the inflation. They were so familiar, in fact, that they came to be thought of as being the problem itself. They were not. They were only by-products of the American inflation.

Foreign exchange rates are an incredibly complex mechanism, governed by incredibly complex forces, much more so than the general price level in a single country. The one important thing to remember about the foreign exchange rate of any currency, however, is that, like prices themselves, it does have at all times a single natural level which it seeks in opposition to all external forces, including exchange rate controls and speculative attack. The exchange rate of any currency cannot be driven arbitrarily high or arbitrarily low without releasing powerful forces pushing it back toward its natural level. Lord Keynes elaborated the theory of foreign exchange rates on a basis of "purchasing power parity," which means that the exchange rate between two currencies must tend to stabilize at the point where the purchasing powers of the two currencies in their own countries are equal to one another. This is logical. If the exchange rate of one country's currency is unnaturally low, making goods and other things relatively cheaper in that country than elsewhere, money would naturally flow in from other countries to buy those things and drive up the exchange rate. And vice versa. The foreign exchange rate of a country's currency is therefore a function of the price level in that country.

Just as foreign exchange rates are a function of price level, *changing* foreign exchange rates are a function of *changing* price levels, more specifically inflation. When one country inflates its money while others do not, its price level will eventually rise, but not immediately; before that, the foreign exchange rate of its currency should fall, because there is more of the surplus money seeking to go out of the country than hard money seeking to come in. Since internal prices are slower to act, this makes the exchange rate unnaturally low at first, and the prices of goods unnaturally competitive, and this in turn brings demand from abroad which helps to drive internal prices up to their new inflated equilibrium. All of this is precisely the sequence of events that transpired in Germany of 1922. Since the falling exchange rate preceded the price inflation, people blamed the falling exchange rate for the price inflation, never noticing that the money inflation had preceded them both and caused them both. Foreign exchange troubles are a product not merely of inflation but of different rates of inflation in one country than in another. If all countries are stable and avoid inflation, there will be no stress on their existing exchange rates, that is plain enough; but they will also be equally free from exchange rate troubles even if they are inflating, provided that they are all inflating at the same speed. The exchange rate crises of the early 1970's were a product of the days when the United States was gaily inflating while other important industrial nations, notably Germany, were resisting. As their resistance was broken down and they all joined in surfing on the inflationary wave, the problem of exchange rates might well go away and leave them only the much greater problem of unchecked worldwide inflation.

Most of the time after World War II and the adoption of the Bretton Woods system, foreign exchange rates of Western nations were not a free market as they were at the time of Germany's inflation, but instead a system of fixed rates which were a form of price control. Fixed exchange rates complicated the problem, and they hampered coping with the problem, but they did not create the problem. Fixed exchange rates for a while introduced some abnormal stability into foreign exchange, but they made the crises worse and they also made it possible for an inflating country like the United States to export its inflation and enjoy the benefits of its inflation at the expense of other countries. Like any other form of price control, fixed exchange rates could not for long prevent exchange rates from answering to natural forces. By 1973 and the onset of the permanent "floating" exchange rates, the system of fixed rates had broken down for all practical purposes. This brought back a freer market for foreign exchange similar to what surrounded Germany. In so doing it brought back the natural falling exchange rate for the inflating currency, the dollar; it brought back the naturally abnormal foreign demand for American goods made cheaper by the falling exchange rate; and it brought back the upward pressure on internal American prices caused by the abnormal foreign demand.

Foreign exchange rates are not as baffling as they sometimes seem. Exchange rates are simply an adjustment mechanism for the problem of inflation, and not a problem in themselves. Exchange rates can adjust correctly for any conceivable combination of forces if they are but allowed to do so. Banishing inflation would be the surest way to banish exchange rate problems. Everyone inflating in unison would also banish exchange rate problems. Failing both of those, nations could also avoid exchange rate problems if they either learned to manage changing exchange rates properly or allowed exchange rates to manage themselves to adjust for differential inflation.

Central bankers, those little-known gnomes who preside over the international relations of money, tend to have several kinds of shortcomings of understanding that impede their ability to do their job. The first is that they do not understand inflation very well, but then no one else does either. The second is an obsession for exports. The third is an obsession for reserves and a balance of payments surplus. And the fourth is an obsession for gold. Among them, these four managed to becloud the vision of central bankers quite completely in the exigencies of the American inflation.

The failure to understand inflation was nothing unique to central bankers. It was important, however. If central bankers had been able to spot money inflation developing in some other country, knowing that a payments outflow and a downward pressure on its exchange rate would soon come, they could have contrived to manage those forces instead of having those forces manage them. But if inflation is difficult enough to analyze correctly in one's own country, it is all but impossible to analyze correctly in someone else's country. So this theoretical possibility was still many years away from becoming a realizable fact.

The obsession for exports was even more important. The obsession for exports translated itself into an affection for reducing the foreign exchange value of one's own currency, which meant *devaluing* it, and a horror of increasing or *revaluing* it. A lower exchange rate made one's own exports more competitive in the world, and that supposedly was good. A higher exchange rate made one's own exports less competitive, and that supposedly was bad. This reasoning was entirely upside down and false, and it was the principal reason for the nations' inability to cope with internationally imported inflation. *No nation can hope to exist free of inflation while inflation rages elsewhere in the world without accepting and even seeking a constantly rising foreign exchange rate for its own currency.* Once a nation learned to accept that fact with equanimity, its problems of exchange rates and imported inflation would be over. Each new upward valuation of its currency would be the signal of success rather than failure, enabling its people to buy abroad more and better things that they like with their good hard money. The rising exchange rate would necessarily foretell increasing competitive difficulty for the nation's own exports in foreign trade, but that kind of competitive pressure placed on its own industries is precisely what holds their prices down and keeps inflation out of the country. Increased demand in the other country or countries resulting from lower exchange rates is precisely what raises prices there and keeps the inflation shut up where it originated. The obsession for exports which are too easily competitive at undervalued exchange rates amounts to giving away part of the value of the national product to the rest of the world for nothing, and it artificially benefits the export sector of the nation's economy at the expense of the rest of its own people. The United States was vivid proof that a nation gains a much easier and richer life by exporting overvalued money than by exporting undervalued goods. The rest of the world, with their zeal for giving away their product and avoiding upward revaluations of their money, made themselves willing importers of inflation from, and exporters of the good life to, the United States.

Central bankers' passion for international reserves was a

cousin to their obsession for exports. Reserves are a nation's international money in the bank. A good corporation treasurer would pride himself on how *small* a bank balance he needed to transact his volume of business, but a central banker prided himself on how *large* a bank balance he could generate. This suggested that there was something wrong with the central banker's view. A nation's reserves arise from a balance of payments surplus, and surpluses come mainly from exporting more and importing less. Both of these are signals that the nation is allowing itself to be victimized. International money coming in is worth only as much as it can buy abroad immediately, and it should be forthwith used for that. A central banker should avoid a payments surplus as ardently as he does a deficit, aiming always at a payments balance which is the absence of either. The most skillful central banker, like the most skillful corporate treasurer, is the one who can manage the largest volume of business on the smallest reserve balance, borrowing when he needs to for covering temporary deficiencies of his working capital.

Gold was the last of the central bankers' anachronistic obsessions, and the most anachronistic of them all. In times past, the passion for accumulating reserves meant more specifically a passion for accumulating gold. Until well into the foreign exchange crises of the 1970's, various nations were constantly injecting the subject of gold into the exchange rate problem, thereby obscuring it as effectively as a morning fog. Other nations tended to point to the inadequacy of the United States' large gold reserve to meet its far larger dollar obligations to foreigners, and say that this was the problem. It was not. If the United States had had no gold at all, the problem would have been no larger; and if it had had more than enough gold the problem would have been no smaller. Some other nations, especially France, tended to urge a return to a gold standard as a solution to the foreign exchange ills, but this absurd notion served only to hide the truth that a currency's value depends on the whole economy that backs it and not on some little pile of hoarded gold. The United States should have sold off all its gold to any nations that wanted it and then, goldless, demonstrated how entirely unimportant was gold to the value of its dollar. As the currency crises wore on with less being heard of gold, the central bankers seemed to be making headway toward shedding the old anachronism. Fifty years earlier Lord Keynes had correctly declared gold to be a barbarous relic, and after fifty years some central bankers might be getting the message.

The root of the foreign exchange problems in the world was inflation in the United States. That bears repeating. If that root were cut, the foreign exchange troubles would wither away like many of the other evil plants of the inflation that appeared to be unconnected growth. But since the thesis of this book is that inflation in the United States virtually could not be permitted to stop, what then for the rest of the world? The choices were clear. The other nations could either erect a wall of defense and contain the inflation in the United States, or they could willingly join in and inflate likewise. Defense against the inflation was entirely possible, but joining the inflation instead was what they had apparently allowed themselves to choose. Defense would have required tight money and tight economics in their own countries along with constantly rising exchange rates for their own currencies against the dollar. Every country's efforts to mount this defense had gradually failed. Shown the way by the inflation they had imported in earlier years, all nations were inflating vigorously for themselves by 1973. The inflation was worldwide, and no end was in sight. That itself was defensive, because no nation can be exploited by inflation if it creates its own share of inflation. If you can't beat it, join it, they say, and that the world had done.

The failure of the rest of the world to defend itself from the American inflation had more melancholy aspects, even for the United States. Having all the world sick would not help the United States get well. Stability in the rest of the world had helped refloat Germany in 1924, but no such stability surrounded the United States in 1973. All of the Western nations could quite possibly descend into an inflationary breakdown together if they chose to, and that was certainly the direction they were going. They were a boatload of sailors at sea in one monetary boat, with all the watertight compartments left open so that a leak sprung in the dollar could impartially flood them all. Inflating together and sinking together, they could not care much longer that the original leak had been in the American dollar.

The American inflation had still broader significance to the United States and the rest of the world than merely economic troubles. The inflationary instability which was impending in the United States posed the gravest potential peril to the peace and security of the world. The damage that could be done to the world's power balance if the American economic system should break down in inflationary turmoil was enormous. Ever since World War II, the United States had been the principal force defending all the Western nations, and not merely itself, from the widening influence of the Soviet Union. Already, as the inflation eroded the economic strength of the United States, the weakening of its hand outside its borders was plain. Military bases were closing, Americans with withdrawing, new military design was disappearing, and the renewal of the American military equipage was running down. The United States was visibly contracting in the world. European nations and other dependents of the United States had loved to tweak the American nose and declare their independence, but the fact was that the American strength had been the sword and buckler of Americans and friends alike. Without it, the sole and final line of defense of everyone would be the benevolence and magnanimity of the Soviet Union. If there were those who thought that the real need for the American defense had been overstated, they might eventually see whether they had been right. Inflation itself was not all there was to fear from the American inflation.

45
Interscript

The American inflation, like most inflations, was rather an absurdity. What the inflation was being permitted to do to the greatness that had been and still could be the nation's was unconscionable. It was a rank absurdity that a nation as great and strong as the United States still was should flush itself down the drain in a flood of money as it was appearing to do. Somewhere in the dense fog of the inflation, it seemed that the nation might very well have passed the crest of its long rise from the beginnings at Plymouth and Jamestown and placed its foot on the slippery slope of decline. It was absurd, and it was unnecessary. A nation doing that to itself resembles not only a man drowning within arm's length of an unseen shore, but one doing so with his strong arms and legs immobilized by the hypnotized belief that they are unable to move. It is absurd, but it is of just such epic absurdities of mass human conduct that the fabric of history is woven.

National rise and national decline seem to be states of mind. The historic declines of one or another culture, compared with the relative durabilities of still others, were functions of the mental capabilities and values of the men that peopled those cultures. Physical circumstances did not seem to matter as much. No mere abundance of resources could make a people great for long, and no mere paucity of resources could make a people small. Leadership by excellent individuals could not lift a people above themselves for long, nor the reverse for poor leadership. In the final analysis, it was the mental and spiritual state of the people that governed. It was the quality of the people that decided.

When we say that the quality of the people decides, we mean the quality of the average of the people and not of selected individuals. A nation cannot nominate a chosen few to take its examinations, because every race and people has at least a few excellent individuals to offer. It is as if the destiny of a nation were to be decided by taking any one of its citizens at random and placing him under the pitiless glare of scrutiny to test how he will respond to the demands placed on the nation. Others who may have thought about and trained themselves for those demands must be content to stand by and observe the test. Just as the people as a whole are the parents of their government, the people as a whole are the often unwitting masters of their own fate. A nation can do only so much as the average of its people will do or allow to be done, and that means that the average of its people either must have the superior intelligence to understand what is before them or, through instinct or inertia or good luck, must act as if they did. History plays no favorites and knows no chosen peoples. It seldom does anything for any people that the average of them does not do for itself.

The inflation presented the American people a test like this. No one could decide for them what to do but only offer them choices. The American people were a unique sort of people. They were a nation of immigrants from all parts of the world. One hundred percent of the people that had made the nation what it was were of immigrant stock. A more heterogeneous collection of people had never been assembled. The United States had probably more of the finest people than any other nation on earth, and also at least its share of the less fine. It had evolved its populace over the course of centuries, and it was not going to have any other. In that time the American collection of people had shown many unusual strengths and very few serious failings. They had met every test.

Every generation of people, however, is a somewhat different people. Every generation is a new test. The national state of mind that had been generated during, and perhaps by, the unrealities of the American inflation was deeply different from the state of mind that had accompanied the American people through their centuries of growth. These unrealities had persisted for more than a generation, and the longer they continued the more deeply would the new state of mind be rooted. It is at least arguable that the new state of mind was not consistent with anything but decline. It is at least a possibility that the only way the United States could back away from the decline opening before it was for its people, acting through either understanding or instinct or luck, to turn and go back. That kind of reversal of national course does not frequently occur in history, but neither is it unknown. What the American people would do with themselves in the inflation was a fascinating mystery.

The weaving of history is a spectator sport. It is a play without a director. No man, not even kings or presidents or prime ministers, is much more than a spectator to the events and sometime bit player. It is reminiscent of Tolstoy's observations on how grand an illusion it was that even the commanding general was in command of the battle. You and I are audience. These final words are not an epilogue, as they would be if the play were over, but a sort of parting word at intermission and a reminder that we may see one another again in the audience to the remaining scenes. There is not much that we can do about the play except to know how we would reply if we were called upon to speak or vote from the audience. After you have thought that out, come and join me in the galleries and we will watch.

NOTES

Notes

Sources which are recurrently cited in these notes are the following:

BLS Prices: Indexes of U. S. wholesale prices and consumer prices are from the U. S. Department of Commerce, Bureau of Labor Statistics, published regularly in its *Monthly Labor Review* and elsewhere. In all cases in this book, wholesale price indexes are for all commodities, including both industrial and agricultural products, and consumer price indexes are the general indexes covering all consumption items and all localities of the United States.

Bresciani-Turroni, *Inflation:* Constantino Bresciani-Turroni, *The Economics of Inflation* (London: Geo. Allen & Unwin, 1937).

Current Business: U. S. Department of Commerce, *Survey of Current Business,* published monthly.

Epstein, *Erzberger:* Klaus Epstein, *Matthias Erzberger and the Dilemma of German Democracy* (Princeton, N. J.: Princeton Univ. Press, 1959).

Fisher, *Purchasing Power:* Irving Fisher, *The Purchasing Power of Money,* (New York: Macmillan, 1911).

F. R. Bulletin: Board of Governors of the Federal Reserve System, *Federal Reserve Bulletin,* published monthly.

Friedman, *Capitalism and Freedom:* Milton Friedman, *Capitalism and Freedom* (Chicago: Univ. of Chicago Press, 1962).

Friedman, *Dollars and Deficits:* Milton Friedman, *Dollars and Deficits* (Englewood, N. J.: Prentice-Hall, 1968).

Friedman, *Monetary Stability:* Milton Friedman, *A Program for Monetary Stability* (New York: Fordham Univ. Press, 1959).

Friedman, *Optimum Quantity:* Milton Friedman, *The Optimum Quantity of Money and Other Essays* (Chicago: Aldine, 1969).

Friedman, *Positive Economics:* Milton Friedman, *Essays in Positive Economics* (Chicago: Univ. of Chicago Press, 1953).

Friedman (ed.), *Quantity Theory:* Milton Friedman (ed.), *Studies in the Quantity Theory of Money* (Chicago: Univ. of Chicago Press, 1956).

Friedman & Schwartz, *Monetary History:* Milton Friedman and Anna J. Schwartz, *A Monetary History of the United States, 1867–1960* (Princeton, N. J.: Princeton Univ. Press, 1963).

Friedman & Schwartz, *Monetary Statistics:* Milton Friedman and Anna J. Schwartz, *Monetary Statistics of the United States* (New York: National Bureau of Economic Research, 1970). The monthly statistics of money quantity (M_1) for which this source is used are taken from Table 1, column 8, pp. 4–53.

Graham, *Hyperinflation:* Frank D. Graham, *Exchange, Prices and Production in Hyper-Inflation: Germany, 1920–1923* (Princeton, N. J.: Princeton Univ. Press, 1930).

Halperin, *Germany:* S. William Halperin, *Germany Tried Democracy* (New York: Crowell, 1946).

Harris, *Kennedy Economics:* Seymour E. Harris, *The Economics of the Kennedy Years* (New York: Harper & Row, 1964).

Helfferich, *Money:* Karl Helfferich, *Money* (New York: Adelphi, 1927). This source is a translation of the sixth and last edition of Helfferich's treatise in German, *Das Geld*.

Heller, *Dimensions:* Walter W. Heller, *New Dimensions of Political Economy* (Cambridge, Mass.: Harvard Univ. Press, 1966).

Keynes, *Economic Consequences:* John Maynard Keynes, *The Economic Consequences of the Peace* (New York: Harcourt, Brace, 1920).

Keynes, *General Theory:* John Maynard Keynes, *The General Theory of Employment, Interest and Money* (New York: Harcourt, Brace, 1936).

Notes

Keynes, *Monetary Reform:* John Maynard Keynes, *A Tract on Monetary Reform* (London: Macmillan, 1924).

Keynes, *Persuasion:* John Maynard Keynes, *Essays in Persuasion* (New York: Harcourt, Brace, 1932).

Labor Statistics: U. S. Department of Labor, Bureau of Labor Statistics, *Handbook of Labor Statistics,* 1972.

National Accounts: U. S. Department of Commerce, *The National Income and Product Accounts of the United States, 1929–1965; The National Income and Product Accounts of the United States, 1964–1969;* and *Survey of Current Business,* July 1973.

Okun, *Prosperity:* Arthur M. Okun, *The Political Economy of Prosperity* (New York: Norton, 1970).

Peterson, *Schacht:* Edward Norman Peterson, *Hjalmar Schacht: For and Against Hitler* (Boston: Christopher, 1954).

Samuelson, *Economics:* Paul A. Samuelson, *Economics* (New York: McGraw-Hill, 7th ed., 1967).

Schacht, *Stabilization:* Hjalmar Schacht, *The Stabilization of the Mark* (London: Geo. Allen & Unwin, 1927).

Standard & Poor's: Standard & Poor's Corporation, *Trade and Securities Statistics, Security Price Index Record,* 1957, 1962, and 1972 editions and current issues. The stock price index used in all cases in this book is the Standard & Poor's 425 Industrials, omitting railroad and utility stocks.

Statistical Abstract: U. S. Department of Commerce, Bureau of the Census, *Statistical Abstract of the United States,* published annually.

Stein, *Fiscal Revolution:* Herbert Stein, *The Fiscal Revolution in America* (Chicago: Univ. of Chicago Press, 1969).

U. S. Budget: Executive Office of the President, Office of Management and Budget, *The Budget of the United States Government, 1974.* The figures of expenditures and deficits for which this source is used are found in Table 20, p. 371.

Page

Foreword

10 History of inflation: Despaux, *L'inflation dans l'histoire* (Paris: "L'Information," 1922); Einzig, *Inflation* (London: Chatto & Windus, 1952), pp. 26–46.

Chapter 1

15 Disastrous prosperity: Coar, "Germany's Disastrous Prosperity," *Independent*, vol. 109, pp. 383–385 (December 23, 1922); Agger, "Building Prosperity on the Sands of Inflation," *Annalist*, vol. 22, p. 597 (November 5, 1923).
Poverty: "The Real Poverty of the German People," *Literary Digest*, September 2, 1922, pp. 22–23.
Starvation: Smedley, "Starving Germany," *Nation*, vol. 117, pp. 601–602 (November 28, 1923).
All the marks in the world: The total German money supply in July, 1922 was 190 billion marks. (The term "billion" is the American usage and compares with "milliard" in the German terminology. A German billion is an American trillion.) This quantity, being about one-fifth of a trillion, become worth about one-fifth of 23¢ at the inflation's end, or less than 5¢. A newspaper then cost 200 billion marks. These figures are found in Bresciani-Turroni, *Inflation*, Tables III, IV, and V, pp. 440–444. Constantino Bresciani-Turroni, author of the book cited in these notes as *Inflation*, was an eminent Italian economist who served in Berlin with the Allied Control Commission during the inflation. He was of the "old-fashioned" money quantity school and he was hostile to Lord Keynes in later years as an inflationist. After World War II, he played a leading part in the Italian economic recovery as president of the Banco di Roma, executive director of the International Bank for Reconstruction and Development, and minister of foreign trade. He died in 1963. See *International Encyclopedia of the Social Sciences* (New York: Crowell Collier & Macmillan, 1968), vol. 2, pp. 149–50.

16 Workers to the bake shops: Peterson, *Schacht*, p. 44; see Stefan Zweig's story, "The Invisible Collection," reprinted in Zweig, *Kaleidoscope* (New York: Viking, 1934), p. 303.
Germany's nine-year cycle: A superior general history of the Weimar period in Germany is Halperin, *Germany*.

Page

Comparison of the combatants: Peterson, *Schacht*, pp. 38-39; Graham, *Hyperinflation*, p. 5 ff. Professor Graham's work is the second of the two principal studies in English of the German inflation. This work contains many keen analytical insights, possibly more than that of Bresciani-Turroni, but Professor Graham's ultimate conclusions seem less sound. He generally subscribes to the Germans' contention that the inflation was not monetary but was thrust upon them by reparations and falling foreign exchange rates of the mark. His complacency with the net effects of the inflation on Germany (see pp. 48-50 of this book and notes) is blood-curdling. Graham spent virtually his entire adult life as an economics professor in Princeton, New Jersey, and died in 1949.

Collection for the war from enemies: This view was that of Karl Helfferich, the finance minister during the war. See pp. 37-38. The war's cost was to be "a ball of lead tied to the feet of future Allied generations," according to Helfferich. Bresciani-Turroni, *Inflation*, p. 289.

Domestic prices and money supply: The wholesale price index (1913 = 1) stood at approximately 1.0 in the first half of 1914, and 2.34 in November 1918. Bresciani-Turroni, *Inflation*, p. 442 Table V. The money supply was 2.0 billion and 18.6 billion marks, respectively. *Ibid.*, p. 440, Table III. The reasons for the low wartime inflation are discussed, *Ibid.*, p. 51, and see p. 54 of this book.

17 German prices, 1920: The wholesale price index was 17.1 in March, 1920, compared with approximately 1.0 in July-August, 1914. *Ibid.*, p. 442, Table V.

German prosperity and foreign recession: Graham, *Hyperinflation*, pp. 247, 287-288; see also p. 19 of this book and note.

German prices, 1920-1921: Wholesale prices did not surpass the March, 1920 level of 17.1 until August, 1921, when they reached 19.2 on their continuous way upward, and in the meantime they had hovered mostly between 13.0 and 15.0. Bresciani-Turroni, *Inflation*, p. 442, Table V.

Money supply doubling: The German money supply was 41 billion Reichsmarks in February 1920 and 80.1 billion in August, 1921, while there had been no increase in wholesale prices. *Ibid.*, p. 440, Table III.

Stimulation, activity, prosperity: Bresciani-Turroni, *Inflation*, pp. 183-186.

18 New fortunes: *Ibid.*, pp. 290-295.

Exports: See p. 32 and notes.

Tourists: Graham, *Hyperinflation*, p. 224.

Mansions in Berlin suburbs: Bresciani-Turroni, *Inflation*, p. 381.

Countryfolk: The remoteness of the countryfolk from the inflation

Page

is evoked in Reyher, "A Tragedy of Thrift," *Century*, vol. 107, pp. 683–695 (March, 1924); and see note, "Comfortable farmers," to p. 22 of this book.

Frugality inconsequential: Bresciani-Turroni, *Inflation*, pp. 51–52.

Crime: *Ibid.*, pp. 332–333. The incidence of property crime like theft increased more than that of crimes against persons.

Unemployment: Graham, *Hyperinflation*, pp. 280, 317; Bresciani-Turroni, *Inflation*, pp. 188–189.

Workers falling behind: Graham, *Hyperinflation*, pp. 203–208; Keynes, *Monetary Reform*, pp. 26–28.

Quality of production: The decreased vitality of workers is noted by Graham, *Hyperinflation*, p. 282. The differences in wages between skilled and unskilled workers narrowed and disappeared, and as a consequence skilled workers too disappeared. *Ibid.*, p. 283 n. 10; Helfferich, *Money*, vol. 2, pp. 579–583; Bresciani-Turroni, *Inflation*, p. 313.

Demoralization: Lichtenberger, "Impressions of Berlin," *Living Age*, vol. 314, pp. 255–262 (July 29, 1922); Bresciani-Turroni, *Inflation*, p. 218.

Disunity: Edwards, "The Financial Status of Germany, V," *Annalist*, vol. 21, p. 13 (January 1, 1923).

19 Office workers and paperwork: Graham, *Hyperinflation*, pp. 246–247; Bresciani-Turroni, *Inflation*, p. 217. The ratio of office workers to production workers increased by 43 percent from 1913 to 1922.

Government workers: Graham, *Hyperinflation*, p. 283. The numbers of government employees rose from 1918 to 1923 by 242 percent in the Reich government, 61 percent in the states, and 27 percent in the municipalities, to reach a total of 4.5 million of a German aggregate labor force of 30 million.

Labor disputes: Bresciani-Turroni, *Inflation*, p. 217.

Middlemen: Graham, *Hyperinflation*, p. 87; Bresciani-Turroni, *Inflation*, p. 215.

New businesses: Graham, *Hyperinflation*, p. 278.

Bankruptcies: *Ibid.*; Bresciani-Turroni, *Inflation*, p. 219.

Stock market speculation: Bresciani-Turroni, *Inflation*, pp. 257–260.

Capital investment: Bresciani-Turroni, *Inflation*, pp. 196–203, traces the extraordinary preoccupation with capital construction, causing the strange condition in which production was high but consumption was low. See pp. 76–77 of this book and note. Graham, *Hyperinflation*, p. 323, thought it somewhat an overstatement to say that almost all of Germany's new investment has been useless.

Notes

Page

Contrast of Germany and neighbors: Edwards, "The Financial Status of Germany, I," *Annalist*, vol. 20, p. 535 (November 20, 1922).

20 "Rationalization" and demolition of factories: Bresciani-Turroni, *Inflation*, pp. 388-90.

Concentration, conglomeration: Bresciani-Turroni, *Inflation*, pp. 203-212; Graham, *Hyperinflation*, pp. 93-94.

Banks: Bresciani-Turroni, *Inflation*, pp. 212-216.

Stinnes: Bresciani-Turroni, *Inflation*, pp. 210, 297; Graham, *Hyperinflation*, pp. 93-94; Hartsaugh, "The Rise and Fall of the Stinnes Combine," *Jour. Econ. and Bus. History*, vol. 3, pp. 272-295 (1931). Ufermann & Höglin, *Stinnes und seine Konzerne* (Berlin: Verlag für Sozialwissenschaft, 1924). Stinnes died in 1924.

Disintegration of the empires: Bresciani-Turroni, *Inflation*, pp. 372-376.

Empire builders: Graham, *Hyperinflation*, p. 274, and Bresciani-Turroni, *Inflation*, pp. 220, 291. See the quotation at p. 75 of this book. The disappearance of the empire-builders after the inflation is recorded by Bresciani-Turroni, p. 374.

"Kings of inflation": Ufermann, *Könige der Inflation* (Berlin: Verlag für Sozialwissenschaft, 1924).

Chapter 2

21 Price rises: The fifteen-month price stability ended with July, 1921, with the wholesale price index at 14.3 (1913 = 1). Within four months, in November, 1921, the index was at 34.2 and by the following July and August was at 100.6 and 192, respectively. Bresciani-Turroni, *Inflation*, p. 442, Table V.

Buyers' strikes: Bresciani-Turroni, *Inflation*, pp. 190-191, and see note to p. 22 of this book.

Constant-value clauses and foreign currency: Graham, *Hyperinflation*, pp. 70-72; Bresciani-Turroni, *Inflation*, p. 221.

Government budget balance: Government taxes and expenditures had a close brush with balance in July, 1922, when the deficit was only a bit over 10 percent of the expenditure but the inflation was still skyrocketing. Bresciani-Turroni, *Inflation*, pp. 61, 438.

22 Price rises: The wholesale price index, 100.6 in July, 1922, increased to 1,154 in November and reached 19,385 in June, 1923.

Total real value smaller than ever: This phenomenon is of the greatest importance and is discussed in detail in Chapter 17 of this book. Helfferich's claim that the phenomenon precluded any question of inflation is in *Money*, vol. 2, p. 599. The idea is rightly rejected

336 Notes

Page

by Graham, *Hyperinflation*, pp. 99–113; Bresciani-Turroni, *Inflation*, pp. 155–160; and Keynes, *Monetary Reform*, pp. 82–83.
Scarcity of money: Bresciani-Turroni, *Inflation*, p. 80.
Vying to buy: "Germans on a Spending Spree," *Literary Digest*, June 17, 1922, p. 18; Bresciani-Turroni, *Inflation*, pp. 190–191.
22 percent interest per day: Schacht, *Stabilization*, p. 159.
20 percent price rise from order to check: "Germany, Land of Perpetual Nightmare," *Literary Digest*, October 13, 1923, p. 40.
Money printing industry: Schacht, *Stabilization*, p. 105; Bresciani-Turroni, *Inflation*, p. 82. The private money issues are described, *ibid.*, pp. 80–81.
Comfortable farmers: Benvenisti, "Rural Germany and the Towns," *Contemporary Review*, vol. 125, pp. 600–606 (May, 1924); Graham, *Hyperinflation*, p. 286.

23 Boston Symphony Orchestra conductor: Ross, "The Passing of the German Middle Class," *Amer. Jour. of Sociology*, vol. 29, pp. 529–538 (March, 1924). Absorbing studies of the final agony are this article and Mitchell, "Germany," *Atlantic*, vol. 131, pp. 534–543 (April, 1923).
Descent into poverty: Bresciani-Turroni, *Inflation*, pp. 326–330. Along with malnutrition and disease, prostitution and pawnshops thrived, and horsemeat and dog meat replaced other meats for eating.
Unemployment: See note to p. 18.
Grinding to a halt: The turmoil of the climactic months of the inflation is described in Halperin, *Germany*, chapter 18.
85 dead in Hamburg riot: The riots occurred on October 23 and 24, 1923. New York *Times*, October 24, p. 1; October 25, p. 2; October 27, p. 1.
"Miracle of the Rentenmark": Bresciani-Turroni, *Inflation*, p. 336.
Stresemann: The appraisal of Stresemann is from Dill, *Germany* (Ann Arbor, Mich.: Univ. of Michigan Press, 1961). See also note to p. 45 of this book.
Dr. Schacht and the Rentenmark: Schacht, *Stabilization*. Dr. Schacht's dark back office, his telephone and his secretary are at pp. 94–95. A worthwhile study of Schacht in this period as well as in his later connection with Hitler is Peterson, *Schacht*.
Rentenmark's imaginary backing: Graham, *Hyperinflation*, p. 12, n. 16.

24 Schacht's appointment to Reichsbank presidency: the supreme irony was that Schacht's opponent for the Reichsbank presidency was the one man who had done most to cause the catastrophe, Karl Helfferich. (See p. 38 of this book.) The Reichsbank governors voted against Schacht, but Helfferich was political poison to the

Notes 337

government headed by Chancellor Stresemann, which approved Schacht. Peterson, *Schacht*, p. 50–52.

Schacht and stabilization: The difficulties and achievements of the stabilization are perceptively and correctly analyzed by Graham, *Hyperinflation*, p. 289–291, and further discussed in Bresciani-Turroni, *Inflation*, pp. 344–353.

Hard times: The economic problems of the post-stabilization crisis are treated in Bresciani-Turroni, *Inflation*, chapter X.

Almost 400,000 government workers discharged: Peterson, *Schacht*, p. 54. The number was 397,000.

"Inflation Reichstag": Halperin, *Germany*, p. 308. The results of the election are discussed *ibid.*, p. 291.

25 Elections of December, 1924: Halperin, *Germany*, pp. 308–309.

Chapter 3

26 Total mortgage debt: Graham, *Hyperinflation*, p. 241.

27 Debtors' gain: *Ibid.*, p. 242; Keynes, *Monetary Reform*, p. 10. The constant ability of borrowers to profit, even at 100 percent per month rates of interest, was observed by Keynes, *ibid.*, pp. 18–24.

Creditors' loss: Bresciani-Turroni, *Inflation*, pp. 314–320.

German profit on marks from foreigners: Graham, *Hyperinflation*, Chapter X.

German national product: Comparisons with Germany's national product are based on an estimate of roughly 40 billion gold marks per year. Graham, *Hyperinflation*, pp. 317–320, estimates Germany's total production at 36.6 billion gold marks in 1920, 46.0 billion in 1921, 48.0 billion in 1922, and 30.2 billion in 1923.

Trustees' investments: Keynes, *Monetary Reform*, p. 8.

Charitable institutions: Bresciani-Turroni, *Inflation*, pp. 314–320.

Financial institutions: Bresciani-Turroni, *Inflation*, pp. 280–282.

Industrial stocks: Bresciani-Turroni, *Inflation*, Chapter VII. The index of industrial stocks stood at 200 in paper marks (1913 = 100) in February, 1920, was at 936 by November, 1921, twenty-one months later and just before the crash. The market then fell to 731 and was still only 897 in July, 1922, by which time the real value of stocks, discounted by the factor of wholesale price inflation, had fallen from 27.40 to 8.92. Real value continued downward to a bottom of 3.64 in October, 1922. Stock indexes are tabulated in Bresciani-Turroni, *Inflation*, pp. 452–454, Table XII.

28 327 cars: Bresciani-Turroni, *Inflation*, p. 265.

Investors slow to grasp: Graham, *Hyperinflation*, p. 177. One cause for the eventual recovery of the stock market was the prohi-

338 Notes

Page

bition by law in October, 1922 of Germans' investing in foreign currency. Bresciani-Turroni, *Inflation*, p. 270. This was the month in which the real value of stocks at last turned upward. See note to p. 27 of this book.

Workers no permanent loss: Graham, *Hyperinflation*, p. 242.

Middle class: Graham, *Hyperinflation*, p. 242.

29 Keynes, "Lenin is said to have declared . . .": Keynes, *Economic Consequences*, p. 235.

Hitler, ". . . once the printing presses stopped . . .": Heiden, *Der Fuehrer* (Boston: Houghton Mifflin, 1944), p. 131.

Chapter 4

30 Needs for money: Karl Helfferich, minister of finance during the war and principal architect of the inflation (see pp. 37-8) was the principal spokesman of the official line:

"The President of the Reichsbank, Havestein, with whom the author, as Secretary of State for the Treasury . . . was in closest contact during those years, steadfastly held the view that there could be no question of any 'inflation' . . . in view of the increased demand, due to the rises of prices and wages, conditioned by the War and independently of currency policy." *Money*, vol. 2, p. 595.

There were, of course, those Germans who were even then speaking out against the inflation of money quantity, including Schacht (Peterson, *Schacht*, p. 30) and the great Austrian economist Ludwig von Mises (Bresciani-Turroni, *Inflation*, p. 93).

31 Keynes, "These 'profiteers' . . .": Keynes, *Economic Consequences*, pp. 236-237.

Speculation: Bresciani-Turroni, *Inflation*, pp. 100-103; Graham, *Hyperinflation*, pp. 48-56.

"Pathological" foreign holdings of marks: Graham, *ibid.*, p. 321.

Rush to get out of the mark: The flight from the mark is recorded by Bresciani-Turroni, *Inflation*, p. 88-90.

Balance of payments: Bresciani-Turroni, *ibid.*, pp. 86-87. The reversal of Germany's payments deficit into surplus occurred in mid-1922, at the same time as the desertion of the mark as an investment by both Germans and foreigners.

32 Exchange rates: Graham, *Hyperinflation*, pp. 117-173.

Exports: *Ibid.*, pp. 209-212. The estimated loss of 10 billion gold marks on underpriced exports is made at *ibid.*, p. 276.

33 Keynes' polemic: *Economic Consequences*.

Reparation demand: Halperin, *Germany*, p. 202.

Notes

Page

Ruhr invasion and passive resistance: Halperin, *Germany*, pp. 248–254.

Reparations payments: The reparations figures are from Graham, *Hyperinflation*, p. 247. The comparison with foreigners' losses on marks refers to p. 27 of this book.

34 Helfferich's apologia, "But claims were put forward . . .": Helfferich, *Money*, vol. 2, pp. 597–598.

35 Controls: Keynes, *Monetary Reform*, p. 26, spoke as follows:

"A host of popular remedies vainly attempted to cure the evils of the day; which remedies themselves—subsidies, price and rent fixing, profiteer hunting, and excess profits duties—eventually became not the least part of the evils."

As usual, controls were partially effective to dampen the apparent rate of inflation in some sectors, but had no effect whatever on the underlying inflationary forces. See Helfferich, *Money*, vol. 2, p. 577.

Rent control and housing shortage: Graham, *Hyperinflation*, p. 79.

Appeals to patriotism, condemnation of flight: Bresciani-Turroni, *Inflation*, pp. 89, 96.

36 Support with gold: Graham, *Hyperinflation*, pp. 85–87; Keynes, *Monetary Reform*, p. 54.

Chapter 5

37 Helfferich and Erzberger: Epstein, *Erzberger*, recounts Erzberger's life and, in chapters XIII and XIV, his brief career as finance minister and his feud with Helfferich. See also Halperin, *Germany*, pp. 169–171. The comparison of Helfferich to Lord Keynes is by Epstein, *Erzberger*, p. 350. The person most directly responsible for the money inflation would have had to be Rudolf Havenstein, who was president of the Reichsbank throughout the war and until his death in the very month (November, 1923) when the inflation was ended. Havenstein seems to have been largely under the influence of Helfferich, however, who was much the stronger figure both intellectually and politically.

38 *Das Geld* in print: *Das Geld* is the German original of Helfferich, *Money*. *Books in Print, 1973* (New York: Bowker, 1973), p. 1155.

Helfferich and the Rentenmark: Peterson, *Schacht*, pp. 47–49. Helfferich was also defeated as candidate for the Reichsbank presidency against Schacht. See note to p. 24 of this book. Helfferich died in a train crash in Switzerland in 1924.

Helfferich, money creation and price inflation: Helfferich, *Money*, vol. 2, pp. 446–447, 592–598.

Cold, arrogant, pharisaical: Epstein, *Erzberger*, p. 351.

39 Blunt, tactless, impulsive: Halperin, *Germany*, pp. 169–170.

Page

War debt 153 billion marks: The figure is from Epstein, *Erzberger*, p. 331.

Tight money: The period of genuinely tight money lasted for only five months, June through November, 1919, in which the money supply rose only from 30 to 31.9 billion marks. Bresciani-Turroni, *Inflation*, p. 440, Table III. In comparison with prices, however, money was reasonably tight from the Armistice to price stability in 1920, rising only 140 percent (from 18.6 billion marks to 45.2 billion marks) while wholesale prices were rising by 630 percent (2.34 to 17.1). *Ibid.*, pp. 440, 442, Tables III, V.

40 Comparison of price factor and money factor: Wholesale prices in March, 1920 were 17 times the August, 1914 level. Money supply in November, 1919, when the period of tight money ended, had also been about 17 times the base level of 2 billion marks at the beginning of 1914. Bresciani-Turroni, *Inflation*, pp. 440, 442, Tables III, IV.

Real burden of war debt cut by five-sixths: Prices increased by about six times from approximately 2.5 at the end of 1918 to approximately 15 in the spring of 1920. Bresciani-Turroni, *Inflation*, p. 443, Table V.

Erzberger-Helfferich warfare: Epstein, *Erzberger*, pp. 349–369.

41 Exchange value: Bresciani-Turroni, *Inflation*, pp. 30–32. The exchange rate of the mark against the dollar more than doubled.

Stock market rise: See p. 27 and notes.

Money supply doubling: See p. 17 and note.

Taxes reduced and deficits increased: The floating debt of the Reich increased by about 8 billion gold marks in the period April, 1920 through July, 1921, which was the era of stable prices. Bresciani-Turroni, *Inflation*, pp. 437–438.

Assassination of Erzberger: Epstein, *Erzberger*, pp. 384–389; Halperin, *Germany*, p. 205.

Chapter 6

42 Marxist insurrection: Halperin, *Germany*, chapter 8; Watt, *The Kings Depart* (New York: Simon and Schuster, 1968).

Kapp *Putsch:* Halperin, *Germany*, chapter 12.

Labor legislation: *Ibid.*, pp. 110–112.

43 Workers and intellectuals: Bresciani-Turroni, *Inflation*, p. 331.

Blocking all adequate taxes: Bresciani-Turroni, *Inflation*, pp. 58–60.

Murder of Luxemberg and Liebknecht: Halperin, *Germany*, pp. 121–122; Watt, *The Kings Depart* (New York: Simon and Schuster, 1968), pp. 271–272.

Page

Social Democrats: The suppression of the Marxists was accomplished by an alliance of the majority workers' party SPD, led by Ebert, and the arch-reactionary former Army forces of the Frei Korps, with whom the Social Democrat Gustav Noske served as liaison and chief suppressor. An interesting study of the SPD in the Weimar era is Hunt, *German Social Democracy 1918–1933* (New Haven, Conn.: Yale Univ. Press, 1964).

44   Erzberger: See pp. 37–41.

Stresemann: See note to p. 45.

Cuno government and industrialists: Halperin, *Germany*, pp. 244–246, 252–254, 258. The constant opposition of industrialists to effective anti-inflationary action is described in Bresciani-Turroni, *Inflation*, pp. 104–105.

Stresemann's dictatorial power: Long, "Stresemann's Economic Dictatorship," *Fortnightly Review*, vol. 120, pp. 939–950 (December, 1923); Halperin, *Germany*, pp. 266–267. Hitler's comparable enabling act is discussed in Shirer, *The Rise and Fall of the Third Reich* (New York: Simon and Schuster, 1959), pp. 196–200.

45   Stresemann: A brief study of Stresemann is found in Craig, *From Bismarck to Adenauer* (Baltimore: Johns Hopkins Press, 1958), pp. 70–83. Stresemann won the Nobel Peace Prize for his work on the Treaty of Locarno in 1925. Stresemann was said to be more celebrated among foreigners than among Germans. Even among foreigners, his memory has suffered something of an undeserved decline since World War II and the disclosure of private papers showing a degree of dissembling underlying his overt efforts toward international cooperation. Germans sometimes say that Stresemann was all things to all men and no one liked him *very well*, but possibly that is the truest measure of a man who is doing the best that can be done.

Fall of Stresemann as chancellor: This happened on November 23, 1923. Halperin, *Germany*, p. 283.

Chapter 7

47   Fingertip sensitivity: Peterson, *Schacht*, p. 56. Schacht also averred that monetary policy was not an exact science but an art.

48   Stinnes speech: New York *Times*, December 17, 1922, Section 1, Part 2, p. 8.

Capital taxes: Keynes, *Economic Consequences*, p. 280, *Monetary Reform*, p. 64; Schacht, *Stabilization*.

49   Inflation evaluation: Graham, *Hyperinflation*, pp. 320–326.

Pensioners returned to labor force: *Ibid.*, p. 246.

Elections of 1932: The NSDAP, or Nazis, received 13.7 million votes, or 37 percent, and 230 Reichstag seats of 608. The Democrats,

Page

Catholic Center, and People's Party had polled 12 million votes in 1920 but virtually disappeared, except for the Catholics, by 1932. The mighty and reactionary Nationalists also joined the Nazis. The Social Democrats, still second in size to the Nazis, weakened in favor of the Communists, but not nearly as much as in the first 1924 elections. Shirer, *The Rise and Fall of the Third Reich* (New York: Simon and Schuster, 1959), pp. 166, 186.

50 Graham, "With all these reservations . . .": Graham, *Hyperinflation*, p. 324.

Chapter 8

53 Dollar lost 70 percent of value: The wholesale price index (1967 = 100) stood at 39.7 in January, 1939 and 136.7 in June, 1973. All American price indexes cited in these notes are found in the sources described as *BLS Prices*.

54 Federal debt: The $269 billion figure was as of June 30, 1946, the end of the government's fiscal year in which the last of the wartime expenditure occurred. *Statistical Abstract, 1969*, p. 392.

Gross national product: The GNP for the year 1946 was $208.5 billion. All references in this book to American gross national product, national income, and related concepts, except as otherwise noted, are taken from the combination of sources described as *National Accounts*.

Monetary expansion: The 3.5 times expansion is derived from money supply totals of $32.3 billion in January, 1939 and $113 billion in September, 1947. Friedman & Schwartz, *Monetary Statistics*. In all cases in this book, "money" is taken to include only currency plus demand deposits, seasonally adjusted, or "M_1" in the monetarist shorthand. See note to p. 102. Figures for money quantity are taken from Friedman & Schwartz, *Monetary Statistics*, for periods through 1946 and comparisons to those periods; from *F. R. Bulletin*, December, 1970, pp. 895–898 for periods from 1947 through 1958 and comparisons to those periods; from *F. R. Bulletin*, February, 1972, pp. 72–73, for periods from 1959 through 1972; and from monthly issues of *F. R. Bulletin* for dates in 1973.

Prices: The wholesale price index increased from 39.7 (1967 = 100) in January, 1939 to 58.2 in June, 1946, or only about 47 percent. Wholesale prices are generally considered more useful in this book than consumer prices. In the same period, the consumer price index increased from 41.8 to 55.9, or 34 percent.

Real value of dollar two-thirds of apparent value: This statement rests on the fact that money supply expansion had already been so much greater than price inflation, and also makes use of hindsight by observing how much farther prices actually did rise, more than

Notes 343

Page

money supply, before the two reached an equilibrium in 1948. See the discussion following.

55 **Letting the inflation happen:** Stein, *Fiscal Revolution*, p. 217: "The country ended the inflation by having it." Stein's work is an excellent historical record of the course of economics in theory and practice in the United States from the Depression through the 1960's, although its purpose is to record sympathetically a "fiscal revolution" to which this book is fundamentally unsympathetic. See Chapter 26 of this book.

Plea to extend price controls: See note to p. 56.

July wholesale prices: The indexes were 58.2 in June and 64.4 in July, a rise of 10.7 percent.

Two years following price controls: In total, wholesale prices increased from 58.2 in June, 1946 to 84.3 in August, 1948, or 45 percent, consumer prices from 55.9 to 73.4, or 31 percent. Wholesale prices were thus a bit more, consumer prices somewhat less, than twice those of January, 1939.

Money growth deceleration: The money expansion abated somewhat immediately after the end of the war in September, 1945. Before that, monthly gains had been almost invariably above an annual rate of 12 percent to 15 percent. From September, 1945 to September, 1947, money supply increased only from $102.4 billion to $113 billion, or 5.2 percent per year. From 1947 until May, 1950, money supply did not move much above the $113 billion level and moved downward at times to as low as $111 billion.

56 **Recession:** The annual rate of GNP was declining from quarter to quarter throughout 1949, from a level of $264 billion in the fourth quarter of 1948 to $255 billion in the fourth quarter of 1949. Similarly, the index of industrial production declined from 69 in October, 1948 to 62 in October, 1949. *F. R. Bulletin*. October, 1969 was also the low point of the monetary contraction.

June 1946 plea for stronger price controls: President Truman's veto message of June 29, 1946, is at *Congressional Record*, vol. 92, p. 8092. His signature to the eventual price control act, with reluctance and misgivings, on July 25, 1946, is at *ibid.*, vol. 92, p. 10162.

Plea to joint session for new controls: *Congressional Record*, vol. 93, p. 10702 (November 17, 1947).

Pure luck: The analysis of the remarkable stability of money supply in 1947–1950, and of the fortuitous reasons for it, is in Friedman & Schwartz, *Monetary History*, pp. 577–585.

57 **Keynes, practical limit on debt:** *Monetary Reform*, p. 64.

Repudiate, capital levy, or inflate: *Ibid.*, p. 65.

German debt burden cut by five-sixths: See note to p. 40.

Page

58 **U. S. war debt reduced to 90 percent of national product:** In 1950, the Federal debt had been reduced to $257.4 billion. That year's GNP was $284.8 billion. In 1968, when GNP was $929.1 billion, Federal debt had risen to $347.6 billion.

Inflation the way most wars are financed: A noteworthy exception was Napoleon's conduct of his own wars. France suffered no inflation at all under Napoleon's tenure, while all the nations allied against him suffered bad inflations. Napoleon passed up some opportunities for military adventure because of cost. Einzig, *Inflation* (London: Chatto & Windus, 1952), pp. 40–41.

Chapter 9

59 **Absence of Federal budget deficit:** During the four years from July 1, 1950, through June 30, 1954, the Federal budget showed an aggregate net surplus of $1.2 billion, representing a substantial surplus in fiscal 1951, a balance in 1952, and small deficits in 1953 and 1954. *U. S. Budget.*

Money supply expansion: The increase of money supply was 16.2 percent, represented by an expansion from an average of $111 billion in 1949 to about $129 billion prevailing in the latter part of 1953.

Price increases: The 13 percent increases in prices were from 78 to 88 in wholesale prices and from 71 to 80 in retail prices from the steady levels of late 1949 to those of 1953, at which point both sets of prices stopped rising.

The Korean War inflation: Wholesale prices increased to a peak of 92.5 in February, 1951, after which they slowly but steadily declined to the range of 87 to 88 by the end of 1952. They held there after the inauguration of President Eisenhower and the release of price controls. Money supply in February, 1951 had only increased to $117.1 billion, or only 5.5 percent since 1949 as compared with 18.6 percent for wholesale prices, but money supply continued its expansion to $129 billion in 1953 where it made rendezvous with prices.

60 **Federal Reserve management of money:** The conduct of monetary policy and events leading to the Accord of 1951 are well described in Friedman & Schwartz, *Monetary History*, pp. 610–638, and Stein, *Fiscal Revolution*, chapter 10. Economists of the Keynesian liberal camp were unanimous in their prophecies of doom to come from anything so catastrophic as a free market in interest rates. Friedman & Schwartz, *Monetary History*, p. 624 n. 21.

61 **Budget deficits:** The fiscal year ended June 30, 1946 had shown a deficit of $18.2 billion. Apart from that year, the fiscal years 1947 through 1953 for which President Truman was responsible showed

Page

an aggregate net surplus of $17.1 billion. President Eisenhower had one bad deficit of $12.9 billion in fiscal 1959 and showed an aggregate net deficit of $2.8 billion for the seven other fiscal years from 1954 through 1961. *U. S. Budget.*

Money supply and prices 1 percent per year: From late 1953 to September, 1962, money supply increased from $129 billion to $146.7 billion, or 13.7 percent in nine years. In the same period, wholesale prices rose from 88 to 94.8, or 7.7 percent, and consumer prices from 80 to 91.2, or 14 percent.

Seven-year price stability: Wholesale prices stood at 95.0 in March, 1958 and 94.9 in December, 1964, and in the interim rose no higher than 95.2 and fell no lower than 94.0.

62 **Monetary oscillations, boom and recession:** Money supply increased only 0.7 percent per year, from $127.4 billion to $128.6 billion, in the sixteen months from December, 1952 to April, 1954. The stock market was deflated and there was recession. Then the money supply increased an average of 3.9 percent per year, from $128.6 billion to $136.9 billion, in the twenty months from April, 1954 to December, 1956. The stock market rose from around 26 to as high as 52 (Standard & Poor's) and there was boom. By the end of 1956, both wholesale prices and consumer prices were rising at about 3 percent per year. In the calendar year 1957, money *decreased* from $136.9 billion to $135.9 billion, or 0.7 percent. The stock market fell and there was recession. Prices stopped rising by early in 1958. After that, money *increased* at a 4.0 percent annual rate for nineteen months, December, 1957 to July, 1959; *decreased* at 1.2 percent for eighteen months, July, 1959 to January, 1961; *increased* again at 2.9 percent for fifteen months, January, 1961 to April, 1962; and *decreased* again at 0.7 percent for five months, April, 1962 to September, 1962, with the effects described in the text. After the stabilization in 1958, prices changed little.

Presidential election of 1960: Nixon, *Six Crises* (Garden City, N. Y.: Doubleday, 1962), pp. 309–311.

63 **Monetary non-growth of 1953–1954:** This period deserves close examination because, of all periods since 1928, it approached closest to what a monetary policy for non-inflationary stability should be. It was more representative than 1947–1950 because special postwar influences had been present in that earlier period. From December, 1952 to April, 1954, money did not contract outright but grew by only 0.7 percent per year. Both wholesale prices and consumer prices were essentially motionless throughout this time (and indeed for more than a year after it ended). But prosperity was poor. Industrial production was sinking little by little almost throughout the period. The GNP likewise drifted downward from the last quarter of 1953 through the first half of 1954. The stock market

Notes

was stagnant in this time and during the preceding year of 1952. See note to p. 307.

Chapter 10

64 "Get the country moving again": Televised speech at Philadelphia, Pennsylvania, on October 31, 1960, about a week before the election. New York *Times,* November 1, 1960, p. 29.

Kennedy intellectual credentials: Harris, *Kennedy Economics,* p. 17.

65 Employment Act of 1946: Public Law 79-304, February 20, 1946. This law did nothing very positive except to declare high employment to be a worthy goal. By way of specific action, it created the Council of Economic Advisers, the annual economic report of the President, and the Joint Economic Committee of Congress, a trinity of thoroughly mixed blessings.

Heller and the Kennedy economics: The more or less inside story of the Kennedy economics, published with manifest self-satisfaction before the backlash of these economics had set in, can be found in Heller, *Dimensions;* Harris, *Kennedy Economics;* and Stein, *Fiscal Revolution.* The observation that five of six economists at random would have done the same is by Stein, not himself a Kennedy economist, *Fiscal Revolution,* p. 380. Besides Heller and his associates of the Council of Economic Advisers, other unmantled but possibly even more influential advisers to President Kennedy were, Cantabrigians all, Professors Galbraith, Samuelson, and Harris.

66 Kennedy preoccupations: The Bay of Pigs invasion by Cuban emigrants, with American complicity, began and ended in abject failure in April, 1961. President Kennedy met Nikita Krushchev of Russia in Vienna, with poor results, in June, 1961. The Berlin wall crisis, which involved calling up military reserves and the like, began in August, 1961. The crisis caused by Russian construction of missile launching sites in Cuba, developing over many months, culminated in successful American naval blockade in October, 1962.

Longest and steepest monetary inflation: In September, 1962, the money supply was $149.4 billion. In the first twelve months, it increased by only 3.8 percent, to $155.1, but by April, 1966, it had increased to $175.3 billion for an average annual rate since 1962 of 4.6 percent. Then followed the brief credit crunch of 1966, in which the money supply was essentially unchanged during the nine months from April until January, 1967. After that the money supply increased to $205.7 billion in April, 1969, for an average annual increase after 1966 of 7.2 percent.

67 Revenue Act of 1962: Public Law 87-834, *Statutes at Large,* vol. 76, p. 960 (October 16, 1962). The earlier liberalization of de-

preciation was made by Revenue Procedure 62-21, 1962-2 *Cumulative Bulletin,* p. 418 (July 12, 1962).

68 Budget deficits: President Kennedy achieved deficits in every year, amounting to $7.1 billion, $4.8 billion, and $5.9 billion in fiscal years (ending June 30) 1962, 1963, and 1964. President Johnson fought off threatening budget balances with rising success; his deficits were $1.6 billion, $3.8 billion, $8.7 billion, and at last $25.2 billion (a peacetime record) in 1965, 1966, 1967, and 1968. *U. S. Budget.*

Big tax cut: Revenue Act of 1964, Public Law 88-271, *Statutes at Large,* vol. 78, p. 17 (February 26, 1964).

Stock market: The stock market (*Standard & Poor's*) rose from a low of 55.10 in June, 1962 to a high of 117.8 in December, 1968, interrupted only by a sharp setback from 98.69 to 79.52 in the tight money period of 1966.

"Fine tuning" rued: Friedman and Heller, *Monetary vs. Fiscal Policy,* (New York: Norton, 1969), p. 34. Professor Heller is doing the rueing.

Accommodation by the Federal Reserve: Harris, *Kennedy Economics,* pp. 106-121; Okun, *Prosperity,* p. 53. Professor Harris in particular recites the veiled threats emanating from Kennedy and Martin toward one another.

Prices: Prices very slowly began rising in 1963 and 1964. The twelve-month increase in consumer prices was 1.6 percent by the end of 1963, 2.9 percent by April, 1966, was never lower than the 2.5 percent of April, 1967 in spite of the tight money and recession, and was 5.4 percent by April, 1969. Wholesale prices in general were slower to rise and responded more immediately to tight money. Their twelve-month rate of rise reached 3.6 percent by April, 1966, fell to no increase in April, 1967, and rose again to 3.8 percent by April, 1969.

69 Comparison of money and prices: The average annual rate of growth of money from September, 1962 ($149.4 billion) to April, 1969 ($205.7 billion) was 5.0 percent. This compares with the rates of price inflation stated in the preceding note. The wholesale price index was 105.5 in April, 1969, compared with an average of 94.8 in 1962 for an increase of 11.3 percent. The consumer price indexes were 108.7 and 91.2 in the same months, for an increase of 19.2 percent. These comparisons as a measure of unrealized inflation are discussed in chapter 21.

Chapter 11

70 GNP increase of $360 billion: The gross national product was $864.2 billion in 1968 and $503.7 billion in 1960. It had been $398.0 billion in 1955. *National Acounts,* Tables 1.1.

348 *Notes*

Page
71 **11 percent population, 16 percent price inflation:** The total American population was 180.7 million in 1960 and 200.7 million in 1968. *Statistical Abstract*, 1972, p. 5. The implicit price deflator for gross national product was 103.3 in 1960 and 122.3 in 1968. *National Accounts*, Tables 8.1.

72 **27 million production workers:** The totals were 27.7 million in 1960 and 27.8 million in 1968. The totals include all workers in farming and transportation and nonsupervisory or production workers in mining, construction, manufacturing, communications and utilities. Agricultural employment is from *Statistical Abstract*, 1972, p. 240. Nonagricultural employment is from *Labor Statistics*, pp. 89, 92.

Production workers' earnings: Overall personal income per capita in constant dollars is based on *National Accounts* and *Statistical Abstract*, 1972, p. 315. Production workers' real earnings are based on average hourly earnings of nonsupervisory and production workers in all private employment (*Labor Statistics*, p. 220, Table 97), discounted for consumer price indexes from *BLS Prices*. By May of 1973, the average annual increase since 1960 of production workers' real hourly earnings had fallen to 1.7 percent.

73 **Profit margins:** The average profit margin for all private industries was about the same in 1968, a boom year, as in 1960, a recession year. The relevant profit margins in nonagricultural industries are calculated from corporate net profits before taxes, as a percentage of corporate sales, set forth by industry in *National Accounts*, Tables 6.13 and 6.19. For farming, net operating income as a percentage of gross receipts from farming is set forth in *Statistical Abstract*, 1972, p. 596.

Average price inflation: These comparisons are based on average implicit price deflators by industry, weighted according to shares of total output in 1968, as set forth in *National Accounts*, Tables 1.21.

74 **Volume of trading:** *Statistical Abstract*, 1972, p. 456.

Securities industry: *National Accounts*, Tables 1.12.

Capital gains: Internal Revenue Service, *Statistics of Income 1968, Individual Tax Returns*, Tables 1.18 and 8.5. The combined national income arising from farming and the gas and electric utilities in 1968 was $35.5 billion. *National Accounts*, Table 1.12.

Keynes, "In one of the greatest investment markets . . .": *General Theory*, pp. 159–160.

75 **Conglomerate mergers:** *Statistical Abstract*, 1972, p. 484.

"Production is abandoned . . .": Graham, *Hyperinflation*, p. 247. As to the phenomenon in Germany, see p. 20 of this book and notes.

"Up to now the idea has been . . .": *Fortune*, April, 1969, p.

Notes

Page

148. Ironically, the quotee is, of all things, a young *German* investment adviser.

76 "In the acutest phase . . .": Bresciani-Turroni, *Inflation*, p. 197. As to Germany, see pp. 19-20 of this book and notes.

$37 billion increased construction: Capital investment, representing only construction of industrial, commercial, and utility plant and manufacture of private producers' durable equipment, increased from $41.9 billion in 1960 to $80.8 billion in 1968. *National Accounts*, Tables, 5.2, 5.4.

Housing: New residential construction in constant (1957-1959) dollars was $23.6 billion in 1955, $20.8 billion in 1960, and as low as $19.4 billion in 1967, even while the population had increased by 19.7 percent. *Statistical Abstract, 1971*, p. 658.

77 12 million more workers: From 1960 to 1968, nonproduction workers in manufacturing, mining, and construction increased from 4.8 million to 5.9 million; active military personnel, from 2.5 million to 3.5 million; government employees, from 8.3 million to 11.8 million; wholesale and retail employees, from 11.4 million to 14.1 million; and financial and service workers, from 10.1 million to 14.0 million. Military personnel are from *Statistical Abstract, 1971*, p. 252; private and government employment, from *Labor Statistics*, pp. 89-102. The 11.8 million government workers were about 15 percent of the total work force of 76.2 million, exactly the same percentage as German government employees in 1922. See note to p. 19 of this book.

Government expenditure: Expenditure of all governments was $151.3 billion in 1960 and $282.6 billion in 1968. *Statistical Abstract, 1972*, p. 410.

Wholesale/retail distribution: National income arising in wholesale and retail trade increased from $64.4 billion in 1960 to $106.1 billion in 1968; in financial, legal, and miscellaneous business services from $53.6 billion to $94.4 billion. *National Accounts*, Tables 1.12.

78 Average price inflation: See note to p. 73.

81 Education: Total public and private expenditure on education was $24.7 billion and $54.9 billion in school years ending 1960 and 1968, respectively. *Statistical Abstract, 1970*, p. 104. Private and governmental employment in education was 3.6 million and 6.3 million, respectively. *National Accounts*, Tables 6.3. Total public and private expenditure in higher education was $6.8 billion and $20.3 billion, respectively. *Statistical Abstract, 1971*, p. 127. In 1960, 3.6 million students were 10.7 percent of the population aged 18 to 34; in school year 1969, 8.3 million students were 18.3 percent. *Statistical Abstract, 1970*, p. 108. The difference, 7.6 percent of the 1969 population, is 3.4 million students.

350 Notes

Page
83 Entertainment: In constant dollars, the real value of personal consumption expenditures for admissions to spectator amusements declined constantly from a high of $2.9 billion in 1946 to $1.2 billion in 1968, passing through $1.5 billion in 1960. *National Accounts*, Tables 2.6.

Crime: *Statistical Abstract*, 1972, p. 143.

Civil disturbance: *Ibid.*, p. 148.

Labor strife: *Labor Statistics*, p. 387.

Chapter 12

87 Viet Nam war: Defense expenditures in fiscal 1969 of $81.2 billion was 9.0 percent of GNP, while defense expenditure in fiscal 1959 of $46.6 billion had been 9.9 percent of GNP. *Statistical Abstract*, *1971*, p. 240. As we have seen, price inflation began to roll smartly from the beginning of 1965, but Viet Nam cost only $103 million and $6.1 billion in fiscal 1965 and 1966, respectively, while space research cost $5.1 billion and $5.9 billion in the same years. *Statistical Abstract*, *1969*, p. 377. Laying the blame for inflation on the war is exemplified by a book, *Prosperity*, by Arthur Okun, chairman of the Council of Economic Advisers at the time.

88 Pension funds: See p. 181 and note.

Balance of payments: The German problem is discussed at pp. 31–32 and notes. The continuous outflows of billions of dollars per year are recorded in U. S. Department of Commerce, *Balance of Payments—Statistical Supplement*, *1963*, and *Current Business*, June and September, 1970, March, 1971. Legislative efforts to stanch the hemorrhages were principally the Interest Equalization Tax Act of 1964, Public Law 88–563, which imposed a penalty tax on American purchasers of foreign securities, and the Foreign Direct Investment Regulations authorized by President Johnson's Executive Order 11387 (January 1, 1968), which imposed quota-type restrictions on investment by American corporations in their foreign subsidiaries. These efforts found no success, and the United States continued to suffer ever larger payments deficits every year through 1972.

Dollars held by foreigners: See p. 314. Germany's reversal of its balance of payments deficit into surplus is discussed at p. 31 and note.

89 Foreign exchange rates: See pp. 315–318.

90 Overvalued currency as subsidy: The effect of unnatural foreign exchange valuations, as a subsidy by one sector of a nation to another sector of the same nation (such as a subsidy by export industries to all other sectors in a high-inflation nation) is noted by Shoup, *Public Finance* (Chicago: Aldine, 1969), p. 455. The im-

portance of this effect to the lives of individuals in every country is enormous but very little noticed.

91 Keynes: See p. 31 and note.

Chapter 13

94 No New Economist heard to recant: A disarming expression of humility is that of Arthur Okun, Chairman of President Johnson's Council of Economic Advisers, in his book *Prosperity*. Of this beguiling confession, Leonard Silk said, "Economists are modest today because they have much to be modest about." New York *Times*, March 9, 1970, p. 53.

Chapter 14

97 Junius Paulus: The Roman Junius Paulus in the third century is cited by Fisher, *Purchasing Power*, p. 14, n. 1, as affirming the money-quantity explanation for price inflation.

Keynes' preface: *General Theory*, p. v.

Chapter 15

102 Supply and demand: See Samuelson, *Economics*, pp. 57–72. Professor Samuelson quotes an anonymous source as follows:

"You can make even a parrot into a learned political economist —all he must learn are the two words 'supply' and 'demand.' " *Ibid.*, p. 57.

Quantity of money: The definition of money limited to dollar bills, coins, and checking accounts is known as "M_1".

The Federal Reserve System publishes a weekly release showing estimated total quantities of money as M_1 as well as other components and totals. These figures are both absolute and seasonally adjusted, and they are recapitulated by week and for recent months in *F. R. Bulletin*. This book uniformly uses M_1, seasonally adjusted, for prevailing quantities of money supply.

103 Equation: The equation is a modification of the "equation of exchange" developed especially by Irving Fisher (see note to p. 104).

104 Quantity theory: Jean Bodin, *Response to the Paradoxes of Monsieur de Malestroict* (Paris: Jacques du Pays, 1568; reprinted Washington, D. C.: Country Dollar, 1947); Fisher, *Purchasing Power*, who also on p. 14, n. 1, lists Locke, Hume, Adam Smith, Ricardo, Mill, and Marshall, along with Junius Paulus of 200 A.D., among the endorsers of quantity theory; Pigou, "The Value of Money," *Quarterly Journal of Economics*, vol. 32, pp. 38–65 (November, 1917).

Notes

Milton Friedman: Examples of Professor Friedman's statements and restatements of the quantity theory of inflation are in Friedman (ed.) *Quantity Theory; Monetary Stability; Dollars and Deficits;* and *Optimum Quantity.*

Foolish to deny: Keynes, *Monetary Reform,* p. 42. At *ibid.,* p. 74, Keynes further observed that quantity theory's "correspondence with fact is not open to question."

Helfferich: *Money,* vol. 2, pp. 446–463.

Chapter 16

107 Delayed response of price inflation to money inflation: No better statement exists than Keynes' in *Monetary Reform,* pp. 74–86. Acknowledging the money-quantity theory that in the long run prices must conform to quantity, Keynes added that "in the long run we are all dead." In other words, quantity changes will affect other things before prices, and perhaps price changes will be postponed permanently. This is undeniably a true possibility.

109 "Cost-push, demand-pull": See, for example, Samuelson, *Economics,* pp. 332–334. Milton Friedman notes that governments have loved to blame cost-push forces for inflation at least since the Emperor Diocletian. *Dollars and Deficits,* p. 97.

110 Inflation always and everywhere a monetary phenomenon: Friedman, *Dollars and Deficits,* p. 98.

Fighting against quantity theory: An interesting example of Keynesians' reaction against quantity theory is the book review by Joan Robinson, an associate of Keynes at Cambridge, of the English translation of Bresciani-Turroni, *Inflation. Economic Journal,* vol. 48, p. 507 (1938). Mrs. Robinson called Bresciani-Turroni's money-quantity interpretation "old-fashioned," dismissed the instant and simultaneous halt of money inflation and price inflation as evidence that money quantity had been causing the inflation, and insisted that rising wages (or cost-push) had caused it. Lord Keynes' own contemporaneous views, as set forth in *Monetary Reform,* had however corresponded perfectly with those of Bresciani-Turroni.

Chapter 17

113 Liquidity preference: Keynes, *General Theory,* chapter 15.

114 Korean War inflation: See pp. 59–60 and notes.

"Income velocity" and "transactions velocity": Useful discussions of the alternative measures of velocity and their deficiencies are Selden, "Monetary Velocity in the United States," reprinted in Friedman (ed.), *Quantity Theory;* and Garvy and Blyn, *The Velocity of Money* (Federal Reserve Bank of New York, paperback, 1969).

Page

The ratio of checking account payments to balances ("transactions velocity") is published monthly in *F. R. Bulletin*. Tabulated past data are found in Board of Governors, Federal Reserve System, *Banking and Monetary Statistics* (1943), p. 254, and *1966 Supplement*, p. 12, and *F. R. Bulletin*, July 1972, pp. 634–635.

The hybrid and invalid nature of income velocity is affirmed by Keynes, *A Treatise on Money* (New York: Harcourt Brace, 1930), vol. 2, p. 24:

"It is as though we were to divide the passenger miles travelled in an hour by passengers in trams by the aggregate number of passengers in trams and trains and to call the result a 'velocity.'"

115 **Rate of increase of velocity:** Income velocity (GNP divided by money supply) ws 1.9 in 1946 and 4.9 in second quarter 1973, for an increase of 158 percent. Transactions velocity (as measured in banks outside New York and six other leading cities so as to exclude in a rough way the distortive effects of purely financial transactions) was 14.1 and 53.4 for an increase of 279 percent or a compounded rate of 4.8 percent per year for 27 years. The rate of increase of transactions velocity was more than twice as high if financial-center banks were included. Furthermore, the rate of increase of velocity was accelerating, averaging almost 7 percent per year from 1964 to 1973.

Money, velocity and GNP: Money quantity increased from $108 billion in 1946 to $260.7 billion in second quarter 1973, a factor of 2.41. The factor of 2.41 multiplied by that of 3.79 for velocity (preceding note) is a factor of 9.1 for aggregate demand. Gross national product in constant (1958) dollars increased by only 2.58, from $312.6 billion to $834.3 billion.

Quantity leads and velocity follows: These usual relationships between movements of money quantity and money velocity are observed in Keynes, *Monetary Reform*, pp. 82–83, and at many places in Milton Friedman's writings.

116 **Velocity in the German inflation:** Bresciani-Turroni, *Inflation*, pp. 166–172. The income velocity of marks declined steadily from .92 in 1914 to .43 in June, 1919, at which point the first postwar inflation was already raging. Velocity then rose to a peak of 1.85 in February, 1920, the point at which prices were stabilizing; velocity declined gradually throughout the stable-price era while money supply was expanding, and velocity reached the low level of .99 in July, 1921, the last month of stable prices. Velocity next began to rise smartly, though somewhat irregularly, to reach 2.97 in July, 1922. It then leaped up to 9.01 in November and remained mostly between 5 and 10 through the larger part of 1923. Velocity rose to almost 18 (forty times its postwar low) in October, 1923, and was unmeasured but astronomical after that.

Notes

Page

Cagan, "The Monetary Dynamics of Hyperinflation," in Friedman (ed.), *Quantity Theory*, examining the German inflation and other extreme European inflations, finds that velocity inflations were never spontaneous but always came as a psychological reaction to past quantity and price inflations.

Keynes, *Monetary Reform*, pp. 45–48, also observed that increasing velocity and a diminishing real value of the money supply were the normal and not extraordinary results of past quantity inflation.

117 Velocity falling when inflation stops: The delicate task of feeding in just the right (large) amounts of new money quantity to offset velocity plummeting back to normal when inflation ends, a perfectly necessary and proper expansion of money quantity, is well analyzed in the German case by Bresciani-Turroni, *Inflation*, pp. 345–349, and Graham, *Hyperinflation*, pp. 289–290.

118 Price equation criticized as a tautology: See, for example, Samuelson, *Economics*, p. 270.

Chapter 18

120 Price declines, nineteenth century: Friedman & Schwartz, *Monetary History*, chapter 3, pp. 89–134.

Supply of values equated to gross national product: This fundamental error is illustrated in Samuelson's basically unsympathetic treatment of the equation of exchange, *Economics*, pp. 269–272.

121 Two money supplies: Among those who have mentioned in passing but not deeply explored the employment of money in markets other than GNP are Keynes, *A Treatise on Money* (New York: Harcourt Brace, 1930); Helfferich, *Money*, vol. 2, pp. 448; and Fisher, *Purchasing Power*, chapter IX.

The Great Depression, which was caused by the Federal Reserve's money contraction, probably resulted from its misunderstanding of money quantity and velocity in the two markets. The Federal Reserve began to contract overall money quantity in 1928 in order to dampen speculative fever and price inflation in the stock market. But there was no real money inflation or price inflation elsewhere, and overall money quantity should not have been contracted. Total money quantity was stable and so were prices of national product. A purely velocity inflation was occurring in the capital market which probably would have passed over of its own accord, like most velocity inflations, or at worst could have been punctured simply by tighter securities credit without any money deflation.

122 Money requirements in capital markets: For stock sales on exchanges, see note to p. 74; money supply, note to p. 66; GNP, note to p. 70.

$3.2 trillion of money claims: *Statistical Abstract, 1972*, p. 438.

Notes

Page

This figure represents total financial liabilities, less money supply and corporate stocks.

High velocity in financial centers: In 1973, the ratio of annual payments from checking accounts to account balances in New York was about 230 (compared with about 250 business days in a year), while it was 53.4 in the rest of the nation. *F. R. Bulletin*, August, 1973, p. A14.

124 Money and stocks in Germany: See pp. 17–18, 27–28, 41 and notes.

Chapter 19

128 National wealth: The national wealth in tangible assets was estimated to be of about $3 trillion in value in 1968, and of this total $715 billion was land, $1.5 trillion was buildings, and $610 billion was equipment. *Statistical Abstract*, 1972, p. 337.

129 Money wealth $3.2 trillion: See note to p. 122.

131 Other uses of money supply: Besides capital markets and paper wealth, there are several other important uses of money which absorb money quantity and purchasing power although they do not add to the supply of real values. One is *intermediate transactions*. Gross national product only measures final products, but does not measure how many purchases and sales of intermediate products and services were necessary for each dollar of final sales. A rough estimate of the magnitude of intermediate transactions can be obtained by comparing corporate *sales* ($1.8 trillion in 1972) with corporate *gross product* ($644 billion in 1972) for a ratio of total sales to final sales of about three to one. *Current Business*, July, 1973, Tables 1.14 and 6.19. If this ratio held good for all national product, intermediate sales would require about twice as much money as final sales or gross national product itself. Similarly, large sums of money are needed each year for non-sales transfers such as taxes and transfer payments by governments to citizens. These money requirements, while large, are relatively invariable and therefore not likely to absorb at first and later disgorge inflationary potential as capital markets do.

Chapter 20

132 Government deficits: The strange evolution of the budget deficit as a magic talisman is well traced in Stein, *Fiscal Revolution*. See Milton Friedman in his two-man symposium with Walter Heller, *Monetary vs. Fiscal Policy* (New York: Norton, 1969).

133 Open market operations: When the Federal Reserve sells government bonds, it also absorbs money from the money supply which Treasury sales do not do more than momentarily. The deflationary

Page

effect of Federal Reserve sales is therefore twice as pronounced as that of Treasury sales, but this does not destroy the basic similarity of effect.

135 **Government surplus to fight inflation:** This futile defense was also the liberal Keynesians' first line of defense in the later 1960's, and it failed like the Maginot Line with predictable completeness. See Okun, *Prosperity,* admitting the failure but still not understanding it.

Chapter 21

137 **Prices and money, 1939 to 1948:** Money increased by a factor of 3.5, prices by only 2.0. See pp. 53–56 and notes. Velocity in nonfinancial centers declined from 19.5 in 1939 to a low of 13.5 in 1945 and recovered to 16.6 in 1948. See sources cited in note to p. 114. Gross national product increased from $209.4 billion to $323.7 billion in constant (1958) dollars, and Federal debt from $40 billion to $252 billion (*Statistical Abstract,* 1969; p. 392).

138 **Correspondence of prices and money, 1948 to 1962:** See pp. 55, 59, 61–62, and notes. The average annual increase of money from late 1949 to September, 1962 was 2.2 percent, that of wholesale prices 1.5 percent, and the difference is the 0.7 percent annual money growth which apparently could be tolerated without producing price inflation.

Velocity increase 4.8 percent per year: See p. 115 and notes.

139 **Index of Latent Inflation:** The Index of Latent Inflation is calculated as follows, using December, 1968 as an example. The factor of money expansion since September, 1962 ($201.6 billion divided by $149.4 billion, or 134.9 percent) is first determined and then divided by a non-inflationary factor of increase based on 0.7 percent compounded per year (104.5 percent), yielding an *equilibrium price factor* of 129.1 percent of 1962. Since wholesale prices in December, 1968 (103.6) had been only 109.3 percent of the average in late 1962 (94.8), the equilibrium price factor was 18.1 percent higher than the actual wholesale price index, and this was the Index of Latent Inflation. By December, 1972, this Index of Latent Inflation calculated in the same way had increased to 22.8 percent.

Chapter 22

142 **Gold as money:** The superiority of valueless fiat money to any kind of commodity currency, including gold, is endorsed by both Keynes (*Monetary Reform,* p. 172, referring to gold as a "barbarous relic") and Friedman ("Commodity-Reserve Currency," reprinted in Friedman, *Positive Economics*).

Value of money: Helfferich's dissertation of whether money has

Page

value in itself is in *Money*, vol. 2, pp. 493–509. The correct idea that money itself is a perfect cipher among real values derives from John Stuart Mill's epochal work, *Principles of Political Economy* (Ashley ed.; New York: Longmans, Green, 1929), Book III, ch. 7, sec. 6, p. 488.

Chapter 23

146 **Constant value:** The objective of holding prices constant as the ideal goal of money management was espoused by Keynes, *Monetary Reform*, pp. 17, 40, 156, and Helfferich, *Money*, vol. 2, pp. 620–623.

Milton Friedman, chief critic of the Federal Reserve: Professor Friedman's harping on the duty of monetary policy simply to stop being a source of instability itself, as it has constantly been in the past, rings throughout Friedman's works, especially *Monetary Stability* and *Optimum Quantity*, and practically always falls on deaf ears.

147 **Money components:** In June, 1973, when the money supply unadjusted was $261.3 billion, only $59.4 billion was currency compared with $201.8 billion of demand deposits in the hands of banks. As backing for the demand deposits (and other deposits), banks also had reserves of Federal Reserve deposits equal to $25.8 billion. The only government money was the $85.2 billion sum of the currency and bank reserves, and this was less than one-third of the total money supply of $261.3 billion. *F. R. Bulletin*, August, 1973, pp. A5, A16.

148 **Non-monopoly by government of German money creation:** Keynes, *Monetary Reform*, p. 60, n. 1: "The profits of note printing were not even monopolized by the Government, and Herr Havenstein continued to allow German banks to share in them." See also Cagan, "Monetary Dynamics of Hyperinflation," in Friedman (ed.), *Quantity Theory*, and Friedman, *Dollars and Deficits*, p. 37.

Thirteen billion dollars: In the one-year period from June, 1972 to June, 1973, total money supply increased from ˙$243.2 billion to $261.3 billion, or $18.1 billion. The sum of currency in circulation and reserve deposits (i.e., government money), however, increased by only $4.5 billion from $88.9 billion to $93.4 billion. The difference between the $4.5 billion government money increase and the $18.1 billion total money increase was the $13.6 billion that was donated by the government to the banks by allowing them to create it. This flow of gifts to banks had been going on continuously throughout the money inflation since 1962.

150 **Fractional reserves and World War II inflation:** Friedman, *Optimum Quantity*, pp. 165–170.

100 percent reserves: A sampling of the literature advocating 100 percent government reserves against bank demand deposits: Hart, "The 'Chicago Plan' of Banking Reform," *Journal of Economic Studies*, vol. 2, p. 104 (1935); Fisher, *100% Money* (New York: Adelphi, 1935); Simons, *Economic Policy for a Free Society* (Chicago: Univ. of Chicago Press, 1948), pp. 62–63; Tolley, "100 Per Cent Reserve Banking," in Yeager (ed.), *In Search of a Monetary Constitution* (Cambridge, Mass.: Harvard Univ. Press, 1962). Professor Friedman also ranges himself on the side of 100 percent reserves, although not with great urgency. *Dollars and Deficits*, p. 96; *Monetary Stability*, pp. 65–76; *Optimum Quantity*, p. 83.

Shifting to a 100 percent reserve system does present some technical problems, but not serious ones. For some reason, the early advocates thought of this reform as a way to retire Federal debt, because banks would be required to turn in interest-bearing Federal bonds in exchange for their new (non-interest-bearing) reserve deposits. But this is manifestly and totally unfair to banks. The only proper way to shift to 100 percent reserves is to leave banks with all their present income assets and simply to donate the new reserve deposits to them, while at the same time immobilizing the new deposits on the books by the 100 percent reserve requirement.

A second problem is how to compensate banks in the future for operating the checking system if checking accounts can no longer be mostly lent out at interest. Either service charges must increase or the government must subsidize or both. Nothing is free. This is a valid point but in no way undercuts the propriety of shifting to 100 percent reserves. The government's subsidy in the past had been grotesquely in excess of the value of the banks' services. In 1972, for example, when the subsidy to banks was $13.6 billion, commercial banks' total annual operating expenses for such things as salaries, utilities, rent, depreciation and the like were less than $18 billion (*F. R. Bulletin*, May, 1973, pp. A96–A97), and only a minor part of their total operating expenses could be allocated to their simple checking account operations. Whatever service subsidy to the banks might be necessary would be very, very small.

152 **Money issued to the government:** Milton Friedman advocated this radical policy in *Monetary Stability*, p. 59. It is breathtaking to imagine how easily and quickly the monetary problem of the Great Depression could have been solved if this power to issue money to the government, intelligently used, had been available. As we see in chapter 25 of this book, both money quantity and money velocity fell by one-third each in the Depression, and thus aggregate money demand by five-ninths, thus causing the Depression. Massive money expansion by the government would have offset these tendencies, but try as it might the government could not get money to expand. The banks were awash in free reserves, but bankers would not lend and borrowers would not borrow. If the

Page

government could just have issued the right amount of money to itself and spent it, or even given it away to the people, the monetary stringency could have been cured overnight. See pp. 162–163.

Chapter 24

154 **Keynes, involuntary unemployment:** The definition is from Keynes, *General Theory*, p. 15.

155 **Friedman and Schwartz:** The work is cited in these notes as *Monetary History*.

156 **Steady rate of money growth:** This central theme of Professor Friedman's writings appears in one formulation or another in most of them, but is perhaps best stated in *Monetary Stability* (1959) pp. 90–92, and later *Optimum Quantity* (1969), p. 48.

Original proposal 3 to 5 percent per year: Friedman, *Monetary Stability* (1959), p. 91. This proposal was based on an assumption of 3 percent real growth per year, which was not unreasonable, and a *decline* of money velocity of 1 percent per year. In fact, however, money velocity continued to increase at its postwar trend of more than 4 percent per year. See p. 115 of this book and notes.

As to the 3 percent rates of both money expansion and price increases associated with the 1954–1956 inflation and boom, see pp. 62–63 and notes.

157 **Change of mind to 1 or 2 percent per year:** Friedman, *Optimum Quantity* (1969) pp. 46–48. Professor Friedman still said that either 2 percent or 5 percent growth of money, if steady, is better than fluctuation, but only because even a constant inflation, if steady, is less damaging than instability. Friedman, *Dollars and Deficits*, pp. 46–60.

As to the economic conditions resulting from less than 1 percent money growth in 1953–1954, see note to p. 63 of this book.

Chapter 25

158 **Keynes' historic milestone:** The work is cited in these notes as *General Theory*.

We are all Keynesians today: Friedman, *Dollars and Deficits*, p. 15. Professor Friedman was at pains to make clear that he also added, "in another sense, no one is a Keynesian any longer."

159 **Present problems presently:** Keynes' putting aside the possible future problem of inflation when depression is the existing evil is exemplified by this quotation:

"A large amount of deflationary slack has first to be taken up before there can be the smallest danger of a development policy leading to Inflation. To bring up the bogy of Inflation as an

Notes

Page

objection to capital expenditure at the present time is like warning a patient who is wasting away from emaciation of the dangers of excessive corpulence." *Persuasion*, pp. 124–125.

160 **Last conversations:** Keynes was quoted as saying that Keynesians were pushing easy money too far, and that inflation would become the present problem presently, by Williams, "An Appraisal of Keynesian Economics," *American Economic Review*, May, 1948, p. 283, n. 33; and Wright, "Mr. Keynes and the 'Day of Judgment,'" *Science*, November 21, 1958, pp. 1258–1262.

161 **Prices and inflation:** *General Theory*, chapter 21. This was the last theoretical chapter of the book. Keynes said:

"So far, we have been primarily concerned with the way in which changes in the quantity of money affect prices in the short period. But in the long run is there not some simpler relationship? This is a question for historical generalisation rather than for pure theory." *General Theory*, p. 306.

In short, Keynes shrugged off the question of money inflation causing price inflation without an answer.

162 **Government budget deficits:** See chapter 20 of this book.

Monetary inflation a legitimate tool: Compare Friedman, *Dollars and Deficits*, p. 38.

Money quantity and velocity contractions of one-third: Friedman & Schwartz, *Monetary History*, pp. 301–305.

164 **Keynes, "In the long run. . .":** *Monetary Reform*, p. 80. See note to p. 107 of this book.

Supply of values: The gross national product in constant (1958) dollars was $203.6 billion in 1929 and about the same in 1937 and 1939, but only $141.5 billion in 1933 and still only $169.5 billion in 1935. *National Accounts*, Tables 1.1.

Chapter 26

166 "... emphasis on the prefix *general*. . .": Keynes, *General Theory*, p. 3.

167 *Economic Possibilities:* Keynes, "Economic Possibilities for Our Grandchildren," reprinted in *Persuasion*, pp. 358–373.

171 **Tax paid by incautious person caught holding money wealth:** A similarity suggests itself to Keynes' sprightly analogy of stock market speculation to a game of Musical Chairs or Old Maid, the loser being he who is caught without a chair or holding the tainted card. *General Theory*, pp. 155–156.

1962 money inflation $6 billion or 4 percent: See note to p. 66.

Inflating by 4 percent, 3 percent tax: An absolute annual money expansion at 4 percent would be the equivalent of 3.3 percent of

Page	
	inflationary potential, after deducting the 0.7 percent expansion which is assumed to be allowable without inflation. An inflation rate of 3.3 percent produces a tax rate of only 3.2 percent, for the same reason that a price increase of 50 percent reduces the value of money by only 33.3 percent.
	Money wealth and revenues: Total money wealth (debt) in 1962 of $1.8 trillion was well over ten times the money supply of about $149 billion. By 1971 the taxable money wealth had increased from $1.8 trillion to $3.2 trillion. See note to p. 122.
	There is an important qualification to be made in gauging the tax effect as the inflation rate multiplied by the money wealth. The inflationary tax revenue is measured by *net* debt and not *total* debt. If one man is a creditor for $10,000 worth of pension benefits and also a debtor for $10,000 on a home mortgage, the inflationary tax harms him and benefits him in equal amounts, the effects cancel out, and the $20,000 of total debt involving him is in effect eliminated from the inflationary tax base. Net debt in this sense is not capable of close estimation, but it is undoubtedly considerably smaller than total debt. The tax base is still very large.
172	**The inflationary tax:** The quotation is from Keynes, "Inflation as a Method of Taxation," *Manchester Guardian Commercial*, July 27, 1922, pp. 268–269, revised and reprinted in *Monetary Reform*, p. 42. The inflationary tax is also cogently studied by Friedman, *Dollars and Deficits*, pp. 35–39, and Cagan's article in Friedman (ed.), *Quantity Theory*, p. 77. Carl Shoup, *Public Finance* (Chicago: Aldine, 1969), p. 459, says of the inflationary tax:
	"The overriding distributive feature is . . . the absence of any need ever to make an explicit decision on how the burden shall be distributed, even initially. It is this freedom from the need to make up one's mind in order to reach an explicit compromise that is so attractive in a turbulent political environment. Inflationary finance is rarely found under dictatorships, for dictators do not have to compromise; they find it easy to decide where the burden shall rest."
	Professor Shoup somewhat overestimates the real practical power of dictators, considering that Diocletian and Hitler, as examples, were the authors of terrible inflations. His assessment that inflation taxation is a product of government weakness is, however, sound.
173	*A Tract on Monetary Reform:* This work is cited in these notes as *Monetary Reform*.

Chapter 27

178	**Monetary inflation causes high interest rates:** This is one of Milton Friedman's frequent themes. See, for example, *Optimum Quantity*, pp. 99–101; *Dollars and Deficits*, pp. 161–164. Interest

Page

rates were rising almost continuously in the United States after 1946, when they reached historic lows of 2.37 percent for corporate bonds and 2.17 percent for Federal bonds. There were spells of temporarily declining interest rates just after the close of tight money periods, when recessions reduced demand for loans at the same time that easy money increased the supply, as in 1949–1950, 1954, 1958, 1960–1963, and 1971. Each time the rise of interest rates resumed and redoubled as inflation returned.

179 Real interest: The difference between nominal interest and real interest was remarked by Keynes, *Monetary Reform*, p. 20, who also noted at p. 29 the blurring of the distinction between income and capital in inflationary conditions of high nominal interest rates. See also Friedman, *Optimum Quantity*, p. 101.

180 "Euthanasia of the rentier": Keynes, *General Theory*, p. 376.

". . . continuously disinheriting fortunes . . .": Keynes, *Monetary Reform*, p. 10.

". . . rentier aspect . . . transitional": Keynes, *General Theory*, p. 376.

181 Continuous loss of value of money wealth: In Germany, the ability of borrowers to take value from lenders until the bitter end of the inflation, even at fantastically high (but not high enough) interest rates, was recorded by Keynes, *Monetary Reform*, pp. 20–24.

Rentiers not rich men: In 1971, the total assets of life insurance companies were $222 billion, virtually all in money obligations. *Statistical Abstract*, 1972, p. 461. Savings and loan associations held $206 billion and mutual savings banks $90 billion. *Ibid.*, pp. 448–449. Public and private non-insured pension plans added another $242 billion of book value, of which $160 billion was in money obligations. Securities and Exchange Commission, *Statistical Bulletin*, vol. 32, no. 8 (April 4, 1973).

Helfferich's observation that, in Germany too, the losers of the money wealth were the smaller citizens is in *Money*, vol. 2, p. 546.

182 Maximum burden of real debt: Keynes, *Monetary Reform*, p. 64.

183 Inversion of interest rates and common stock yields: In 1950, common stock yields averaged 6.3 percent and corporate bond interest 2.86 percent. By 1968, however, corporate bonds yielded 6.5 percent and common stock 3.2 percent. *Statistical Abstract*, 1972, p. 456. Corporate stock yields remained remarkably steady just above 3 percent from 1962 on.

Fixed interest a barbarous relic: It was gold that Keynes called the "barbarous relic," *Monetary Reform*, p. 172, but in the same work, pp. 1–17, he linked the heyday of fixed-interest capital to the historically unprecedented era of stable prices from the Napoleonic Wars to the end of the nineteenth century.

Page
184 **Constant-value loans:** Marshall, "Remedies for Fluctuations of General Prices," *Contemporary Review*, March 1887, reprinted in Pigou (ed.), *Memorials of Alfred Marshall* (London: Macmillan, 1925), p. 188. Fisher, *Purchasing Power*, also devoted chapter X to this subject. As to Germany, see note to p. 21 of this book.

Chapter 30

197 **Excessive saving, insufficient consuming:** Chronic oversaving and underconsumption can fairly be taken as the main thrust of Keynes' entire *General Theory*, and the one which is generally disregarded by all latter-day economics including "Keynesian" economics.

199 **Capital taxes:** Many of the ideas of this book regarding the need for capital taxes and its reasons are intimated in Alan A. Tait's excellent work, *The Taxation of Personal Wealth* (Urbana: Univ. of Illinois Press, 1967).

Chapter 31

204 **Net worth taxes:** Shoup, *Public Finance* (Chicago: Aldine, 1969), ch. 14; Netzer, *Economics of the Property Tax* (Washington: Brookings, 1966), Table 1–4, pp. 14–15.
Yield of $30 billion: Total privately-owned property was estimated to be about $2.46 trillion in 1968. Two percent of that would have been $49.2 billion, less the $27.7 billion of real estate taxes already being realized in that year. The resulting $21.5 billion net yield, multiplied by a factor of 1.33 for rising prices from 1968 to 1973, would have produced a net yield of $28.6 billion in 1973. Figures from *Statistical Abstract*, 1972, pp. 337 and 415.
Real estate taxes: Netzer, *Economics of the Property Tax* (Washington: Brookings, 1966). The estimate of 1.4 percent average real estate taxes is at p. 103, Table 5–4.

205 **Inheritance tax revenue:** The figures are for 1970. States also collected less than $1 billion in inheritance taxes. *Statistical Abstract*, 1972, p. 412.

206 **Inheritance tax authorities:** Shultz, *The Taxation of Inheritance* (Boston: Houghton Mifflin, 1926); Eisenstein, "The Rise and Fall of the Estate Tax," *Federal Tax Policy for Economic Growth and Stability*, 84th Cong., 1st Sess. (1955).
"The estate tax ... desirable. ... :" Hoover, *Memoirs* (New York: Macmillan, 1952), Vol. 2, p. 29.
"Its inadequacies methodically increase. . .": Eisenstein, *op. cit.*, p. 833.
Inheritance versus income: Mill, *Principles of Political Economy*, (Ashley ed.; New York: Longmans, Green, 1929), bk. 2, ch. 2, pp. 219, 228–229; Keynes, *General Theory*, pp. 373–374. Keynes

also had this to say in "Am I A Liberal?" reprinted in *Persuasion*, p. 327:

"I believe that the seeds of the intellectual decay of Individual Capitalism are to be found in an institution which is not in the least characteristic of itself, but which it took over from the social system of Feudalism which preceded it,—namely, the hereditary principle. The hereditary principle in the transmission of wealth and the control of business is the reason why the leadership of the Capitalist Cause is weak and stupid. It is too much dominated by third-generation men. Nothing will cause a social institution to decay with more certainty than its attachment to the hereditary principle."

207 Simons, inheritance as income: Simons, *Personal Income Taxation* (Chicago: Univ. of Chicago Press, 1938), p. 125.

Exemptions and deductions: It seems clear that the deduction for charitable bequests should be kept lest charitable organizations be abolished too. It also seems clear that some reasonable exemption for inheritance by surviving spouses or other dependents-in-fact should be kept, especially where the tax will otherwise be made to apply to much smaller estates than formerly.

35 percent tax, $35 billion yield: If the total private non-institutional wealth is estimated to be $3.2 trillion in 1973, based on $2.4 trillion in 1968 (see note to p. 204) multiplied by a price factor of 1.33, a 35 percent tax would yield $35 billion per year if the total wealth was transferred by death or gift only every 32 years on average. As much as $700 billion of the private wealth could be effectively removed from the tax flow by dependency deductions and ownership by charitable organizations, without reducing the tax yield, if the average rate of transfer was once every 25 years.

208 Capital gains taxes: Blum, "A Handy Summary of the Capital Gains Arguments," *Taxes*, vol. 35, p. 247 (1957); Simons, *Personal Income Taxation* (Chicago: Univ. of Chicago Press, 1938), pp. 148 ff.

209 Keynes, transfer taxes: *General Theory*, p. 160.

Inflation adjustment and ordinary income: Corbin, "New Proposals for Capital Gains Taxation," *Taxes*, vol. 34, pp. 663 (1956).

Revenue loss: If *all* revenue from capital gains taxes in 1970, for example, were lost, the total would be no more than about $3.5 billion. *Statistical Abstract*, 1972, p. 393.

210 Elimination of corporate taxes: Friedman, *Capitalism and Freedom*, p. 132.

211 Loss of revenue: If net corporate income for 1969 had been taxed at 35 percent, the net loss from actual tax yield would have been

Notes

Page

about $5 billion. *Statistical Abstract*, 1972, p. 396. Taxable dividends were $15 billion, so that another $5 billion or so might be lost by eliminating that tax. *Ibid.*, p. 393.

Progressive income taxes: The best analysis of progressive income taxes is probably Blum and Kalven, *The Uneasy Case for Progressive Taxation* (Chicago: Univ. of Chicago Press, 1953). See also Smith, "High Progressive Tax Rates," *Univ. of Florida Law Review*, vol. 20, pp. 451–463 (1968); Friedman, *Capitalism and Freedom*, pp. 172–176.

Produced very little revenue: In 1970, the total tax revenue from individual income taxes was only an average of 20.9 percent of total taxable income (*Statistical Abstract*, 1972, p. 393), which was precisely the same effective rate of tax that a single taxpayer would pay on only $10,000 of taxable income.

"The moment you abandon. . .": Blum and Kalven, *op. cit.*, p. 45, quoting McCulloch, *Taxation and the Funding System* (1845), p. 142.

213 **Single-rate tax, $100 billion per year:** Total taxable income of individuals plus personal exemptions added back in was $508 billion in 1970. Thirty-five percent of that would have been about $178 billion, compared with actual income tax revenue of about $84 billion. *Statistical Abstract*, 1972, p. 393.

Every taxpayer more cash in hand: A family of two adults and two children would approximately break even under the 1973 tax structure as compared with a flat 35 percent tax plus national dividend of $1200 for adults and $600 for children at the level of $27,000 gross income before exemptions, which is the point above which additional income was taxed at more than 35 percent in 1973. In either case, this family would have about $21,000 left after taxes. A higher-income taxpayer would do better under the flat 35 percent tax than under the 1973 structure. A lower-income taxpayer would also do much better because the national dividend would become proportionately more important. At $10,000 gross, for example, a family of this size would have only $8,810 left after taxes under 1973 taxes but would have $10,100 at a 35 percent tax rate plus national dividend. Personal deductions are disregarded here on the assumption that none would be abolished and no tax increase would result.

Chapter 32

218 **National dividend replacing all distribution systems:** It seems obvious that Social Security benefits already being paid which were larger than the national dividend would have to be preserved until such time as the national dividend could exceed them.

220 **Cost of national dividend:** The lowest population projection for

Notes

Page

1975 was 77.1 million below age 20 and 138.6 million above that age. *Statistical Abstract, 1972*, pp. 8-9.
Social Security, etc.: Costs of social welfare plans are for 1972 and are from *Current Business*, July 1973, p. 35. Costs of subsidy programs are Federal programs only, exclusive of tax subsidies, for the year 1970 from *Statistical Abstract, 1972*, p. 390. State and Federal payroll taxes for Social Security and unemployment also amounted to $30 billion in 1970, much of which would no longer be needed after a national dividend superseded those programs.

221 Rhys-Williams, *Something to Look Forward To:* London: Mac-Donald, 1943.
Friedman: *Capitalism and Freedom*, ch. 12, pp. 190–195. See also Green, *Negative Taxes and the Poverty Problem* (Washington, D. C.: Brookings, 1967).

Chapter 33

225 Lack of need for work: Keynes treated this situation in "Economic Possibilities for Our Grandchildren" (1930), reprinted in *Persuasion*, p. 358.
226 "Phillips curve": Phillips and Lipsey, "The Relationship Between Unemployment and the Rate of Change of Money Wage Rates in the United Kingdom, 1861–1957," *Economica*, vol. 25, p. 283 (November 1958), and vol. 27, p. 1 (February 1960).
227 Keynes' definition of full employment: *General Theory*, p. 15.
229 No involuntary unemployment: Possibly the involuntary unemployment might not be so fully eliminated by free market forces as this suggests for the reasons argued by Keynes' *General Theory*. If not, there is no objection to the government's serving as "employer of last resort," offering some kind of useful work to everyone who cannot find it in the private free market, so long as the wages the government offers in this employment are lower than those in the free market and do not compete with that market.

Chapter 35

241 Conventional liberals impostors: Friedman, *Capitalism and Freedom*, pp. 5–6. Schumpeter, *History of Economic Analysis* (New York: Oxford Univ. Press, 1954), p. 394:
"As a supreme, if unintended, compliment, the enemies of the system of private enterprise have thought it wise to appropriate its label [i.e., *liberalism*]."
244 Keynes, "Am I A Liberal?": Reprinted in *Persuasion*, p. 323.
245 Keynes, "The Conservative Party ought . . .": *Ibid.*, pp. 326–327.

Page

Keynes, "I am ever more convinced. . .": "Democracy and Efficiency," *New Statesman and Nation*, vol. 17, p. 121.

247 Lysenko: Joravsky, *The Lysenko Affair* (Cambridge, Mass.: Harvard Univ. Press, 1970).

Poincaré, war too important: Friedman, *Dollars and Deficits*, p. 173. Friedman also attributed the same saying to Clemenceau. *Ibid.*, p. 94.

248 Epidemic of mathematics: Compare Keynes, *General Theory*, pp. 297–298:

"Too large a proportion of recent 'mathematical' economics are mere concoctions, as imprecise as the initial assumptions they rest on, which allow the author to lose sight of the complexities and interdependencies of the real world in a maze of pretentious and unhelpful symbols."

249 Friedman, rules rather than men: *Dollars and Deficits*, pp. 177–194.

Benjamin Strong: *Ibid.*, pp. 187–188; Friedman, *Monetary History*, p. 692; Snyder, *Capitalism the Creator* (New York: Macmillan, 1940), p. 203.

250 ". . . economists . . . dentists. . .": Keynes, "Economic Possibilities for Our Grandchildren" (1930), reprinted in *Persuasion*, p. 373.

Chapter 36

254 Index of Latent Inflation: See p. 139 and note. Wholesale prices were 6.5 percent higher than a year before in December 1972, compared with only 2.8 percent higher in December 1968.

255 Budget deficit: The deficit for the fiscal year ended June 1968 had been $25 billion. *U. S. Budget.*

Price inflation: Wholesale prices in December 1968 were 2.8 percent higher and consumer prices 4.7 percent higher, than a year before.

Money inflation: Money supply in December 1968 was 7.8 percent larger than a year before. The peak rate in the Korean War was about 5.8 percent in early 1952.

256 Balanced budget: The deficit was reduced to a low $2.8 billion in fiscal 1970.

Money inflation dropping: In April 1969, money supply was $205.7 billion, or 8 percent higher than a year before. In April 1970, it was $213.6 billion, or only 3.8 percent higher.

Stock prices: The *Standard & Poor's* index peaked at 115.64 in the week of May 16, 1969, fell to 99.50 in the last week of July, and continued to a bottom of 79.42 in the week of May 29, 1970.

Notes

Page

Interest rates: Banks' prime rate, which had been near 6 percent in 1968, reached 8½ percent by June, 1970. Prime commercial paper which had been below 6 percent in 1968, also exceeded 8 percent by June 1970. *F. R. Bulletin.*

Business recession: The index of industrial production, which had averaged 110.7 for 1969, sank as low as 102.6 in November 1970. *F. R. Bulletin.* The gross national product in constant dollars was lower in every quarter of 1970 than a year earlier. *Current Business,* July 1973, p. 18. Unemployment, from 3.5 percent in 1969, reached 6.2 percent in December 1970. *F. R. Bulletin.*

Prices: Wholesale prices, which had been 3.8 percent higher than the year before in May 1969 when the tightness began, were also 3.7 percent higher in May 1970 when it ended. The comparable rate of consumer price increase actually rose from 5.4 percent to 6.2 percent. In both cases, the rate of increase abated a little for a few months around the end of 1970 when the brief recession was at its worst, but quickly accelerated again in 1971.

258 Budget deficit: The government's deficit was back up to more than $23 billion in each of the next three fiscal years, 1971, 1972, and 1973. *U. S. Budget.*

Renewed money inflation at 6.5 percent: The August 1970 money increase was a full $1.3 billion, and the total increase in the next twelve months was actually over 8 percent, from $216 billion to $234.1 billion. After that it tapered down to a steady 6.5 percent from 1971 to 1973.

Chapter 37

259 6.5 percent annual money increase: See note to p. 258. From July 1971 to July 1973 money increased from $234.1 billion to $264.6 billion, or 6.5 percent per year. It was seldom less than 6 percent or more than 7 percent above the preceding year for longer than a month or two.

260 Stock market: The *Standard & Poor's* index rose from its bottom of about 80 in July 1970, just before the money expansion began, to 115.35 in the week of April 30, 1971, a rise of over 44 percent to a level about as high as its 1968–1969 peaks.

Interest rates: Rates on prime commercial paper, which had been above 8 percent in July 1970, rapidly declined to less than 6 percent by the end of 1970 and less than 4 percent by early 1972. *F. R. Bulletin.*

Prosperity returned: The rate of annual gain of gross national product in constant dollars from the previous year accelerated in every quarter after 1970, from a decline in 1970 to a gain of 1.9 percent in the first quarter of 1971 and 7 percent in the last quarter of 1972.

Notes

Page

Price inflation: See note to p. 256. Both wholesale prices and consumer prices had moderated their inflation a bit in the winter but were worse than ever by summer. Wholesale prices were especially worrisome, having risen at a 6.1 percent annual rate in the first six months of 1971 from 111.0 in December to 114.3 in June.

August 15, 1971 price controls: New York *Times*, August 16, 1971, pp. 1, 14–15.

262 Keynes, "not least part of evils": See note to p. 35.
263 Korean War comparison: See pp. 59–60 and notes.
265 Paid hardly half the cost: See notes to pp. 138–139. In December 1972, when the money supply was $255.5 billion, the money expansion since September 1962, after discounting for an assumed non-inflationary rate of 0.7 percent per pear, was still an inflationary expansion of 59 percent; while the wholesale price index, at 122.9, had increased by only half that or 29.6 percent. Since President Nixon's entry in January 1969, the discounted monetary inflation had been about 23 percent, while wholesale prices, at only 19 percent, still had not risen as much as money inflation. The raging inflation that broke out in 1973 when controls were loosened greatly reduced the Index of Latent Inflation and was the only healthful thing that was happening in 1973. By June 1973, when wholesale prices had increased a full 11 percent in six months, the Index of Latent Inflation had accordingly fallen to only 13.4 percent, which was somewhat lower than it had been when President Johnson turned the mess over to President Nixon.

266 Helfferich, "crises and catastrophes": See note to p. 34. John E. Sheehan, a member of the Board of Governors of the Federal Reserve System, pleaded much the same helplessness as Helfferich: "If you listen to Milton Friedman, all we have to do is choke back on the money supply and we can squeeze inflation out of the economy. Sure, we can do that. But the economy will start downhill on a toboggan, and people will be out of work. The day is past when the American people will tolerate high unemployment as socially acceptable." *Wall Street Journal*, May 7, 1973, p. 19.

Chapter 38

268 President Truman's special message: See p. 56 and note.
269 Equilibrium 168 percent of 1962 prices: See notes to pp. 138–139 and 265. At the established 6.5 percent rate of expansion, money supply in December 1973 would be $272 billion, or 182 percent of September 1962. Discounted for a permissible growth of 0.7 percent per year, that would give an equilibrium price index of 168 percent of September 1962. This would be 30 percent higher

Page

than wholesale prices of December 1972, which were 129.6 percent of September 1962.

Zero money growth: Zero money growth is relative, not absolute. It depends on what velocity and the supply of values are doing. According to all past history, an absolute money growth of about 0.7 percent per year would be a zero money growth relatively.

270 **100 billion new dollars:** See note to p. 269. If the money supply in December 1973 was $272 billion, an addition of $100 billion would represent a 37 percent increase to $372 billion. That in turn would be 249 percent of the $149.4 billion of September 1962, or, discounted for permissible growth at 0.7 percent per year, an equilibrium price level of 230.1 percent. Equilibrium prices at that level would be 77 percent higher than in December 1972, when they stood at 129.6 percent of 1962.

"Immense access of inflation": Graham, *Hyperinflation*, p. 289; Bresciani-Turroni, *Inflation*, pp. 337–340.

Chapter 39

278 **Stabilized inflation:** Friedman, *Dollars and Deficits*, pp. 46–60. See pp. 173–174 of this book.

280 **Friedmanite steady trend:** See note to p. 156.

As 1973 wore on: Interest on prime commercial paper and the prime rate both increased from less than 6 percent in January to more than 9 percent in August. The stock market (*Standard and Poor's*) declined from 133.92 in the week of January 13 to 113.73 in the week of August 24. Price controls were somewhat relaxed (Phase III) by President Nixon in January; wholesale prices rose by 11 percent in the six months to June; another freeze (Phase III½) was temporarily imposed; food shortages developed; and revised controls (Phase IV) were substituted for the freeze in August. Although slowdown and recession were being widely anticipated, by summer of 1973 there was not yet any outward sign of deteriorating business.

282 **Keynes foreseeing U. S. inflation:** "The Economic Consequences of Mr. Churchill" (1925), reprinted in *Persuasion*, p. 265, n. 1.

283 **Comparison of latent inflations:** See p. 140.

284 **Shakespeare's Mercutio:** *Romeo and Juliet*, Act III, Scene 1.

Chapter 40

286 **Inflation the plague of weak governments:** See note to p. 172.

Chapter 41

294 **"Parliamentary bedbugs:"** Hitler, *Mein Kampf* (Boston: Houghton Mifflin, 1943), p. 104.

Page

Lenin's judgment: See p. 29 and note.
Fisher's aphorism: Fisher, *100% Money* (New York: Adelphi, 1935), p. 200.

Chapter 42

300 Total debt 3.2 trillion: See note to p. 122.
301 "Indexed" debt: See pp. 184–186.
302 Germany: The Christian Democrats (CDU) remained the plurality party through 1973, but in 1966 Chancellor Erhard was forced out and the CDU forced to accept the Social Democrats (SPD) into a "grand coalition," with Karl Schiller of the SPD becoming the very dominant Minister of Economics. Following the elections of 1969, the Social Democrats, though still second in strength, formed their own coalition and took over. German industrial wholesale prices had increased by less than 5 percent *in total* in the seventeen years from 1951 to 1968, but by 1973 they were increasing by more than that in a single year. German money supply increased at more than 10 percent per year from 1966 on, compared with only 6.8 percent per year 1961 to 1966. These figures are derived from International Monetary Fund, *International Financial Statistics*, September 1973 and *1972 Supplement*.

Hardly any nation: No industrial nation was even in the running. The only nation reporting to the IMF which in 1973 had averaged no more than about 2 percent per year price inflation since 1963, was still close to that, and was not letting its money supply explode with danger for the future, was Senegal. Venezuela and Morocco were marginal, with price inflation not serious yet but money expansion substantially faster than in earlier years. Examples of countries that had stood fast up to about 1969 to 1971, but then slipped into rapid money expansion followed by price inflation, were the Dominican Republic, Malaysia, and all the Central American states of Guatemala, Honduras, Costa Rica, and Nicaragua. In May of 1973, the *average* consumer price inflation over the year-earlier month in the United States, Canada, Japan, and industrial Europe was over 8 percent, and at the close of 1972 the average one-year increase in money supply had been over 16 percent. These data are from International Monetary Fund, *International Financial Statistics*, September 1973, pp. 34–35.

303 Farmland: The index of value of farmland increased by a factor of 5.7, from 23 to 107, between 1939 and 1968, compared with a factor of only 2.6 for the wholesale price index in the same period. A large part of that rise occurred between 1943 and 1951, when the land value index more than doubled, while it did not double again until 1966. Prices that farmers received trebled from 1939 to 1951, but they were never again as high as in 1951 until the inflationary

Page

frenzy of 1973. Farm prices that rise high in inflationary blowoffs have a way of falling back sharply, as they did from-1919 to 1921, or from 1951 to 1956. The only years since 1913 in which farm income was above 100 percent of parity (the ratio of farm prices received to expenses paid in 1910–1914) were the extreme inflationary years of 1916 to 1919 and 1942 to 1951, and the years after 1960 and before 1973 were mostly in the range of 70 percent of parity, the same range as the depression years of 1934 or 1938. U. S. Dept. of Agriculture, *Agricultural Statistics*, 1972, pp. 502–503, 553.

Chapter 43

307 Stock market and money inflation: The monetary interpretation of the stock market is also made by Sprinkel, *Money and Markets* (Homewood, Ill.: Richard D. Irwin, 1971).

No capital gains without inflation: This is moderately an overstatement. If a growth in the real value of the nation resumed, such as it enjoyed up to 1960, there would be net increases in real capital values, but they would be rare and precious as gold.

1948 and 1954: The stock market index (*Standard & Poor's*) stood at 14.65 in September 1946, 14.55 almost three years later in July 1949, and in between varied no lower than 13.88 and no higher than 16.65. The accompanying stability is described at pp. 55–56 and notes. For the 1952-1954 period, the index was at 26.29 in December 1952, 26.72 in March 1954, and mostly between 24 and 26 in the interim. It had reached 24 in September 1951. The accompanying stability is discussed in note to p. 63.

309 Stock market bottoms and money supply: The low of the stock market (*Standard & Poor's*) of 79.42 in the week of May 29, 1970 was 42.2 percent above its low of 55.85 in the week of June 29, 1962. The money supply in May 1970 was $214.6 billion, or 43.2 percent higher than the $149.9 billion in June 1962.

311 As had been true in Germany: A most illuminating study of which businesses did well and which did not after the stabilization in Germany is in Bresciani-Turroni, *Inflation*, pp. 368–383.

Chapter 44

314 Foreigners' holdings: Federal Reserve Bank of St. Louis *Review*, January 1973, p. 5; F. R. *Bulletin*, July 1973, p. A76.

321 All nations inflating: See p. 302 and notes.

Author Biography

Ronald H. Marcks (Jens O. Parsson) wrote "Dying of Money" in 1974, at the height of the double-digit inflation then raging. Working with Federal Reserve statistics, he observed trends and relationships between inflation and the money supply analyzing its causes and accurately predicting its future. He self-published his book under the pen name Jens O. Parsson and used his former Massachusetts corporation Wellspring Press as the publisher's name.

A former Navy pilot, Ron graduated from Dartmouth College (Phi Beta Kappa) in 1952 and Harvard Law School in 1960. He was a partner in the Boston, MA, law firm Goodwin, Procter & Hoar, before becoming the General Counsel at Norton Company in Worcester, MA.

Through the years he has participated in numerous business and philanthropic organizations, including his local conservation commission. Retired, he and his wife live in suburban Boston, enjoying opera, theater, family and outdoor activities, and his interest in economic matters.

In the last few years, some have begun to take notice of his work. In the summer of 2010, the British newspaper the Telegraph published an article observing that London bankers were scrambling to get copies of Dying of Money. Thirty six years after he wrote the book and long after Ron thought the book had been forgotten, the world has begun to take notice of his prescient thesis.